CHANGING DIMENSIONS OF BANKING IN INDIA

K. Srinivasa Rao

INDIA · SINGAPORE · MALAYSIA

Notion Press Media Pvt Ltd

No. 50, Chettiyar Agaram Main Road,
Vanagaram, Chennai, Tamil Nadu – 600 095

First Published by Notion Press 2022
Copyright © K. Srinivasa Rao 2022
All Rights Reserved.

ISBN 978-1-68494-195-7

ACKNOWLEDGEMENT

I am thankful to my revered parents for the inspiration, guidance and imparting the culture of perseverance and commitment to live up to the family values. I gratefully acknowledge their blessings. Equally so, I am grateful to my research guide Prof. M.N. Mishra, Banaras Hindu University (BHU), Varanasi for providing the foundation to pursue academic work. Post my research, the inspiration to pursue writing and publication comes from my father-in-law Prof. RVR Chandrashekhar Rao, an eminent academician himself having pursued his research studies from London School of Economics (LSE) and post-doctoral studies from Yale University. He closely tended my academic orientation to scale it up to work towards publishing.

My son Chy. K. Vishwanath Chandrashekhar and my daughter in law Ms. Shruti working with Ernst and Young (E & Y) are my young friends always adding innovative fervor to my thoughts and orientation. They spared abundant time to fine tune my working to sync with the demographic shift of readers, their likings and their way of understanding subjects. My loving thanks go to them for their contribution.

My wife Mrs. K. Udaya Lakshmi always stays behind me in my endeavors. She is engrossed in making me comfortable and runs home – an arduous task without any need for me to spare my time. She encourages my engagements with love and affection sharing even my role in the family activities. Her sacrifice is the reason for me to focus on my writing work. I thank her for the valuable role in shaping up this book.

While lamenting over the irreparable loss of my two elderly iconic personalities in our family in the recent past – Mrs R. Prathibha

Annapoorna (attagaru), my mother-in-law and my elder sister Mrs C. Indira (Babyakka). I acknowledge their support, care and affection that I enjoyed in their protective long association. I therefore dedicate this book in their honor – a humble way to express my gratitude to them.

My siblings, near and dear cousins keep encouraging me by reading and commenting on my essays/publications making valuable contributions to strengthen my opinions, express their views to add to the creativity. I thank them for their constructive role. My thanks also go to my mentors and colleagues in Bank of Baroda, National Institute of Bank Management (NIBM) – Pune, National Institute of Banking studies and Corporate Management (NIBSCOM) – Noida and Institute of insurance and Risk Management (IIRM) – Hyderabad. I gratefully thank to all those, whom I could not name but had their role in my task. Finally, my thanks go to Notion Press, Chennai, the publishers and its team for the cooperation, understanding and coordination during the publishing process.

Hyderabad

15th October, 2021 K. Srinivasa Rao

DEDICATED TO

Ms. Ravikanti. Prathibha Annapoorna,

My mother-in-law (Attagaru)

&

Ms. Chatti Indira

My elder sister (Babyakka)

Previous Book of the Author

Transformation of Public Sector Banks in India

ISBN: 978-1646785889

Date of publication: 17 September 2019

Link: https://www.amazon.in/Transformation-Public-Sector-Banks-India/dp/1646785886

Publishe : Notion Press; 1st edition (17 September 2019)

CONTENTS

Preface   *9*

Abbreviations   *15*

1. Bank Strategies – Beyond 2021   25

2. Emerging Banking Sector Growth & Opportunities   37

3. Policy Implications of Union Budget 2021-22   57

4. Financial Inclusion in India – Progress and Prospects   67

5. Corporate Governance   83

6. Banks Board Bureau   108

7. Revised PCA Framework   116

8. Merger of PSBs   124

9. Privatization of Public Sector Banks   136

10. Digital Transformation   149

11. Digital Literacy   167

12. Changing Lending Appetite of Banks   176

13. Asset Quality Management   184

14. 'Project Shashakt' – A debt Resolution Model   200

15. Insolvency and Bankruptcy Code (IBC) – 2016   211

16. NPA Management – Recognition to Resolution   224

17. Managing Credit Delinquency   239

18. Bad Bank – Long Term Implications   251

19. Policy Innovations in MSME Sector   268

20. Reinventing MSME Sector   278

21. Changing Credit Risk Management Policy   290

22. Risk Management in Financial Sector   299

23. Developments in Lending Rates   306

24. Implications of LIBOR Transition   313

PREFACE

The metamorphosis in banking sector in India has been rapid in the post reform era. More so, after digital penetration began to change the way banking services are delivered and accessed. The stakeholders are systematically gearing up to fine tune financial sector infrastructure to serve the growing needs of the economy. With the fast-integrating financial system with rest of the world, the nuances of risks are challenging due to proliferation of complex financial products. Amid the changing dimensions, risk management will assume greater significance in the years to come. The onus of risk management is not only on the financial intermediaries but also on its users. The business constituents using the financial system also should be able to appreciate that if they are not prudent in their business risk management, they make the financial system vulnerable challenging their ability to provide sustainable service.

Risk management is the collaborative and collective task of financial intermediaries, its users, regulators and all stakeholders to identify, measure and mitigate them for the safety and sustainability of the financial system. The financial system witnessed many instances of failure of big financial entities with mammoth collateral damage to customers and co-entities due to lack of enterprise risk management. The weaknesses in corporate governance systems are more than obvious. They could have been averted if risks in setting pace of growth beyond the risk appetite was considered necessary and proper checks and balances were maintained. The regulatory apparatus has its own limitations in guiding the market participants to stay sustainable within the boundaries of manageable risks.

If the entity is not sensitive towards ramifications of risk taking and is not self-regulated, it becomes difficult to avert the inevitable collapse when the risk eats into the fundamentals of the entity. It is therefore essential to understand how the financial and banking system has evolved, what changes have taken place and how the landscape of banking is evolving. This book precisely provides the trace of changes that can help decision makers to cope with the changes and balance the business priorities keeping the risks well under control. Information and track of regulatory and business changes can be the harbinger of risk mitigation. Many institutional, regulatory and operational changes in banking industry has taken place at various points of time that can catapult growth opportunities to those that can map its pathway and use the knowledge for developing creativity and innovations in financial sector.

As a curious observer of financial sector developments, it will be interesting to capture recent changes in the present edition for the benefit of readers. I have drawn upon my experience as a career banker for close to four decades in articulating my thoughts and sharing my perspectives and interpretations for the particular benefit of next generation leaders of the financial system.

The present book on *"Changing Dimensions of Banking sector in India"* is planned to provide an overview of how changes have taken place to shape a vibrant and competitive banking sector. In order to bring clarity of thoughts, the contents are arranged in sequential. Readers can pick all or any of the major subject of interest and each chapter is fulfilling in itself while providing continuity in the spectrum of developments. In discussing chapters, the readers may find some information/data repetitive but it was thoughtfully retained to bring the perspective together, or else readers will have to go back to past chapters to connect the dots. There are 24 crisp chapters beginning with how banking growth potentiality is evolving in pre and post covid scenario. Most of it is drawn from recent changes to keep it relevant and interesting.

Structural changes of mergers in PSB space, entry of new set of banks, the impact of non-banks including fintechs. How their systemic controls and regulatory norms are getting attuned to the volume shift. How the corporate governance is getting fine-tuned and the increasing role of stakeholders. This chapter while looking to the past is more futuristic with cross functional institutional integration taking shape.

Digital innovation is the catalyst to take the banking services from branch driven silos to virtual space with widening internet bandwidth and spreading access through the trinity – JAM (Jandhan, Adhaar and Mobile). Offline financial transactions will also be forming part of delivery of electronic remittances for hinterland that suffers from lack of internet connectivity all the time. RBI is taking initiatives to evolve an ecosystem of offline delivery. The services through technology are mesmerizing to the users but one need to be very mindful about the risks coming along with it. Institutional risk management capability. Cyber security and invincibility of fire walls will gain more prominence stronger technology – the machine learning and artificial intelligence – the game changers.

Right from the inception of banking system, credit delivery and asset quality management has been an enterprising function with credit origination, monitoring and recovery integrated into a combined task of managing risks at every level. With borrower community exposed to enhanced business risk, banks have to constantly upgrade their risk management skills with the help of technology to manage own risks keeping the risk profile of the borrower in view. With the historic formation of a National Asset Reconstruction Company Ltd (NARCL) – Bad Bank and Insolvency and Bankruptcy Code – 2016 taking deeper roots in debt resolution, the credit risk management can find new tools. Despite these developments and empowerments, unless banks acquire the skill sets to originate good quality credit, maintain a grip on the asset quality, these external nuances may not be able to help banks to run their business models on sustainable basis. The chapter on credit and asset quality management captures the past and present which may look like a monotonous storyline but credit risk management needs sustained efforts and collaboration with borrowers.

While sectoral balance in shaping up business mix is the prerogative of each financial institution/bank, yet MSME sector is the most vital sector for unleashing growth potentiality of the economy. Several facilitating policy changes and ease of doing business enablers have been consistently put in place for strengthening MSME sector. But in operationalizing them, the financial system is not able to reach out to them in sufficient measure creating a void in institutional credit. With financial inclusion shaping up fast with PMJDY and technological innovation, financial intermediaries will have to work out collaborative path for outreach, more importantly in providing institutional credit to entrepreneurs at the bottom of the pyramid. This will be in the long-term interest of the economy. The wider potentiality of growth lies in medium and micro industries that has immense export capability and employment intensity.

With NBFCs fast coming into the mainstream of financial services with RBI providing more autonomy, banks will have to engage with them including Fintech outfits to derive the full synergy. Since the risk management architecture in NBFCs are yet to evolve on a scale necessary to provide the range of newly allowed services, banks while collaborating with them have to be more sensitive in managing risks. With the global financial system transiting from LIBOR to alternate reference rates, the risks have to be carefully managed. Keeping these sectoral aspects in mind, the book is well diversified yet made into divisible parts to suit the interest of readers to quickly grasp the relevant information.

The task of writing a book is a fascinating journey of providing shape to imagination and creativity in a bid to provide ready tool to the readers to refer and proceed in practicing financial sector business. It is difficult to assure an error free writing of a long script but a humble attempt is made to capture the recent changes in the area of banking into compact chapters put in the right part of the book. Suggestions are always welcome. Learning from reader's views will be another objective of my unending journey and quest to upgrade my capacity to disseminate knowledge. Happy reading.

Hyderabad

15th October, 2021 K.Srinivasa Rao

ABBREVIATIONS

ATM	Automated Teller Machine
POS	Point of Sale Terminal
PSB	Public Sector Bank
NPA	Non-Performing Assets
PCR	Provision Coverage Ratio
RBI	Reserve Bank of India
NBFC	Non-Banking Financial Company
CLM	Co-Lending Model
PPI	Prepaid Payment Instrument
KYC	Know Your Customer
DICGC	Deposit Insurance and Credit Guarantee Corporation
DPI	Digital Payment Index
RTGS	Real Time Gross Settlement
NEFT	National Electronic Fund Transfer
NACH	National Automated Clearing House
QR	Quick Response
SMS	Short Message Service
PA	Payment Aggregators
DIC	Digital India Corporation
MSME	Micro Small and Medium Enterprises
DSB	Door Step Banking
EASE	Enhanced Access Service Excellence
TDS	Tax Deducted at source
CRPF	Central Reserve Police Force
SBI	State Bank of India
RPA	Robotic Process Automation

AI	Artificial Intelligence
WFH	Work from Home
CORE	Centralized online Realtime Exchange
NARC	National Asset Reconstruction Company
GDP	Gross Domestic Product
UB22	Union Budget 2021-22
UB & SPs	Union Budget and Stimulus Packages
IL & FS	Infrastructure Leasing and Financial Services
DHFL	Deewan Housing Finance Ltd
PMCB	Punjab and Maharashtra Cooperative Bank
HDIL	Housing Development Infrastructure Ltd
IBC	Insolvency and Bankruptcy Code -2016
NDTL	Net demand and time liabilities
LCR	Liquidity coverage ratio
HFCs	Housing Finance Companies
NHB	National House Bank
WALR	Weighted average lending rates
YoY	Year on Year
PMAY	Pradhan Mantri Awas Yozana
RERA	Real estate Regulatory Authority
PMGSY	Pradhan Mantri Gram Sadak Yozana
PPP	Public Private Partnership
GST	Goods and Service Tax
MCA	Ministry of Corporate Affairs
RIDF	Rural Infrastructure and Development Fund
MUDRA	Micro Units Development and Refinance Agency
MSE	Medium and Small Enterprises
MSEFC	MSE Facilitation Council
TReDS	Discounting of trade receivables of MSMEs
PSU	Public Sector Units
GeM	Government e-Marketplace
ADF	Acceptance Development Fund
MDR	Merchant Discount Rate

UPI	Universal Payment Interface
PMJDY	Pradhan Mantri Jan Dhan Yozana
FBs	Foreign Banks
HSBC	Hongkong and Shanghai Banking Corporation
UK	United Kingdom
BIS	Bank for International Settlement
WOS	Wholly Owned Subsidiary
SBM	State Bank of Mauritius
LVB	Lakshmi Vilas Bank
SCB	Scheduled Commercial Bank
PSLC	Priority Sector Lending Certificate
HNI	High Net-Worth Individual
NGO	Non-Government Organisation
FSR	Financial Stability Report
CAR	Capital Adequacy Ratio
SPV	Special Purpose Vehicle
ARC	Asset Reconstruction Company
IBA	Indian Banks' Association
TARP	Troubled Asset Relief Program
DFI	Development Financial Institution
IIFCL	Infrastructure Finance Company limited
NaBFID	National Bank for Financing Infrastructure and Development
CAPEX	Capital Expenditure
GFCF	Gross Fixed capital formation
FDI	Foreign Direct Investment
LIC	Life Insurance Company
ANBA	Atma Nirbhar Bharat Yozana
PLI	Production Linked Insurance
MITP	Mega Investment Textile Park
NSFR	Net Stable Funding Ratio
FI	Financial Inclusion
FIP	Financial Inclusion Policy

BC	Business Correspondent
IIBF	Indian Institute of Banking and Finance
BSBDs	Basic Savings Bank Deposit Accounts
KCC	Kisan Credit Card
GCC	General Credit Card
FIF	Financial Inclusion Fund
IPPB	Indian Post Payment Bank
DOP	Department of Posts
IFSC	Indian Financial Systems Code
CBDC	Central Bank Digital Currency
NMFI	National Mission for Financial Inclusion
JAM	Jandhan Adhaar and Mobile
PMSBY	Pradhan Mantri Suraksha Bima Yojana
PMJJY	Pradhan Mantri Jeevan Jyoti Yojana
APY	Atal Pension Yojana.
PMVVY	Pradhan Mantri Vaya Vandana Yojana
PMMY	Pradhan Mantri Mudra Yozana
FLCs	Financial Literacy Centres
NCEF	National Centre for Financial Education
NSFE	National Strategy for Financial Education
FIDD	Financial Inclusion and Development Department
P2PL	Peer to Peer lenders
DBT	Direct Benefit Transfer
GFIX	Global Financial Inclusion Index
EIU	Economic Intelligence Unit
BRICS	Brazil, Russia, India, China and South Africa
NSFI	National Strategy for Financial Inclusion
FIAC	Financial inclusion advisory Committee
NCLT	National Company Law Tribunals
CG	Corporate Governance
DFS	Department of Financial Services
ESOP	Employee Stock ownership Plan
CVC	Chief Vigilance commission

CBI	Central Bureau of Investigation
RTI Act	Right to Information Act
BIC	Bank Investment Committee
CEO	Chief Executive Officer
PE	Private Equity
AQR	Asset Quality Review
PCA	Prompt Corrective Action
BBB	Banks Board Bureau
DPG	Discussion Paper on Governance
CFSL	Centrum Financial Services Ltd
SFB	Small Finance Bank
SEBI	Securities and Exchange Board of India
CRO	Chief Risk Officer
CCO	Chief Compliance Officer
HIA	Head of Internal Audit
CIV	Chief Internal Vigilance
WTDs	Whole Time Directors
NED	Non-Executive Directors
MD	Managing Director
NRC	Nomination and Remuneration Committee
ID	Independent Director
RBS	Risk Based Supervision
CAMELS	Capital Adequacy, Asset Quality, Management quality, Earnings, Liabilities and Systems and Controls
RRBs	Regional Rural Banks
PBs	Payment Banks
BCBS	Basel Committee on Banking Supervision
NOFHC	Non-Operative Financial Holding Company
GRAF	Governance, Reward and Accountability Framework
FY	Financial year
NNPA	Net Non-Performing Assets
GNPA	Gross Non-Performing Assets
ROA	Return on Assets

IBBI	Insolvency and Bankruptcy Board of India
SMA	Special Mention Accounts
PNB	Punjab National Bank
D-SIB	Domestic Systemically Important Bank
S&P	Standard & Poor
CRAR	Capital to Risk weighted Assets Ratio
JLF	Joint Lenders Forum
CRILC	Central Repository of Information on Large Credit
SDR	Strategic Debt Restructuring
BOI	Bank of India
CET	I-Common Equity Tier-I
OTS	One Time Settlement
TLs	Turnaround Leaders
OBC	Oriental Bank of Commerce
UBI	United Bank of India
BOB	Bank of Baroda
VB	Vijaya Bank
DB	Dena Bank
NAE	New Amalgamated Entity
IRAC	Income recognition and asset classification
ICAAP	Internal Capital adequacy Assessment Policy
SLR	Statutory liquidity Ratio
CRR	Cash Reserve Ratio
CMD	Chairman and Managing Director
EDs	Executive Directors
BCG	Boston Consulting Group
CBI	Central Bank of India
IOB	Indian overseas Bank
DIPAM	Department of Investment and Public Asset Management
VRS	Voluntary Retirement Scheme
NPS	New Pension Fund
AM	Alternative Mechanism
ICT	Information, Communication and Telecommunication

CAGR	Compounded Annual Growth Rate
NPCI	National Payment Corporation of India
AGM	Annual General Meeting
TAT	Turnaround Time
ML	Machine Learning
IO	Internal Ombudsman
BSBDA	Basic Savings Bank Deposit Account
OTP	One Time Password
DWs	Digital Wallets
FLCCs	financial literacy and credit counselling Cells
Disha	*Digital Saksharta Abhiyan*
NDLM	*National Digital Literacy Mission*
NIELIT	National Institute of Electronics and Information Technology
NDLM	National Digital Literacy Mission
CVV	Card Verification Value
TLTRO	Targeted Long Term Repo Operation
CCB	Capital Conservation Buffer
ECLGS	Emergency Credit Line Guarantee scheme
SMC	Sunil Mehta Committee
SOP	Standard Operating Procedure
ICA	Inter Corporate Agreement
PCA	Public Credit Registry
CAP	Corrective Action Plan
CDR	Corporate Debt Restructuring
SDR	Strategic Debt Restructuring
COC	Committee of Creditors
CIRP	Corporate Insolvency and Resolution Process
NCLAT	National Company Law Appellate Tribunal
IRPs	Insolvency Resolution Professionals
EoDB	Ease of Doing Business
OECD	Organisation of economic cooperation and Development

SARFAESI	Securitization and Reconstruction of Financial Assets and Enforcement of Securities Interest (SARFAESI)
DRT	Debt Recovery Tribunals
NIM	Net Interest Margin
DRT	Debt Recovery Tribunal
CRM	Credit Risk Management
IMF	International Monetary Fund
R D D B F I Act	Recovery of Debts Due to Banks and Financial Institutions Act
AIF	Alternate Investment Fund
CERSAI	Central Registry of Securitisation Asset Reconstruction and Security Interest of India
IDRCL	India Debt Resolution Company Ltd
GVA	Gross Value Added
IOS	Industrial Outlook Survey
BEI	Business Expectations Index
PMI	Purchasing Managers' Index
IFC	International Finance Corporation
SDG	Sustainable Development Goals
CGT MSE	Credit Guarantee Fund Trust for Micro and Small Enterprises
SIDBI	Small Industries Development Bank of India
UN	United Nations
SSI	Small-Scale industries
SIDO	Small Industries development Organization
KVIC	Khadi Village Industries Commission
NSIC	National Small Industries Corporation (NSIC)
NIMSME	National Institute for Micro, Small and Medium Enterprises
MGIRI	Mahatma Gandhi Institute for Rural Industrialization
RIDF	Rural Infrastructure Development Fund
MCA	Ministry of Corporate Affairs
ANBC	Average Net Bank Credit
CSR	Corporate Social Responsibility

SHGs	Self Help Groups
FSB	Financial Stability Board
SAARC	South Asian Association of Regional Cooperation
NBFI	Non-Banking Financial Institutions
GRC	Governance, Risk and Compliance
HFCs	Housing Finance Companies
UCBs	Urban Cooperative Banks
BPLR	Benchmark Prime Lending Rate
MCLR	Marginal Cost of Funds Based Lending Rate
RLLR	Repo Linked Lending Rate
CASA	Current and Savings Accounts
LIBOR	London Interbank Offered Rate
ICE	Intercontinental Exchange
IBA	International Benchmark Administrator
BBA	British Bankers Association
RFRs	Risk Free Rates
CFTC	Commodity Futures Trading Commission
IOSCO	International Organization of Securities Commissions
ARRC	Alternate Reference Rate Committee
SOFR	Secured Overnight Financing Rate
ARR	Alternate Reference Rate
FCA	Financial Conduct Authority

CHAPTER – 1

BANK STRATEGIES – BEYOND 2021

The banking sector is gearing up to look beyond the pandemic to harness growth potentiality. The nuance of challenges in continuing the journey of bank reforms is now compounded with unprecedented Covid induced stress and its ramifications. Based on the operational results of banks of FY21, banks are well set to be stronger efficient and resilient. A look at the evolving landscape of financial sector to work out future strategies in banks will be interesting. Amid the rapid financial sector changes, banking sector too has been rapidly coping with the evolving ecosystem. The metamorphosis in banking is further led by technological innovations and regulatory interventions making way for faster transformation. In addition to traditional bank branch network pegged at 1, 50,207 in March 2021, the alternate delivery channels are fast outpacing brick and mortar presence and strengthening the infrastructure and capacity building on a durable basis providing greater customer convenience on go.

The proliferation of off-site technology driven outlets is significantly rising. By June 2021, the network of ATMs has reached 2,13, 766. Points of sale Terminals (POS) are at 4.6 million. The mobile/internet banking is supported with 906 million debit cards and 6.30 lakh credit cards. A host of virtual debit cards and digital wallets supplement the infrastructure to intensify digital financial transactions. These are the sequential developments as part of modernization of financial sector, a journey in perpetuity. Increased proactive adoption of digital mode by bank customers due to the covid-induced compulsion has provided the much-needed shift – a digital penetration level that could have taken years of efforts of banks to reach. As a result, customers could perceive the enhanced operational efficiency, competitive pricing and significant customer centricity. Demonetization and the onset of pandemic has prompted customers to increasingly rely on digital mode.

In reaching these digital milestones, private banks had lesser challenges as they started new with their own state of the art technology, trained industry-ready manpower and other infrastructure but Public Sector Banks (PSBs) had to transform its conventional banking practices and adopt integrated technology to compete with private peers. The ongoing shift of PSBs from 'sellers' market' to 'buyers' market' is a big leap that is yet to shape up fully. The Covid induced stressful experience added multidimensional nuances that is painful in near term but can accelerate speed of transformation in the medium to long term.

Despite navigating through the large-scale disruptions since the onset of pandemic, banks are able to shape up well at a pace better than earlier. The recent financial stability report of RBI – July 2021 highlighted that bank have relatively improved by March 2021. The ratio of non-performing assets (NPAs) of banks have gone down to 7.48 percent, capital adequacy ratio increased to 16 percent and provision coverage ratio (PCR) has gone up close to 70 percent. These improved performance parameters need to be sustained in the years to come using the ongoing policy reforms. Reserve Bank of India (RBI) has been proactive in guiding the banks by aligning the regulations and readjusting its lens enabling banks to support faster revival of the economy. The government, the majority owner of PSBs too is calibrating bank reforms balancing its intent and socioeconomic needs. In order to work out future strategies, it will be pertinent to recapitulate some notable policy changes, particularly initiated in the last 2-3 years that tend to shape the future of banking system.

1.1 Competition from non-banks:

As a proactive central bank, RBI has been working towards continuously and consistently strengthening financial institutions and creating healthy competition by (i) deepening the bank reforms and (ii) provided breakthrough support since March 27, 2020 to fight the catastrophic impact of *'once in a century'* kind of black swan event – the pandemic. It created reinforcing pillars of policy support to the three strategic arms of the financial sector – PSBs, Private banks and non-banks so as to supplement and draw their synergy for innovative and well-balanced covid induced timely action. In order to complement comparative advantages of banks and Non-Banking Financial Companies (NBFCs), greater operational flexibility was provided to the lending institutions. A "Co-Lending Model" (CLM) has been evolved by RBI permitting banks and NBFCs to come together to lend jointly to improve the flow of credit to the un-served and underserved sectors of the economy. It is intended to make available funds to the ultimate beneficiary at the bottom of the pyramid at an affordable cost. The banks can claim priority sector lending status in respect of their share of credit while engaging in the CLM. Collaboration between banks and non-banks is an inevitable tool to coexist in competitive markets.

Coming to fintech start-ups, RBI permitted setting up regulatory sandbox, or innovation hub, to help them launch innovative products at lower costs. It enabled live testing of new products or services in a controlled/test regulatory environment. In order to promote digital transactions while making it mandatory for Prepaid Payment Instruments (PPIs) to move towards interoperability with mandatory full – Know Your Customer (KYC) compliance. RBI hiked the limit of outstanding balance permitted to be held in wallets to Rs. 2 lakhs. Earlier, the limit was Rs. 1 lakh for any wallets or cards. The deposit-taking limit of payment banks is increased from Rs.1 lakh to Rs. 2 lakhs. Now that the deposit insurance is raised to Rs. 5 lakhs, payment banks have been persuading RBI to increase the permitted limit of deposits to Rs.5 lakhs from the increased level of Rs. 2 Lakhs. When smarter financial intermediaries encounter with new age techno savvy customers, even the thin margins of profitability will logically flow to smart winners.

For wide spread and adoption of digital payments in a safe and secure manner, the RBI increased the limit for contactless card transactions to Rs 5,000 from Rs 2,000 per transaction from January 1, 2021. As a result, PSBs, private banks, differentiated banks and non-banks including fintech and neo banks are spearheading the diversified growth of digital products/delivery channels. The rapid transformation of banks is indicating that what has happened in the last 30 years can be just the beginning and more innovative customer centric banking is fast shaping up.

Following the raising of deposit insurance from Rs. 1 lakh to Rs. 5 lakhs in February 2020, the Deposit Insurance and Credit Guarantee Corporation (DICGC) Act 1961 has been recently amended. After the amendment, insured depositors can access funds from DICGC within 90 days unlike in the past when depositors had to wait endlessly till the bankruptcy process comes to an end to get insurance funds. This is a big relief to small depositors where they can get the deposit insurance funds faster.

1.2 Mining digital Power:

Banks have been focusing on shifting customers to technology mode. It is evident with the uptick in digital payment index (DPI) of RBI conceived in 2018 as a base year from 100 at the time of start to reach 270.59 by March 2021 indicating a three-fold rise in digital transactions. It is poised to rise further with the recent thrust on developing interoperable digital infrastructure in a big way. (i) Real Time Gross Settlement (RTGS)/ National Electronic Funds Transfer (NEFT) is now available round the clock (ii) the bulk payment system driven on National Automated Clearing House (NACH) will be available on all days of the week from August 1, 2021. (iii) The launch of Quick Response (QR) Code/ SMS string based prepaid, contactless e-rupi on August 2, 2021 was another digital innovation that can not only make goods and services reach the intended beneficiary without any leakage of subsidy but can eventually tag even non-bank customers to formal digital world opening up for greater financial inclusion. E-rupi is designed to deliver subsidy/stimulus to be provided in commodity form with built-in end-use verification. (iv) RBI is also enforcing enhanced cyber security features – one example is, neither the authorized Payment Aggregators (PAs) nor the merchants on-boarded by them can store customer card credentials within their database or server from January 2022 and hence card holders can be protected against compromise of data, if any due to data breach.

The digitization of banking operations is fast transcending to multiple areas. It has begun to progressively cover parts of digital lending. Work from home, remote access to customers, video – e-KYC, webinars and digital connectivity with the borrowers of banks will bring more intense monitoring of credit through digital mode. Digitally driven auto alerts for credit monitoring are fast developing. Banks are already working towards simplification of lending procedures to go green – accepting many documents on digital mode. The DigiLocker of Digital India Corporation (DIC) will also be explored to verify the authenticity of documents submitted by bank's constituents. The threshold of lending automation will get expanded to service more micro small and medium enterprises (MSME)/retail loans. Thus, the digital powered convenience, speed and efficiency is proactively at work.

1.3 Doorstep Banking (DSB):

Though not as an outcome of Covid19 stress, government has impressed upon the banks to introduce door step banking (DSB) as part of the ongoing Enhanced Access and Service Excellence (EASE) bank reforms. DSB initiative is designed to provide convenience of banking services to customers at their doorstep through the universal touch points of call centre, web portal or mobile app, and through other digital remote modes. The proposed DSB services will be rendered by the doorstep banking agents deployed by the selected service providers, initially at 100 identified centres across the country. In order to introduce DSB as a mode of delivery more aligned to the senior citizens and others who cannot visit branches, it will start with non-financial services and will be expanded to cover financial services.

The range of services will include accepting request for standing instructions, request for account statement, delivery of non-personalized cheque book, demand draft, pay order, acknowledgement, etc., Delivery of Tax Deducted at Source (TDS) / Form 16 certificate issuance, delivery of pre-paid instrument / gift cards will also be delivered to customers under DSB. Customers can also track their service request through these channels. These services can be availed by customers of PSBs at nominal charges. The services shall benefit all customers, particularly Senior Citizens, Defense personnel, Central Reserve Police Force (CRPF), widows, Divyang individuals, Students, Salaried employees, corporate clients, retail shopkeepers, street vendors who cannot leave their business unit/home due to their nature of business/limitations in mobility.

It can be recalled that EASE reform agenda was aimed at institutionalizing clean and smart banking. It was launched in January 2018, and the subsequent edition of the program ☐ EASE 2.0 built on the foundation laid in EASE 1.0 and furthered the progress on reforms. Reform Action Points in EASE 2.0 aimed at making the reforms journey irreversible, strengthening processes and systems, and driving outcomes. Now EASE 4.0 model is implemented which calls for more improved services. These kinds of long-term reforms will be shaping up the banking in the coming years. Hence, reference of it will have direct bearing on future strategies. DSB is proposed to be managed as a separate line of business to generate profitability and DSB agents may not necessarily be staff of the bank.

1.4 Enhancing people competency:

With automation and DSB type of innovations and nuances of ongoing bank reforms covering more activities at off-site points, banks will have to work out strategies to decongest branches to make them smart 'sales and service' outlets. It requires manpower to change their attitude, more so in PSBs to move from desk to market for more qualitative business expansion with intense outdoor activities. Staff will have to be trained to monitor and maintain infrastructure and understand the nuances of operational risk. They need to be groomed to better manage credit risk at branch level where the business originates. Deployment of manpower for specialized activities will call for skill centric training and up gradation of qualitative standards that will be the driving differentiator. The branch staff has to play a more active role as a first line of defence in risk management of the bank. They need to be made competent to understand the nuances of risk management and all software applications in use at the branch to avoid dependence on vendors.

They should also be well groomed to build up communication and negotiation skills to provide advisory, credit and entrepreneurial counselling services. Upkeep, presentability and orientation for marketing, cross-selling and grasping customer relationship management data and peer market analysis. It will be essential to make the most out of the changing landscape of banking. Unlike the past practice to focus on table work, the staff should now be more outbound, tech savvy and customer centric.

With automation of many activities of front and back office, desk work at branches shall come down, more significantly in coming years. Even many processes of lending are hived to offsite-centralized hubs. Optimization of staff deployment through retraining, reskilling re-deployment is an opportunity to improve productivity. Lateral recruitment of experts in risk, technology, marketing, legal, economic intelligence and project management may be a good move in near term to provide a blend of experience and lateral expertise but eventually the internal skill sets have to be aligned to suit the new requirements.

1.5 Internal branch architecture:

Besides rationalization of branch network to derive the synergy of amalgamation of PSBs, the banking system is now on coordinated move with NBFCs and Fintech joining the banks in a big way. The resultant technological innovations, adoption of new branch business models to work in coordination and co-origination format will need changing the internal edifice to meet the new needs. In the midst of emerging development, the number of outlets may not necessarily come down in the long run but they need to be redesigned to disseminate knowledge and skill-based services of a non-routine nature. For example, after amalgamation, Bank of Baroda merged 1310 branches, Punjab National Bank – 430 branches, Canara Bank – 105 branches, Union Bank of India – 275 branches and Indian Bank -203 branches until March 2021.

As a result, both as an outcome of mergers and rationalisation of business positioning by banks in general, the trend of branch relocation, closure and mergers will continue in potentially evolving banking structure but customer connectivity will stay in a different form but more widely. The proposed privatization of two PSBs though may not materialize during FY22 but whenever happens will eventually lead to branch network realignment and reset of business priorities. Digital intensity is fast replacing human interventions in banking. The rise of neo banks (virtual banks with no branch presence) like 811 by Kotak Mahindra, Yono by State Bank of India (SBI), Razorpay, Open, NiYo and many more similar upcoming entities coupled with fintech activism are setting standards for a branchless banking environment. This trend may not reduce the number of bank branches in near term will call for realignment of physical model of bank presence. Many innovations must be in making to reduce operational costs but more effectively reachable to customers.

In such emerging digitally driven work environment, archaic huge brick and mortar branch infrastructure will have to be redesigned with smaller spaces but better aligned to serve customers. Digital kiosks/ Point of sale terminals/Business correspondents and customer service centres are capable to meet many of the day today services. The covid induced work culture is expected to sustain in the long run because it suits everyone to reduce physical presence in the bank branches.

The footfalls at branches is set to move to be more selective to obtain specific credit and advisory form of services with routine activities moving to digital format.

Moreover, as far as customer queries are concerned, routine customer enquiries are now increasingly moving to chat bots and virtual interactive assistants and many other innovative forms are in offing. Hence, the need for human presence within the branch for rudimentary banking services may come down providing more quality time for staff to spend on marketing. The use of robotic process automation (RPA) and application of a combination of robots and Artificial Intelligence (AI) to replace and augment human operations in banking is already taking roots signalling more human replacement. Work from home (WFH) is a new way in banks to cut costs. Bank of Baroda is the first PSB to consider making WFH a permanent policy for a section of its employees. The bank has also appointed management consultancy firm McKinsey & Co to help implement a strategy for a post-Covid world. Similar initiatives are in the offing in many banks paving way for a different mode of more effective working with reduced staff strength.

Some of the digital capabilities of using video conferencing during pandemic times should be further developed as cost cutting strategies. Banks that do not plan taking the pandexit strategies to the next level will be behind the competitive curve. Looking to the scale of digital banking, many of the activities hived off to centralized processing hubs, banks may not need any more the kind of elaborate branch architecture and huge space that prevails in banks now.

Banks will need compact well-digitized branches manned by trained specialists to handle the selective customers who visit branches for obtaining specialized services. More people will be needed in debt resolution, negotiating recovery deals and handling of quasi legal affairs in loan recovery. Customers may not step into branches for depositing petty cash or withdrawal of funds or buying a draft, not definitely in urban and metro centres. Hence, it will be a right strategy to resize the existing branches into smarter and well-decked branches. Even the idea of shared workspaces like co-working architecture on the lines of polyclinics can also be explored.

1.6 Lending automation:

Many banks have undertaken extensive business process reengineering to shift mode of lending from the manual system to digital. Many internal processes have been reoriented to work in alignment with the Centralized online Realtime Exchange (CORE) Banking technology. But the benefits of process improvements have been more focused on the liability products and ancillary services. Though lending automation and centralization of loan processing is moved to hub and spokes model in many banks but borrowers have not been fully benefitted. It has been focused on internal process reforms to hasten the turnaround time. Going forward, the secondary market for corporate loans now formed would lead to diversification of credit risks, provide market-based credit products for a diversified set of investors, and can potentially improve transparency in banking. Formation of a separate National Asset Reconstruction Company (NARC) to function on the lines of bad bank could trigger more reforms in lending and asset quality management.

The borrowers are normally required to visit the bank branches many times and have to submit physical documents to satisfy bank needs. Keeping legal and regulatory norms, banks can prescribe documents that can be obtained on digital mode and innovate methods to avoid repeat visits of potential borrowers. The loan document needs should be transparent and kept minimum hosted in the website to keep the prospective borrowers aware about the process. Taking the process reforms forwards, banks will have to work out methodology to reduce the footfalls of borrowers for completing paper formalities. It is important to shun the drudgery of borrowing process from the user point of view. The next move is to innovate simplification of loaning process. More than the loan policy reforms, the operational processes have to be reviewed. Borrowers should be able to experience a seamless process to obtain bank loans at fair interest rates and service charges in a competitive working ecosystem. More risk sharing in lending with small finance banks and cooperative banks could also be explored as they have better grass root level connect and deliverability.

1.7 Strategy view of experts:

Even many strategy experts propagate the need to capture the evolving business ecosystem to work out well-aligned strategies. It will be interesting to look at what the Canadian strategist, Mr. Mintzberg recommends. According to him, breaking down management roles and responsibilities and organizing the workplace to simplify complex concepts that helps to better organize commercial entities and it allows each member to develop their own skills. Adjusting work space to the customer needs and reskilling people will be the hallmark of future banking.

Even Mr. Michael E. Porter, another globally acclaimed strategist avers that the essence of strategy is to understand and cope with competition and should focus on five competitive forces – competitors, customers, suppliers, potential new entrants and substitute products. In the context of banking of future – neo banks, fintechs are the aggressive competitors. The new age customers will need delivery of banking services with the click of mouse. Technology providers as vendors will have their way in pricing key software essential for financial entities in running their operations. The recent working group of RBI had already recommended to allow large NBFCs with asset size of over Rs. 50,000 crores to be granted banking licenses as and when they enter the banking space, the financial sector will look more competitive with deeper penetration. Substitute products are already in the financial system with corporate sector aggressively accessing bond/debt markets.

In view of the changes taking place prior to Covid19 and during the pandemic period, it is clear that, going forward some of the changes will be an integral part of the banking system. Banks have reinvented many technological processes and the way of conducting the businesses. The evolving trend points towards all the five forces that Mr. Michael Porter dealt with that are emerging fast providing cue to banks to rework on their organizational and structural challenges to be able to adopt to these changes. With future of banking driven on technology, the nuances of strategies should be profit centric so that the benefit of reforms flows equitably to all stakeholders. Lot of homework is needed in coming up with new set of business strategies to compete in post covid banking environment.

It is the right opportunity to reform and modernize bank branches to pursue profitable business in the coming years when the economy will unleash its adrenaline and animal spirit from the Gati Shakti master plan in the offing. The roll out National Monetisation Pipeline – 2021-25 and National Infrastructure Pipeline – 2020-25 are the big game changers that can be unleashed by the banking system to grow big. Hence, the growth of banks in future can be in geometric progression and can catch up exponential levels for visionary banks who can visualize the changes and set the barometer of action plan now.

CHAPTER – 2

EMERGING BANKING SECTOR GROWTH & OPPORTUNITIES

In the backdrop of articulation of a clear vision to increase the size of the economy to US $ 5 trillion by 2025 on its way to reach US $ 10 trillion by 2030, Union Budget 2021-22 (UB22) brought out many reinforcing policies despite the marked slowdown of GDP due to the impact of ongoing pandemic. These targeted years for achievement of GDP milestones may get postponed but government is on way to implement many developmental projects to realise the goals. Notwithstanding such near-term disruptions of Covid19, the potential spurt in the size of the economy would open up multiple opportunities to different sectors, more importantly to banks that are meant to undertake speedy and efficient financial intermediation. Banks can take a cue from the most important intentions and aspirations outlined in the economic survey, union budget, series of stimulus packages and more significant is the proposed mergers, privatization of PSBs and privatisation of state-owned insurance company that can have a spill over impact on the financial sector. These could pose both challenges and opportunities to banks to move to a higher growth trajectory.

But realization of growth objectives by banks will be contingent upon coordinating synergy of large number of players that have an umbilical connect with non-banks, fintech companies and peer to peer lenders and so on. Going by the same logic, deposits of the banking system now at Rs.155 trillion and bank credit at Rs.109 trillion (August 27, 2021) should be close to double its size by 2025. The stronger and fewer PSBs in new dispensation can look forward to handle business size far higher than they handle today. The capacity of risk appetite will be increased with improved capital adequacy ratio and synergy of technology. With consolidation and big banks in fray, better economies of scale can be attained. The 27 PSBs at one point of time are now trimmed to 12 should be able to make them more potentially capable to handle larger chunk of business. Smart sizing the banks will be one way to make them efficient. But in order to tap such newer opportunities, organizational preparedness need to be improved to work out future growth strategies for different lines of business.

2.1 Emerging opportunities for banks:

In order to start the journey of uphill trek to reach GDP target of US $ 5 trillion, the road map and resource algorithm in union budget and stimulus packages (UB&SPs) are well calibrated with continued thrust on fiscal prudence. But expansion capital expenditure and higher tolerance for fiscal deficit is essential in near term to revive the economy and catch up pre-covid level normalcy. It is the right opportunity for banks, more importantly the stronger and bigger PSBs whose market share has been declining after the asset quality review of RBI and its aftermath. PSBs need to reinstate their strategic role in supporting the economic growth and help attain the sustainable development goals set out by Niti Ayog.

Overcoming the near-term disruptions, achieving a sustained real GDP growth of 8 percent per annum will be necessary to inch up close to the long-term growth objectives. It may look to be a tough challenge to realize the broad vision of growth but banks can sense huge opportunities in the new measures of relief. In a bank led economy, the efficiency of financial sector will be critical for ensuring seamless monetary transmission and flow of credit. Many thoughtful measures built in the set of UB&SPs for strengthening banking sector and rescuing NBFCs can lead to development of robust financial sector ecosystem.

The upfront infusion of Rs. 20000 crores of capital into select PSBs can shore up capital adequacy and create more lending space. The impact of these relief measures on how the financial sector groaning under the weight of ailing NBFCs and continued asset quality woes will be able to work will depend on the strategies designed and implemented with full vigour.

In order to unleash such opportunities, banks will have to work out strategies to overcome the series of shocks and collateral damage caused to the financial sector. It began with Infrastructure Leasing and Financial Services (IL&FS) fiasco in September 2018 with its ramifications on Dewan housing Finance Ltd (DHFL) and other interconnected NBFCs. It exacerbated with the fallout of fraud in Punjab and Maharashtra Cooperative Bank (PMCB) perpetrated in connivance with Housing Development Infrastructure Ltd (HDIL). These adverse developments weakened the sentiments in financial intermediation impeding the growth.

2.2 Consolidation of PSBs:

When 18 PSBs eventually converged into 12 large and more capable PSBs, they can compete with large private peers and pose challenge to other financial intermediaries. In the process, the customers can look forward for improved quality of customer service with fine-tuned risk-based pricing policies. Realizing the need for strong capital base to comply with Basel – III standards by March 2020 that had to be postponed due to pandemic. Government has infused capital in many PSBs assessing their specific needs. It is in addition to Rs.2.5 trillion already provided to PSBs in the last five years. The enhanced capital allocation can restore lending appetite. The slowdown in credit growth in the last three years due to large-scale bad loans is also being tackled by amending several clauses of Insolvency and Bankruptcy Code -2016 (IBC) to make it strong and pragmatic.

Near term disruption in the working of 10 PSBs now formed into 4 large banks cannot be ruled out but it need to be minimized with suitable proactive plan of action. But more important is to derive the synergy of amalgamation in the long term which seem to be happening now and its impact will be seen more in coming years. With the merger process completed in March 2020, the newly formed bigger banks are settling down to manage. Out of the newly carved out set of PSBs, six of them will be bigger in size and reach and their role will be significant to decide the future course of financial intermediation.

The 10 newly formed PSBs have a total business share of Rs.55.56 trillion with a branch network of 37663. They together wield significant clout on the banking system. It will be challenging for them to minimize the disruption in the working. The process of amalgamation should not be allowed to mar the prospects of their growth in the intervening period. Formation of separate teams for rolling out amalgamation plans and hiving off lines of responsibilities will be essential. The initial disruptions on account of amalgamation have to be reduced to ensure that the very objective of merger – making them bigger to lend to big projects and building up robust risk appetite is realized.

2.3 Policy impact for banks:

Lot of operational reform are in making to insulate against frauds. Policies are getting aligned to work out methods to prevent other people (other than account holder) to deposit money into bank account. This has become necessary after large-scale deposit of funds by third party into the account belonging to someone else during demonetization that impacted the efficacy of the process. It will help banks check menace of money laundering. It will further scale down cash transactions. As part of ease of providing customer services, banks are expected to harness technology and increase offer of online credit facilities and can roll out doorstep banking. Senior citizens and people needing special assistance and differently abled should also be provided with dedicated services. Door step banking however is coming up in a big way in the next few years. In lieu of such service, fee income can be targeted. It will have dual impact. Customer convenience with potential added income for banks.

Liquidity relief is provided to NBFCs that has caused huge collateral damage to the financial system after IL&FS collapse and its aftermath. The lingering liquidity shortfall continues causing successive default in honouring their financial commitments. Under an arrangement, government had encouraged PSBs to buy high-rated pooled assets of sound NBFCs up to Rs 1 trillion for which the government provided a one-time six-month partial credit guarantee for the first loss of up to 10 per cent.

Banks are also incentivized to support NBFCs by using one percent of their Net demand and time liabilities (NDTL) to be treated as high quality liquid assets for computing their liquidity coverage ratio (LCR). This extra liquidity can be used to extend fresh funding to NBFCs and Housing Finance Companies (HFCs) effective July 5, 2019. NBFCs will also be treated at par with banks in respect of tax breaks on interest received. They will now be able to handle taxes on losses arising out of NPAs.

Government had proposed an amendment to Section 45-IA of the RBI Act 1934 to empower the central bank to supersede the board of NBFCs and enable resolution of financially troubled NBFCs through merger, restructuring or splitting them into viable and non-viable units known as bridge institutions. RBI can now remove auditors, call for audit of any group company of an NBFC and can even decide upon the compensation of senior management. Such comprehensive empowerment can improve public confidence on NBFC sector. RBI will now regulate HFCs, a power that was vested with National Housing Bank (NHB). Out of the 82 HFCs, top five HFCs have a market share of over 90 percent that were more important to be brought under robust regulations.

2.4 Scope for increased flow of credit:

Despite hefty repo rate cuts by RBI in the current rate cycle beginning February 2019, the role of banks in transmitting policy rates has remained subdued. The weighted average lending rates (WALR) on fresh rupee loans hardly decreased by 29 bps and in fact the WALR on outstanding loans increased by seven bps. A further drilling down, the WALR trends will indicate that foreign banks, private banks and PSBs have brought them down by 66, 48 and 25 bps respectively. Similarly, the market share of fresh rupee loans of private banks had gone up to 49.3 percent as against 39.8 percent of PSBs during the fiscal up to August 2019.

Such trend reflects more aggressive role of private banks compared to PSBs that were struggling with high volume of toxic assets. The rest of the market share of 10.9 percent of fresh rupee loans went to other sectors of the economy. Since the bulk of the beneficiaries at the bottom of the pyramid are with PSBs, the flow of credit may not have reached the wider section of the society limiting the revival process. However, with increasing market share of private banks and enhanced lending activism, the benefit is beginning to impact larger segment of borrowers even at lower rung of the society.

Even an overall trend of credit growth of banks did not augur well to push growth prospects. The YOY bank credit growth has been tepid at 10.3 percent as on September 13, 2019 as against 13.5 percent recorded during corresponding period of previous year that reflected marked slowdown in credit off take during current fiscal 2020. The same trend continued even till Q1 of FY22.

Banks can work on new opportunities to increase credit flow based on the recent additional tax concessions extended up to Rs. 1,50,000 on interest on affordable housing loans. The increased allocation under Pradhan Mantri Awas Yozana (PMAY) can open up more scope for retail lending sector. Similarly, the tax concession on home loans now at Rs.2 lakhs will go up to Rs.3.5 lakhs. The added tax concession will be available only to fresh loans to be granted during the financial year 2020. It will increase sudden demand for home loans. With Real estate Regulatory Authority (RERA) institutionalized in many states, construction/housing sector will be better regulated protecting rights of buyers.

With a target of 1.95 crore housing units that were to be constructed in a record time of next two – three years to move towards the objective to provide housing for all by 2022, the sector will get a boost and banks can tap this source which has high cross selling opportunity. But due to pandemic these timelines and targets will get stretched. Similarly, the income tax concession on interest on loans taken to buy electric vehicles can create additional demand for car loans. Eventually even auto industry may gradually shift towards manufacturing electric vehicles to fall in line with the green initiatives. With hardly one percent of people opting for electric vehicles as of now, there will be spurt in buyers in higher tax bracket who can save more. Increase in retail loan portfolio could be possible with the new dispensation. Financing for electric vehicles can be a good source of business for banks in coming years. New modified electric vehicles with innovative features and increased durability of the battery/spare battery are coming into markets creating demand.

Infrastructure sector will be under focus with an expenditure outlay of Rs one trillion to be spent in next five years. Allocation of Rs. 80250 crores for phase – III of Pradhan Mantri Gram Sadak Yozana (PMGSY) for the up-gradation of 1.25 lakh kilometers of road in hinterland will activate many interdependent businesses to boost rural infrastructure. Similarly, under 'National Rural Drinking Water Mission', all rural households are to be provided piped water supply by 2024. Presently, 18 – 20 percent of household has such facility. This will also bring up many rural activities right from laying pipelines, construction of overhead tanks, civil works, job works, and sale of hardware accessories along with job creation. Every such activity brings increased bank collaboration. However, these activities are disrupted due to the spread of virus and local lockdowns.

Proposals to increasingly use of Public Private Partnership (PPP) model by railways and privatization of some of its activities when seen together with increased capex spent of government will benefit many sectors. The proposal to raise foreign currency resources from overseas will open up new opportunities for many sectors of the economy.

2.5 Increased thrust on MSME:

Since MSME and *'Startups'* are known to be critical employment intensive sectors, measures were proposed to increase flow of credit to unleash its potentiality. The angel tax has been addressed and a two percent interest subvention is allowed on fresh loans to be granted to Goods and Service Tax (GST) registered MSMEs for which an allocation of Rs.350 crores is made in UB20. Rationalization of labor laws can help them accelerate formalization of the economy. Corporate tax rate was brought down to 25 percent for firms having turnover of up to Rs.400 crores, raised from Rs.250 crores which will provide relief to 99.3 percent of the 1.5 lakh companies incorporated so far according to the data of Ministry of Corporate Affairs (MCA).

In order to reinforce *'Make in India'* campaign to pump prime manufacturing activity, the import tariffs were calibrated to boost local manufacturing. Increase in customs duty of certain automobile components and electronic devices will increase local manufacturing activities and more so when loans are made available with interest subvention. MSME units will be encouraged to increase production by taking benefit of concessions using digital mode.

When these budgetary sops are seen together with key recommendations of the report of the *'Expert Committee on MSME (Chairman: Mr. U.K. Sinha)'*, it will provide further insight on the emerging potentiality of the sector. Among many far reaching recommendations, the game changing proposals relate to (i) formation of Stressed Asset Fund of Rs.5000 crores for units impacted by change in external environment beyond the control of the entrepreneur (ii) setting up an apex National/State level council for MSMEs (iii) doubling of limits of collateral free loans under Pradhan Mantri MUDRA Yozana and Start up India to increase flow of funds (iv) expansion of scope of SIDBI to be the fulcrum to steer the sector to next level of growth (v) creation of incentives and disincentives to lenders by introducing Rural Infrastructure and Development Fund (RIDF) scheme requiring banks to deposit shortfall in achieving MSME targets. (vi) making it mandatory to source 25 percent of PSU needs from MSME units through GeM portal (vii) expansion of number of MSE Facilitation Council (MSEFC) to help address the delayed payment conundrum of the sector along with strengthening TReDS platform.

At the same time, the government has also directed PSBs to assign credit availability aspects of MSME sector to GM level executive for accelerating flow of credit. It also suggested a well-calibrated monitoring mechanism to institutionalize a weekly feedback in a bid to improve accountability for performance. Despite several expert committees providing guidance and policy interventions from time to time, the plight of MSME continues to be weak. In order to energize the sector, the government had earlier rolled out 12-point MSME outreach initiatives way back in November 2018. One of the most important initiatives was introduction of *'in-principle'* sanction of loans to MSME units up to Rs.1 crore in just 59 minutes. The intending borrower should log into a dedicated website – *'psbloansin59minutes'* which will collect borrower details on line from various digitally connected sources such as income tax department, GST and other sources to provide an in-principal sanction with which the potential borrower can approach any PSB to get the loan. These are some early efforts to speed up credit delivery, if implemented well may facilitate the borrowers.

The demand for external credit of MSME sector is estimated to be in the range of Rs. 37 trillion in 2018 as against formal credit flow of Rs.14.5 trillion that hardly meets half its needs. Bank credit to MSME sector was Rs. 11.7 trillion in March 2015 that could reach Rs.Rs.15.77 trillion by March 2019 working out an annualized growth of 6.9 percent far below the banking industry credit growth. In view of these developments, banks can work towards increasing exposure to MSME sector in a big way and pursue inclusive development.

2.6 Digital banking:

In a bid to encourage digital banking, RBI proposed to increase liquidity support to convert NEFT remittance channel now available up to 7.45

pm into 24/7 mode from December 2019 to remove time limitations in transfer of funds. It is now open 24/7 on all days of the week. A good development in the digital sector. RBI has also proposed an Acceptance Development Fund (ADF) for better servicing of card infrastructure. The government has proposed to levy TDS of two percent on firms that draws cash withdrawals of over Rs.one crore in a year from a bank/post office. It will not apply to government and interbank transactions. This will encourage routing most payments of entities through electronic mode. Henceforth, Merchant Discount Rate (MDR) shall be waived and will not be charged either from member establishment or customers. Banks and RBI will bear the costs from out of potential savings from reduction in transaction costs on account of handling less cash.

It will now be made mandatory for firms with annual turnover of over Rs.50 crores to necessarily provide low-cost digital modes of payment such as BHIMUPI, UPI, Adhaar Pay, debit cards, NEFT and RTGS to its customers to strengthen digital ecosystem. In the backdrop of robust digital infrastructure built in last five years, the digital transactions volume has increased from 796.7 million in October 2016 to 3323.4 million in March 2019. The volume of remittances has increased from Rs.108 trillion to Rs.258 trillion during the period. The ATM base of over two lakhs, 3.8 million POS terminals and a huge debit card base of 825 million at that time in March 2019 can indeed make a big difference to the banking system. These statistics have considerably improved now and have been discussed in later part of the book.

With MDR already waived for transactions up to Rs.2000 and NEFT/RTGS made free, a strong tone for incentivization of digital banking is already set. Next challenge for banks would be to increase use of its strong network of customer base added after financial inclusion agenda was pursued through Pradhan Mantri Jan Dhan Yozana (PMJDY). Just connect with customer through a savings account may not be able to deliver full value. Intense two-way use of bank relationship can only help banks to reduce transaction costs, the ultimate broad purpose of digitization from the point of banks. Efficiency in customer service must however be ensured.

With UB&SPs opening up multiple growth opportunities, banks including PSBs will have to do lot of homework to tap add on business expected from the thrust areas. The corporate tax cuts to the tune of Rs. 1.45 trillion and softened GST rates will make available more funds with entrepreneurs that can plough back into the banking system. In order to unleash digital capability, cyber security standards have to be upgraded keeping the increase in transaction load and customer expectations for safety and security. The vendor interface, after sale service, standard of service level agreements and quality of maintaining the electronic hardware needs more attention. Well-coordinated strategies will have to be put in place to disseminate financial and digital literacy to large mass of customers so that operational risks arising out of intense use of digital mode could be better managed.

Firewalls and protection against fraudulent use of systems will have to be ensured. It may also be a high time to consider institutionalizing a separate loan policy for MSME instead of having a universal loan policy for the bank. The customization of the policy to suit the sector will be in the larger interest to protect the line management. That precisely is the reason that despite several policy innovations, the MSME portfolio is not picking up to its full potentiality. The growth rate of MSME sector more often falls short of industry level credit growth.

The capacity building for human resources in banks in terms of recommendations of Shri G. GopalaKrishna Committee merits full implementation to ensure that efficiency and skill sets of work force improves in specialized areas. Data mining, analytics, economic and market intelligence will have to be used in improving methods of planning resource deployment. Handling business of the levels expected in banking industry in next 3-4 years may not be possible with past methods and practices. Lot of workspace innovation, use of technology such as blockchain technology, AI, robotics, machine learning and deep learning where appropriate will be essential. Banks can take a cue from the economic survey that suggested use of the behavioural economics concept of 'nudge' to encourage desirable social and economic change.

Nudge theory is based on the rationale that human resources often need encouragement or intervention – a nudge – to get going and to enable them to their best. In gist, tapping the umpteen new and innovative sources of business would require equally well-designed business strategies supported by a strong network of implementation and monitoring of performance. Stronger PSBs can stage a comeback to their rightful leadership position in the industry if reforms in internal policies and processes are carried and people competencies are built. Seen from every perspective, the emerging economic slowdown should not be seen as adversity that cannot be tackled but it should be used as a wider growth canvass with potentiality to grow to its full capacity.

More important for PSBs under amalgamation was to make efforts to insulate day- to-day operations from any disruption and continue to put credit growth trajectory intact in the long-term interest of protecting market share and customer patronage. Hence, it is more important to sustain inclusive efforts of banks to revive the economy.

2.7 Citi Bank exit from consumer banking:

In the context of discussing the future growth potentiality of banks, it will be pertinent to discuss the implications of the recent strategic move of Citibank to exit consumer-banking business as part of its global business strategy in Asia and parts of Europe. A commercial call taken by Citi bank that opens up a wide canvass of business opportunities for Indian entities. It intends to exit from 13 international consumer markets including India, Indonesia, China and Taiwan for want of scale of business to compete. The strategic decision to shed consumer banking in these markets is definitely a pointer to host countries to look at the adequacy of their internal ecosystem compatible to retain the global tinge in domestic financial markets. Shying away by global players is an early sign to rejig broader market dynamics. But it will be interesting to find as to why Citi bank decided to exit and how Indian entities could mine this as a business opportunity.

The points of introspection is to see if market players are deprived of an appropriate level playing field to compete and raise the sustainable bar of quality of consumer banking services? Banks deciding to exit a line of business after developing it for decades is a hard option signalling, among others, the likely inappropriateness of domestic operating environment. The related stakeholders need to work in collaboration to create compatible financial markets for coexistence and development of a growth-oriented culture.

It can be recalled that Citibank, the global banking behemoth started India operations way back in 1902. Its umbilical connect with Indian consumers is even older than that of many PSBs. It entered consumer-banking business in 1985. Among foreign banks, Citibank worked hard to develop a consumer base of 2.9 million retail customers. Its credit card base is 2.6 million out of total credit card strength of 61.6 million in February 2021. Its range of credit cards and diversified offerings are popular among the middle- and higher-income groups.

2.8 Consumer banking in India:

There is a clear similarity in the business approach of foreign banks (FBs) in expanding different lines of business, more importantly entry into retail banking that needs granular strategies and wider connect. Dominated by PSBs, domestic banks were operating in a sellers' market integrating concessional/free service costs in their business models itself. As a result, there was a huge gulf between the quality, diversity of products, features, delivery mode, responsiveness and accessibility of services of FBs and other intermediaries. In this league, the services of old generation private banks are considered better than PSBs but their customer connect is highly localized. The cost of services of FBs is considered higher than domestic service providers. Therefore, customer targeting too has a divide with select better placed consumers opting for FBs.

2.9 Impact of bank reforms:

As part of progressive move towards deeper financial sector reforms, the pace of bank reforms and regulatory changes increased creating an enabling environment to grow on a sustainable basis. This change brought domestic banks into play on a greater scale. As part of it, many changes were made that could mature to create new institutions to improve the efficiency of the financial system. For example, the entry of private sector banks with latest technology began to create intense competition to FBs. Joining the journey of reforms, PSBs began to improve their operational efficiency amid technological transformation. Their appetite for retail banking picked up faster pace. With the wide network of PSBs already penetrated well into urban/rural agglomerations with liberal RBI branch expansion policy, augmenting retail customer base was relatively cost efficient with inbuilt cross-selling ability.

The aggression of new generation private banks combined with the newfound inclination of PSBs to compete in retail banking services, debut of differentiated banks – payment banks and small finance banks, expanded network of Non – banks including Fintech companies posed intense competition to FBs. The expanded turf and form of domestic financial market players worked as a tipping point for FBs to reach close to a stage to consider consumer banking business as a *'not so profitable'* line of business.

The post reform phase of banking thus moved consumer banking from a phase of choice for domestic players to necessity to survive amid rising competition. FBs have a choice to wind up any line of business or even exit from overseas markets but not so for domestic financial intermediaries. With such shift in consumer banking landscape, strategies of banks tend to change, particularly when entities have better and more attractive business options.

2.10 Early signs of change:

The shift in business strategies began when competition started stiffening. Having started operations in 1858, even prior to Citibank, the UK based Standard Chartered Bank with 100 branches across 43 cities began to expand different lines of business in India. But in 2015, it decided to scale down its unsecured retail and corporate business in India as a part of its global restructuring move. The phenomenon of expansion and contraction in the lines of business has been a function of forward view of FBs.

The Hongkong and Shanghai Banking Corporation (HSBC) Limited having started its operations in 1853 expanded its foothold in corporate and retail segment. It provided the first ATM services in India in 1987 announcing the shift to alternate delivery mode of banking services. Despite experience of working in India for several decades, in May, 2016, it decided to scale down its retail presence bringing down its branch network from 50 spread across 29 cities to 26 branches across 14 cities. It roped in many of its existing clients on to digital mode to continue relationship.

Recently the only branch of South Africa's second largest lender – First Rand opened in 2009 converted it into a representative office. It did not look too attractive for it to continue its full-fledged branch operations.

Historically, FBs as a group have been low on asset creation but they continue to play a differentiating role by bringing diversity, expansion of financial markets, import of better automation strategies, innovations in introducing risk sharing products and services aligned with risk-based pricing. Despite their low presence, setting better operating standards and seamless digital access has been their main stay.

One of BIS papers points out that 'The entry of foreign banks brings large benefits to host countries' financial systems and economies at large. Benefits stem from efficiency gains brought about by new technologies, products and management techniques as well as from increased competition stimulated by new entrants. Moreover, as foreign banks may have greater access to resources from abroad, they have more stable funding and lending patterns than domestic banks. They also hold a more geographically diversified credit portfolio and hence would not be as affected during periods of stress in the host country'.

Thus, FBs need to be a part of Indian financial markets for cross boarder connect and sharing of best practices. Their consistent move to thin down presence in India needs to be reviewed to set right the policy framework governing financial markets.

2.11 Regulatory shift:

The operational presence of FBs in India has been through branch network while representative offices are meant for building bilateral relationship. Looking to the spill over risks due to interconnectedness and drawn from the experience of global financial crisis – 2008, RBI changed its stance leaning towards domestic incorporation of FBs. Accordingly, in 2013, it urged FBs to adopt the model of incorporating wholly owned subsidiaries (WOS) in India for a near national treatment. The change is aimed to (i) protect local retail depositors, (ii) ease the resolution process, and (iii) afford greater regulatory comfort.

Accordingly, two FBs opted to convert into WOS – (i) DBS Singapore and (ii) SBM (Mauritius). As a result of level playing field extended to it, DBS Singapore could acquire the ailing Lakshmi Vilas Bank (LVB) and gained a wider entry to consolidate its presences in India.

2.12 Presence of FBs:

The total number of FBs stands at 46 with a branch network of 308 in March 2020. Their representative offices engaged in non-transactional businesses are significantly large standing at 37. The share of asset size of FBs to total assets of Scheduled Commercial Banks (SCBs) is placid working out close to 7 percent in March 2020 a notch lower than 7.2 percent recorded in 2010. Their market share of credit in 2000 was at 8 percent that came down to 4 percent by 2020 whereas the market share of private banks in credit moved up from 12.5 percent to 36 percent during the same period, a significant rise compared to FBs.

Though their India footprint has been stable, their India linked credit and investment exposure has been rising outside India. It is bigger than the loan and investment book in India. The synergy of their India foothold is visible from the large number of representative offices and their potential business linkages between host country – India and their home country.

Historically, FBs have never been very keen to expand balance sheet size but the risk appetite for 'off balance sheet exposure' has been better and thrust has been on earning fee-based income. They are accordingly active in derivatives, treasury operations and advisory and ancillary services adding to their 'other income'. Priority sector lending targets meant for FBs were mostly complied indirectly. The introduction of priority sector lending certificates (PSLCs) permitted by RBI in April 2016 encouraged banks to expand lending to priority sector and sell the excess portfolio to banks that have shortfall in achieving the targets. PSLCs helped many banks including FBs to comply with the norms.

2.13 Shift in business strategies:

The move of Citibank provides cue to all stakeholders, more importantly, the commercial banks. A business strategy of any line of banking business is sensitive to changing business environment. Looking initially as potentially attractive business strategy, a line of business grows, develops, earns, peaks and survives but entry of more attractive and paying lines of business can challenge relevance of existing lines of business. Consumer banking business in the case of Citibank is a classic case when more focused persuasion of wealth management and institutional business in the current context looks more promising and attractive.

A line of business may therefore loose sheen when better alternate business opportunities are poised to replace the old line of business. Business models evolve not by the financial entities alone but are an interface between regulations and government priorities. If it turns not so attractive from the long-term perspective, such businesses may get phased out. No commercial entity likes to be in a line of business when better alternatives evolve with time and better macroeconomic settings.

A recent study on the wealthy by Capgemini titled 'World Wealth Report 2020' has revealed that the population of high-net-worth individuals (HNI) in India has increased to 2.63 lakhs in March 2019 up from 2.56 lakh in March 2018. They were just 1.53 lakhs in 2010.

Similarly, the number of Indian middle-class individuals is close to 350 million rising from 160 million in 2010. Such rising upper middle class and HNIs opens up a well-diversified market for wealth management. With globalized corporate sector connect; new business opportunities arise adding to the scope for institutional businesses and cross boarder trade. Such select class of affluent consumers can afford service charges to get benefit of product reengineering and risk sharing value propositions that does not normally exist in consumer banking.

2.14 DBS Bank to pitch:

DBS Bank India Ltd, one of the two WOS of FBs is keen to buy the consumer banking business of Citibank to further consolidate its presence in India. It already gained strength with takeover of LVB. Besides a strong customer base close to 3 million, the retail banking assets are put at Rs.32 billion.

Moreover, the work of decades of Citibank to build relationship with socially better-placed community can provide a perpetual source of business to the buyer. It all depends upon the terms of valuation of the outgoing business for Citibank and incoming business value for intending buyer. Striking a deal with win win value proposition is a challenging task.

It needs to be seen whether all these businesses will be sold together or piecemeal. Also, payment consideration, in cash vs stock, will be a critical determinant to decide the eventual buyer. Since Citi functions in India through a "branch route" versus a WOS, the transaction will mostly be asset sale. As a result, the process of non-disruptive switchover could take 6-12 months until a final deal is shaped up.

2.15 Opportunities from consumer banking:

The consistent move of FBs to move away from consumer banking business in India is an opportunity for Indian entities but it merits a deeper study to find missing gaps in the policies, governance and processes of financial sector. Banks and Non-banks should work in collaboration with regulatory agencies to make consumer banking more cost efficient by moving both processing and delivery to digital mode. Enhancing cyber security, engaging in imparting digital and financial literacy to users will hold the key. In a developing economy any sign of withdrawal by competitors needs to be averted so that a fully developed financial market exist.

The consumer-banking products can be made affordable but more important is to protect its viability in the long run to stay in business. Similarly, the borrower community, non-government organizations (NGOs), trading and business forums should educate and inculcate better loan repayment culture to ensure availability of consumer banking services on sustainable basis. The rising bad loan in the banking system is a social menace that can eat into future potentiality. It may eventually lead to slow decline of risk appetite of lenders even in consumer banking sector. So, the ecosystem for recovery of loans has to be improved by banks while working upon business growth.

May be drawing from the spirit of bank nationalization, mass of consumers tends to develop a psyche that costs of banks are to be socialized. Even levy of actual transaction costs is resisted and many consumer forums look at them as exploitation. Digitization of transaction can be a differentiator. But unless there is social acceptability of actual cost of delivering financial services, there cannot be equitable development of competitive ecosystem. The focus of all stakeholders should be galvanized to improve the long-term sustainability of consumer banking. Unless the wakeup call by FBs is taken up with seriousness at all levels, the Indian consumers will be deprived of global standard of risk-adjusted services that can be paying in the long run.

The future growth of banks will depend on how they act now based on well-articulated strategies and pave a futuristic vision to position growth in next 4-5 years. The knack will depend on the ability of banks to link synergy of business opportunities built around the innovative policies well-articulated in interim budget, union budget, stimulus packages, National Monetization Pipeline, National infrastructure Pipeline and so on with a near term and long-term vision.

The consolidation among PSBs could be used to attain greater economies of scale and efficiency that should lend stability, sustainability and robust growth. Driven by the changes due to pandemic and pent-up demand creating newer opportunities, the regulators have provided many support measures. Government too has been active in standing by the entrepreneurs who have been adversely impacted by the pandemic. All these put together can bolster growth opportunities for banks.

CHAPTER – 3

POLICY IMPLICATIONS OF UNION BUDGET 2021-22

Designed to fight the implications of coronavirus pandemic, the Union Budget 2021-22 (UB22) has been built upon six key pillars – (i) health and well-being, (ii) physical, financial capital and infrastructure, (iii) inclusive development for aspirational India, (iv) reinvigorating human capital, (v) innovation and R&D and (vi) minimum government and maximum governance. Providing a clear precedence to growth over fiscal prudence, the fiscal deficit is allowed to reach a high of 9.5 percent of GDP in 2020-21 and intends to spend Rs.11.7 trillion during the current fiscal taking the total expenditure to Rs. 34.5 trillion that goes to Rs 34.83 trillion in next fiscal creating enough space for building infrastructure and increasing allocations to different sectors of the economy.

Accordingly, more spending under capital expenditure is envisaged during the ongoing recovery phase to pull the economy from the lingering impact of the pandemic shock. An out-of-box approach is adopted to carve out methods to pump prime economic growth to catch up speed going beyond the pre-Covid levels. Such innovative measures create huge opportunities to various sectors of the economy and equally so to financial sector.

It is expected that the fiscal deficit will be slowly reduced to 6.8 percent of GDP by next financial year 2021-22 and eventually stretching fiscal consolidation to 4.5 percent by only 2025-26. With inflation back within the comfort level of RBI to clock 4.59 percent in December 2020, the down side risks to the economy are abating. Since many economies have to push the growth trajectory with increased expenditure to revive activity and employment, India has taken the lead to forge ahead in creating a better development-oriented ecosystem.

Amid the buoyant budgetary measures, right set of opportunities can be identified in UB22 for banking sector. Out of the six pillars, financial sector is focused in second pillar – *'Physical, financial capital and infrastructure'*.

As part of first pillar, the priority of health care and medical infrastructure needs has been identified. A 137 percent rise in allocation is envisaged with budgetary provision of Rs. 2,23,846 crores for health sector. These funds will be channelized among others, to the flagship scheme – pradhan mantri 'AatmaNirbhar Swasth Bharat Yojana'. It is set to strengthen health infrastructure for preventive, curative care and to enhance sustainable wellbeing of the society. In addition, Rs. 35000 crores is allocated for massive vaccine campaign that can infuse confidence and protect people.

The second pillar relates to evolving growth centric stable and robust financial system to play a more significant role in financial intermediation to support ambitious development plans to help overcome the shocks of the pandemic. Hence, looking to the evolving policy priorities many long-term challenges of banking and financial sector are addressed in UB22 with appropriate measures in transforming banks into growth engines of the economy. In order to calibrate such striking measures, UB22 has taken into consideration the state of the banking system.

3.1 Rising stress in banks:

Though banks have been grappling with bad loans for many years, its potential rise due to Covid has suddenly called for urgent action to fight the menace. The financial stability report (FSR) of RBI already alerted banks about the impending deterioration in the state of asset quality.

Though NPAs have come down to 7.5 percent in September 2020, partly due to the standstill clause in the asset classification, they are set to zoom, once it is lifted. NPAs then may shoot to a level of 13.5 percent in baseline stress and to a high of 14.8 percent in severe stress. PSBs having higher share of NPAs may end up having 17.6 percent of toxic assets by September 2021. Rising NPAs shrinks the capital adequacy ratio (CAR) of the banks to a low of 12.5 percent due to rise in risk-weighted assets that will severely limit bank's ability to expand fresh loan portfolio.

Banks were needed to maintain a minimum CAR of 10.875 percent till March 31, 2021 and 11.5 percent from October 1, 2021 in terms of Basel Committee norms. However, its implementation is now postponed to October 2021. Due to rise in NPAs, it is feared that some weak PSBs may even breach the minimum mark of CAR preventing them from lending further. Considering the fragile capital base, UB22 pegged capital infusion at Rs.20,000 crores. Keeping in view the huge impact of the asset quality erosion, capital allocations made in UB22 may not be able to shore up CAR of PSBs to a great extent.

Looking to the huge collateral impact of rising bad loans on the economy due to restricted lending capacity of banks, a quick transformative strategy could be to form a separate entity to transfer the contaminated asset portfolio to enable banks to focus on fresh lending. Taking the practical constraints of banks, UB22 rightly proposed setting up a special purpose vehicle (SPV) – a dedicated Asset Reconstruction Company (ARC) on the lines of a bad bank to take over NPAs of commercial banks. The idea is not new. Such a proposal was mooted by Indian Banks Association (IBA) in 2017 but was not considered, as the magnitude of crisis at that time did not merit its formation.

3.2 Formation of ARC (Bad Bank):

It is a quick opportunity for banks to transfer the burden of NPAs to the proposed specially designed state-owned ARC in one go. The asset size of banks will come down depending upon the volume of NPAs transferred to it. The CAR of the bank – the driving factor to push fresh credit will rise due to reduction in the asset size in the balance sheets of banks. It will create additional space for banks to start fresh lending to the distressed borrowers to hasten recovery. Banks will also be relieved of the rigor of pursuing for recovery of huge stock of NPAs that can now be transferred to the bad bank. Thus, banks could be de-stressed to a large extent reinvigorating better operational efficiency.

More time and effort saved from managing bad loans can be used for fresh lending operations. Banks can also work on preventing accumulation of fresh NPAs by closely following up and nursing the existing borrowers. Globally, setting up bad bank is considered as a quick remedy. Government of Malaysia had set up a bad bank – Danaharta bank to tackle menace of toxic loans arising out of the Asian Financial crisis. The launch of Troubled Asset Relief Program (TARP) program of US Federal Reserve to tackle the global financial crisis in 2008 was also on same lines. If Bad Bank is used as an effective tool to ward off the crisis, it can work well. It will open up many opportunities for banks to participate more actively to revive the economy. The risk appetite and profitability of banks can increase with scope to add new volume of business.

It will also open up an opportunity for banks to look into the reasons for repeated resurgence of asset quality woes and how it can be internally fixed by the banks. Since the banking system has to operate on a sustained business model to remain commercially viable, banks should be well equipped with requisite policies, processes, systemic controls, internal skills and methodology to manage deposits, lend and recover the loans in normal course of banking activity.

Banks having well established credit risk management policy may have to review the systems and plug weaknesses, if any to create a healthy and sustained credit portfolio targeting market driven risk adjusted returns. The economic survey 2020-21 already observed that the slackness on the part of banks and auditors in managing the asset quality have led to build up of huge toxic assets.

Banks need to guard and ensure that formation of a bad bank should not develop any sense of complacency among borrowing community to adversely impact the credit culture of the country. A sound, sustainable and well-regulated banking system is *sine quo non* for an aspiring India. Hence, the ARC to take over bad loans should be used as a space to improve the internal credit management systems and avail the benefit of bad banks as a solution to strengthen its internal credit management skills. Banks should also design appropriate methodology to educate the borrowing community to inculcate responsible borrowing and repaying culture.

3.3 Development finance institution (DFI):

The next strategic move is a proposal to set up a DFI with an initial capital of Rs. 20000 crores, partly funded by the government. It is designed to meet the long-term financial needs of the infrastructure sector. It will be formed with India Infrastructure Finance Company limited (IIFCL) to take a bigger shape. Before subsuming it with IIFCL, its bad debts close to Rs. 4500 crores were to be fully provided so that a clean start of the new entity is possible. The DFI will be known as National Bank for Financing Infrastructure and development (NaBFID) to operate on a larger scale after necessary enabling amendments were made to RBI Act 1934 and Banking Regulation Act 1949. It was expected that it will raise and finance up to Rs. 5 trillion in next 3-5 years to fund long term infrastructure projects without causing disruption to the commercial banking system.

With greater participation of private sector more competition should emerge in lending to infrastructure sector at competitive prices and banks will have to tone up their internal capabilities to join funding for working capital needs. Scope for associating with NaBFID is possible with funded and non-funded products of the banks. Ample opportunity to shore up exchange rate earnings and fee-based income can be tapped.

It is a well-known fact that the business model of banks is built upon the deposits. With the change in the societal spending and saving trends, the duration of term deposits is shrinking – say in the range of 1-3 years and some up to 5 years. Banks are not having enough funds for longer duration. Most of the infrastructure projects are of longer duration with risks of cost and time overruns. Banks are thus exposed to risks of asset liability mismatches in lending to infrastructure projects and formation of a different entity could be a plausible solution. But coordination among these institutions can generate synergy to all stakeholders in the value chain.

After the recent failure of some of the NBFCs on account of liquidity stress, the constraints of lenders have become obvious. Even the risk appetite of banks to lend to large corporate sector borrowers has come down to balance risks. Therefore, a DFI with a suitable mix of long-term liabilities will be better able to balance the credit risk in financing long-term projects.

It can be recalled that based on the recommendations of Mr. S.H. Khan Committee on – 'Harmonizing the role and operations of development financial institutions and banks in India' set up by RBI in 1997, the concept of universal bank entered the banking lexicon ending the term lending institutions. With more focus on building infrastructure now with longer gestation period, increasing shift of preferences of savers towards short term, the increasing risks of asset liability mismatches, re-induction of developmental financial institutions is needed. With diversification, expansion and deepening of investment options, increasing knowledge of optimizing savings, bank consumers prefer to park their savings with banks for shorter duration exacerbating the asset liability risks. With lending space well carved out with formation of DFI, banks can tap the emerging potentiality to derive the right synergy.

3.4 Capex thrust:

Since capital expenditure (capex) has the potentiality to generate employment, revive demand and support livelihood, UB22, even at the cost of fiscal prudence has harped on spending more. Accordingly, it increased capex allocations in various sectors. At 15.9 percent, the capex share allocation in total spend is the highest in over a decade.

The government has not only increased the revised capex budget during the current financial year by 6.6 percent taking it to around Rs.4.4 trillion, UB22 raised it more conspicuously by 25 percent to raise it to Rs.5.54 trillion. In addition, it will also provide Rs.2 trillion to states for spending on capex. Since the private sector investment slowed down, capex has been the main casualty of the pandemic as new projects fell by 87.6 percent.

As the economy recovers from the downturn, private sector too will be expanding fast. Diversification and better capacity utilization shall be providing boost to the private investment that can increase gross fixed capital formation (GFCF) in FY22 and beyond. With thrust on infrastructure development such as roads, ports and highways and health infrastructure, lending opportunities will increase for banks. Thus, these re-prioritized allocations while opening up employment and demand for goods and services will also provide enough opportunities to the financial intermediaries to improve their business volume and profitability.

3.5 Long-term measures:

While successfully articulating methods to tackle the near-term challenges of the pandemic, the medium and long-term measures have also been kept in view. Willingness to push the reform button on several fronts can change the future course of growth. The disinvestment process can transform the overall productivity and transparency in policy can invite larger overseas investments. The intent to privatize two of the PSBs and one state owned insurance company – details of which are yet to unfold will be an effort to improve the corporate governance and to shrink government ownership. Way forward, the government sources have indicated that it is looking for 20 SBI sized banks to be the reckoning force in financial intermediation in a bid to catch up global size.

Similarly, increase of foreign direct investments (FDI) in insurance industry from 49 percent to 74 percent and life insurance behemoth – Life insurance company (LIC) set to access capital market are efforts to dilute government stake and to increase private stakeholder participation. The coordinated role of banks and insurance outfits under private ownership can draw vast synergy for the mutual growth in the reinvented form.

These prospects when seen together with implementation of three editions of 'Atmanirhar Bharat Abhiyaan (ANBA) – self-reliant India with an estimated allocation of Rs. 27.1 lakh crores, banks can look for its multiplier impact on business opportunities on both assets and liability products. Since many of the government-sponsored schemes, affordable housing and real estate projects could not work well due to the lockdown and its aftermath, banks can look forward for their more active participation creating demand for credit.

As further part of ANBA, a Production-Linked Incentive (PLI) scheme was introduced to create global manufacturing champions intended to boost domestic manufacturing for 13 identified sectors. PLI is designed to attract foreign manufacturers to move base to India and to create an inviting ecosystem. The aim of the scheme is to generate more employment and cut down the country's reliance on imports from other countries. The program has an allocation worth Rs.1.97 lakh crore in UB22 with its benefits spread over a period of five years. PLI can go a long way in increasing production activities adding to the scope for banks to lend.

The well designed PLI scheme is to be seen together with proposals in UB22 to shape a Mega Investment Textile Parks (MITP) scheme to be rolled out with seven textile parks in next three years. Increased scope for road construction under the flagship programs of Bharatmala Pariyozana to establish wider road connectivity, setting up National high way corridors and implementation of National Rail plan for India – 2030 are some more long-term policies to create multiple opportunities and employability.

Other long-term proposals having potentiality to open up opportunities include allocation of Rs. 2,87,000 crores to *'Jal Jeevan mission'* to provide water tap connections to 2.86 crore households to be operationalized in next five years. Swachh Bharat, Swasth Bharat scheme gets Rs. 1,41,678 crores for Urban Swachh Bharat Mission 2.0 to be used in next 5 years.

The activated implementation of ongoing schemes such as Smart city projects, PMAY, PMGSY, the employment guarantee schemes, direct benefit transfers etc can provide ample opportunities to banks.

While expanding its spending spree and allocations to different sectors of the economy to tackle the ongoing distress, the benefits of many of the reinforced activities will flow back into the banking sector in one form or other. Taking cue from the respite provided to banks in the form of regulatory relaxations, it will create demand and open up scope for multiple business activities with thrust on lending.

The postponement of implementation of last tranche of Basel – III and net stable funding ratio (NFSR) norms till October 1, 2021 will create necessary elbowroom for banks to cope with Covid19 induced challenges. While taking benefit of the new state-owned ARC – NARC for dealing with the stock of bad loans, banks will get an opportunity to streamline its rigor in credit risk management.

With improvement in the rigor in implementing the debt resolution tools, enhanced regulatory surveillance and robust insolvency and bankruptcy laws, the borrowing community need to be educated to realize that repaying bank loans is essential to remain in business. A bad loan not only prevents banks from recycling funds but it also mars the risk appetite of banks. It prevents growth prospects of future generation of entrepreneurs due to non-availability of credit through formal financial system.

Banks and borrowing community should use this new initiative as an opportunity to mend the credit culture in the long-term interest of growth. The free flow of growth adrenaline through UB22 was hailed as a well-designed historic expansionary policy stance to put India on high growth trajectory. The bold initiative to set up a Bad bank should be able to nudge the banks to shape well. The diversity and expansionary initiatives of UB22 and reforms in financial sector can be a big differentiator for banks to position on sound footing – way ahead.

CHAPTER – 4

FINANCIAL INCLUSION IN INDIA – PROGRESS AND PROSPECTS

Financial inclusion (FI) is increasingly recognized world over as a key driver of economic growth and poverty alleviation. On August 17, 2021, the RBI launched a Financial Inclusion Index (FI-Index) to track the process of ensuring access to financial services, timely and adequate credit for vulnerable groups such as weaker sections and low-income groups at an affordable cost. The FI-Index is a comprehensive index, incorporating details of banking, investment, insurance, postal, as well as the pension sector in consultation with government and respective sector regulators. While the FI-index will serve as a barometer, it will be pertinent to understand the efforts and outcome in the direction.

FI is broadly a process of connecting the society with formal financial system known globally to have multiplier impact to bring about socioeconomic transformation in the society. Access to formal finance can boost job creation, reduce vulnerability to economic shocks and increase investment in human capital. Thus, persuasion of FI is mainly intended to (i) provide access to affordable financial services to the society to enable them to save, borrow, and remit funds to settle financial transactions. FI also covers social security financial products like insurance, pension annuities and bank assurance products. (ii) pool or mobilize money lying with individuals by developing robust financial network through suitable savings schemes and assured returns to the saving community so as to provide finance to enterprises (iii) spread a culture of commercial and business orientation that can add to the economic prosperity and well-being of the society. (iv) eventually develop a well-informed, financially and digitally literate society by optimizing financial resources that can plough back into the economy in the form of increased gross domestic product (GDP) and higher tax collections.

4.1 The genesis of FI:

With the introduction of *'social control'* on banks dating back to 1967, banks began to disseminate services to not merely to the rich and mighty urban class, but also to people at the lower strata of society to uplift their economic well-being. Banks began an arduous journey to move from 'class banking' to 'mass banking' that still continues. The momentum to connect the banking with people gained more prominence after bank nationalization in 1969/1980. It was intended to hasten reach of banking services to masses, a welfare concept enunciated in the social control of banks that was strengthened further with ownership of majority of banks with the government.

During expanding banking services, maintaining minimum balance in the account and need for introduction to open a new bank account was a hurdle in connecting masses with the formal system that were mostly not literate and lacks awareness. RBI then rightly introduced, for the first time, the system of allowing customers to open 'no frill' account, a product designed for propagating mass banking. Such accounts can be opened with *'zero balance'* based on simplified *'Know your customer'* (KYC) norms. These liberalized banking facilities began to spread banking and savings habits.

The expanding form of banks gradually made inroads into hinterland when liberalized branch expansion policy renewed thrust on opening new bank branches. It was the *'Report of the committee on Financial Inclusion'* (2008) (Chairman: Dr. C. Rangarajan) that brought Financial Inclusion (FI) to the centre stage of formal policy making in banks. It was the first time that RBI directed banks to adopt a three-year board approved FI policy (FIP) beginning its first phase from April 1, 2010.

The board of banks is also made accountable to ensure that road maps articulated in the FIP are implemented to achieve the desired FI targets.

In order to facilitate implementation of FI, RBI for the first time, permitted use of intermediaries where banks can engage business facilitators and Business Correspondents (BCs). The BC model allowed 'Cash in – Cash out' transactions at remote location much closer to the rural population to enable last mile reach. In order to strengthen the BC model of delivery and help prospective users to identify BC having good service track record, a BC Registry has been launched under the aegis of IBA. For capacity building and to ensure certain minimum standards of service rendered by the BCs, a BC Certification course through Indian Institute of Banking and Finance (IIBF) has also been introduced.

4.2 Financial Inclusion Policies:

The FIPs articulated by each bank's board aims at keeping self-set targets in respect of rural brick and mortar branches to be opened, BCs to be engaged, coverage of un-banked villages with population above 2000 and as well as below 2000. In the meantime, RBI dispensed the tag of 'no frill' savings bank accounts in 2012 and designated them as Basic Savings Bank Deposit (BSBD) accounts to standardize the spread of banking to far-flung geographies. Relaxed KYC norms have been allowed for BSBD accounts with aggregate balance not to exceed Rs. 50,000 with credits into account not exceeding Rs. One lakh. Adhaar Cards to be accepted as proof of identity as well as for address proof.

RBI also added micro lending products, specifically designed and oriented, more importantly for rural areas to eligible farmers for farm sector enterprise known as Kisan Credit Cards (KCCs) and for general businesses as General Credit Cards (GCCs). RBI has been monitoring implementation of FIPs on monthly basis. In order to effectively implement FIPs, the tasks were disaggregated and disseminated down up to the branch level. Branch level functionaries should ensure that the assigned targets are achieved to speed up the journey of FI.

These 3-year FI policies of banks are expected to create a road map of steps to be taken towards pursuing inclusive banking in villages with population of over 2000. The purpose is to reach banking services to hitherto unbanked areas and to expand outreach.

4.3 Delivery infrastructure:

Liberal expansion of network of bank branches and touch points is essential in the journey of FI. RBI has, from time to time simplified and opened up wider scope to establish new branches with a balanced focus on penetrating rural and hilly terrains. In addition to the classification of branches into Metro, Urban, Semi-urban and Rural, RBI introduced another set of segregation of bank branches into 6 tiers. Under the new policy, domestic banks are permitted to freely open branches in Tier 2 to Tier 6 centres with population of less than 1 lakh under general permission where they can open branches and report to RBI instead of seeking specific centre wise prior approval. In North-Eastern States and Sikkim, domestic banks can open branches without having any permission from RBI.

With the objective of further liberalizing, general permission to domestic banks (other than RRBs) for opening branches in Tier 1 centres, RBI permitted branch expansion, subject to certain conditions. Compulsory requirement of opening branches in Un-banked Villages is put as a condition in permitting opening of branches in Tier – I centre. RBI directed banks to allocate at least 25% of the total number of branches opened at Tier – I centres during a year for opening new branches in un-banked (Tier 5 and Tier 6) rural centres during the year.

RBI has relaxed the branch authorisation guidelines in 2017 wherein fixed-point Business Correspondent outlets serving for more than 4 hours a day and five days a week are treated on par with physical brick and mortar branches. An exclusive fund viz., Financial Inclusion Fund (FIF) has been created to support adoption of technology and capacity building with an initial corpus of Rs.2000 crore.

Further, the entry of new private banks and their branch network has also been added to the banking infrastructure more notably, branches of Small Finance Banks and Payment banks. This is intended to incentivize banks to spread banking in unbanked villages that may not necessarily be lucrative for banks. The idea is to cross subsidize the revenues at the two groups of branches and to spread network of branches across the geography. Among payment banks, Indian Post Payment Bank (IPPB) has the potentiality to leverage the vast network of Department of Posts (DOP) with 1.55 lakh Post Offices, more than 3 lakh postmen and Grameen Dak Sewaks to further scale up FI initiatives in the country.

Thus, the expanded network of branches when seen together with spread of business correspondents and alternate delivery channels created a strong delivery infrastructure more focused on deposits and remittances but are yet to develop in terms of ability to disseminate credit to the mass of customers connected to the banking system. With all the efforts, number of bank branches works out to 147210 by September 2019. Number of bank branches per 100000 works out to 14.72 in 2017 ranking at 76 while the global average is 18.13 branches. Considerable improvement is desired to push FI and to expand scope of access.

4.4 Digital penetration:

In the journey towards FI, in addition to network of bank branches, advancement of technology had a catalytic role. By using integrated core banking technology, banks started developing a strong network of alternate electronic delivery channels at a much faster pace. Increased mobile connectivity, mobile network, Internet services were made accessible and affordable to people at the bottom of the pyramid. As a result, the number of POS terminals increased from 12,11,890 in September 2015 to 45, 89,727 by September 2019 while the number of debit cards increased from 604 million to close to 835 million during the same period. The number of ATMs reached 210086 by December 2019. But still there is lot of scope for increasing the ATM network.

India is having 21.74 ATMs per 100000 adult population ranking at 111 when the global average is 56.11 ATMs per 100000 adult population.

Close to 1200 Fintech companies collaborate with banks to increase digital outreach in different forms. 45 wallet players, 50 UPI – based payments service providers and 142 banks on the UPI platform are actively collaborating with each other to deliver services to customers. E-rupi, a new digital innovation is introduced. It is a QR code or SMS string-based instrument that will be sent to beneficiary through mobile phone. Such digital innovative spread extends to telecom companies, e-commerce entities, banks, Internet companies and even messaging applications. As a result of proliferation of such financial sector touch points, the scope for FI through digital penetration increased significantly.

4.5 Electronic payment Mode:

Coterminous with expanded digital infrastructure, facilities of electronic payment gateways for online payments have also been well developed. As larger part of RBI policy to promote digital inclusion, making online remittances through NEFT and RTGS in savings bank accounts made free from January 2020 is indeed significant. It is also now made available on 24/7 basis facilitating quick fund transfer round the clock. The account number and Indian Financial Systems (IFSC) code is becoming popular to remit funds from one end to other. The MDR – the charges that merchants have to pay to banks on transactions done on debit/Credit were waived while presenting the union budget 2019-20.

Companies with a turnover of Rs.50 crores or more are mandated to provide free facility of payment through Ru-pay debit card and UPI, QR code to customers from January 2020 and tax of 2 percent will be levied on entities drawing cash of over Rs.1 crore during a year. It is intended to discourage cash transactions. In view of recent efforts, digital payment volumes have seen considerable growth. The Central Bank Digital Currency (CBDC) is another possibility with many other countries actively experimenting to replace physical currency.

RBI vision for digital payments and settlement system – 2019-2021 released in May 2019 clearly intended to *"empower every Indian with access to a bouquet of e-payment options that are safe, secure, convenient, quick and affordable".*

In the same realm, the "Report of the high-level committee on deepening of digital payments (Chairman: Nandan Nilekani)" envisaged a tenfold increase in digital payments in the next three years. RBI reinforces easing digital payment foothold with several continuing collaborative measures that can evolve a robust and seamless payment ecosystem.

Enhancing access to financial touch points and reducing cost of access has been the twin drivers of digital inclusion. The recent growth in digital banking infrastructure could bring about a cultural shift in the intensity of use of electronic mode of payments and settlement, more encouraging is its adoption even in hinterland with the active use of POS terminals, QR codes, digital wallets based on rising broad band speed and easy access. Moreover, the introduction of new type of PPIs will go a long way in deepening FI through further digital penetration.

4.6 Game changing initiatives:

The Government initiated the National Mission for Financial Inclusion (NMFI) and introduced a scheme to ensure that every unbanked family to have at least one bank account for connecting people with the formal banking system. Known as PMJDY, the scheme was floated in August, 2014 to provide universal banking services based on the guiding principles of banking the unbanked, securing the unsecured, funding the unfunded and serving un-served and underserved areas.

A digital pipeline has been laid for the implementation of PMJDY through linking of Jan-Dhan account with mobile and Aadhaar [Jan Dhan-Aadhaar-Mobile (JAM)]. The trinity has connected millions of hitherto unbanked families. Banks have measured up to the spirit of FI and opened 380 million savings accounts as on 12/2/2020 of which PSBs have opened 303 million accounts working out close to 80 percent. Involvement of PSBs in making the scheme realize its objective has contributed substantially to take FI forward.

In order to move towards creating a universal social security system for all Indians, especially the poor and the under-privileged, three ambitious Jan Suraksha Schemes or Social Security Schemes were designed. They pertain to Insurance and Pension Sector that were announced by the Government in the Budget for 2015-16. The schemes were launched on 9th May, 2015, for providing life & accident risk insurance and social security at a very affordable cost namely (a) Pradhan Mantri Suraksha Bima Yojana and (b) Pradhan Mantri Jeevan Jyoti Yojana and (c) Atal Pension Yojana. Pradhan Mantri Vaya Vandana Yojana to protect elderly aged 60 years and above was initially opened for subscription for a period of one year i.e. from 4th May 2017 to 3rd May 2018.

Similarly, Pradhan Mantri MUDRA Yozana was rolled out to develop micro entrepreneurship where collateral free loans could be granted by banks up to Rs. 10 lakhs. Under this scheme, borrowers can avail business loans ranging from Rs.50,000 to Rs.10 lakh on the basis of the Sishu, Kishor, and Tarun categories. MUDRA Loans are offered under the Pradhan Mantri Mudra Yojana (PMMY). It is an effort for lending inclusion of entrepreneurs as a broader part of FI.

The purpose is to prompt people to avail small loans and start their own enterprise so that job seekers could be converted into job providers. These flagship schemes can take progress of FI to the next level but the potential beneficiaries should know about them.

4.7 Financial literacy and credit counseling:

Lack of knowledge on using banking relationship for prosperity is one of the key limiting factor in taking FI to the next level – deepening customer connect. The society connected to the banking system is simply unaware of use of banking relationship and about its utility to save, borrow and remit funds. Regulator expects banks to educate customers on how to use the bank account for social well-being. But banks engrossed in their primary responsibility to safeguard stakeholder interest are simply not able to disseminate knowledge to its customers. This gap in information and knowledge is keeping huge banking infrastructure under used.

Realizing this fact, RBI has set up financial literacy centres (FLCs) in select blocks. But RBI efforts in developing an informed society equipped with financial and digital literacy are a far-fetched aspiration. The efforts are still at a nascent stage. RBI has directed that all rural bank branches should develop into financial literacy centres but with the kind of asset quality issues, branches may not be able to fulfil such a tall responsibility.

In order to build capacity and skills, and sensitize the Counsellors of FLCs and rural banks' branch managers for delivering basic financial literacy at the ground level, a two-tier training program on financial literacy was designed. Further, the National Centre for Financial Education (NCFE) has been set up under Section 8 of the Companies Act 2013 to focus on promoting financial education across the country for all sections of the population as per the National Strategy for Financial Education (NSFE).

In this context, the Financial Inclusion and Development Department (FIDD) of the RBI is working as the nodal department for formulating and implementing policies for promoting FI in the country. But the efforts are not adequate to impart literacy to such large population now connected after implementing PMJDY scheme.

4.8 Progress of FI:

In the background of some of the unparalleled policy initiatives taken and implemented since 2010, it will be interesting and noteworthy to look at the progress in the journey of FI.

Progress of financial inclusion in India (2010-2019)

S.No	FI Parameter	End March 2010	End March 2019	End March 2019
1	Banking outlets – Bank Branches	33378	50806	52489
2	Business Correspondents	34174	515317	541129
3	Other touch points	142	3425	3537
4	Total banking touch points	67694	569547	597155
5	Basic Savings Bank deposits accounts (BSBDA) (No of accounts in Millions)	73	536	574
6	BSBDA A/C (Amount in Rs. Billion)	55	1121	1410
7	Kisan Credit Card (No of cards in Millions)	24	46	49
8	Amount of loan outstanding in KCC in Rs. Billion	1240	6096	6680

(Source: Annual report of Reserve Bank of India 2019-20)

The data on FI since March 2010 can quantify the outcome and achievements of the banking system and related stakeholders. Unless a detailed research is conducted, it will be difficult to assess the exact impact of the progress in implementing FI thus far. Out of close to 6,60,000 villages in India, close to 6,00,000 villages have either a brick-and-mortar branch or a BC point. Steep increase in number of banking touch points from a mere 67694 in 2010 to a whopping 5,97,555 has increased easy access to banking services. As a result, the number of BSBD accounts has increased from 73 million to 574 million with deposits in the accounts going up from Rs.55 billion to Rs. 1410 billion by March 2019. These numbers would have gone up by now.

But the borrower base continues to be poor going up from 24 million to just 49 million. It indicates that propensity to borrow from formal banking system is still low. Non-Bank peer-to-peer lenders (NBFC – P2P) and co-origination of loans by banks/NBFCs should bring about some change in the trend. But in all its dispensation, financial literacy efforts need to be accelerated to reach out to millions of newly connected customers to derive the full synergy of FI efforts.

Another big challenge is the large number of inoperative accounts. It is estimated that close to 23 percent of PMJDY accounts and in all 42 percent of deposit accounts do not have turnover or have scanty turnover that does not actually provide any advantage to customers, more so to banks that host these accounts. Lack of cash in the hands of people in the hinterland is known to be a reason but with government routing subsidies through direct benefit transfer (DBT) provides a way to activate the account. Unless financial and digital literacy efforts are increased with greater involvement of village level people, bulk of account holders may not use the banking system defeating the very purpose of connecting them with the mainstream financial system. But there is resurgence of hope, looking to the progress of PMJDY scheme that has now 43.41 crore accounts with deposits in them reaching Rs.1,45,14,077 crores as on 15/9/2021.

4.9 Global recognition of FI policies:

Despite the limitations with which the ambitious policy of FI is pursued, India has been a front-runner in implementing FI. India ascended the global map after PMJDY deposit scheme was implemented beginning in August 2015 and with the digital thrust that came after demonetization.

The Global Inclusion Findex (GFIX) assessed by World Bank began to measure and highlight efforts of economies in implementing FI beginning with its first edition in 2011 that is released once in three years. The latest edition is GFIX – 2017 showed that 515 million adults worldwide opened an account at a financial institution or through a mobile money provider between 2014 and 2017. The next edition is due sometime after 2020. Global Findex also showed that that 69 percent of adults globally have an account, up from 62 percent in 2014 that was 51 percent in 2011. In high-income economies, 94 per cent of adults have a bank account; in developing economies 63 percent do. There is also wide variation in account ownership among individual economies.

The progress is laudable as far as India is concerned. Its GFX was 35 in 2011, 53 in 2014 and 80 in 2017. This reflects a speedy improvement in FI moving from a mere 35 in 2011 to 80 by 2017, a remarkable uptick. The focused Indian FI policies in the last few years have worked out well and have been effective. It is significant to note that GFX – 2017 stands in league at 80 for China, Russia – 76, Brazil -70 and South Africa – 69. GFX – 2014 was 79 for China and 53 for India. The rapid incremental improvement in India's efforts can be considered significant. It is 96 for UK and 93 for US. Looking to the constraints of poverty, illiteracy, lack of spread of banking network, the progress achieved with PMJDY scheme has been a great differentiator in FI space.

The whole inclusion has been further aided by the digital revolution that has also been widely recognized in Global Microscope – 2019 a report on the '*enabling environment for financial inclusion and the expansion of digital financial services*' released by Economic Intelligence Unit (EIU) that ranked India well ahead of its peers among 55 countries studied in the report. It assessed regulatory and policy environment in its approach towards digital inclusion though it did not measure FI outcomes. The progress in five domains considered by the report were related to (i) Government and Policy Support, (ii) Stability and Integrity (iii) Products and outlets (iv) consumer protection and (v) infrastructure.

While increases in countries' scores across the index provide evidence of more favourable environments for FI around the world, Colombia, Peru and Uruguay maintained their rankings at the top. Among the BRICS economies, the ranking of India is considerably ahead. Brazil 9, Russia 19, India 5, China 11 and South Africa at 13. It affirms that India is steadfast in pursuing FI through digital thrust for which infrastructure is getting built and policies are made FI friendly.

4.10 FI impact in the society:

With the FI objectives achieved so far, it has been a game changer for economic transformation and improved social well-being. India has proved to be pioneer in setting standards for pursuing FI. The combination of several sustained policy efforts of RBI and government had a multiplier impact (a) on the development of banking infrastructure – physical and digital well spread in the hinterland (b) due to institutionalized user friendly dependable electronic payment systems introduced for round the clock usage. (c) on the development of well-diversified range of financial products that can meet the needs of every age/income/gender. (d) on the systemic controls that have been designed to provide safety and security against cyber threats. (e) in the area of customer grievance and redressal system that has been ensured by institutionalizing internal and external ombudsman.

As a result, FI efforts pursued so far, the base of the banking system has increased to 195 crores of depositors and 15 crores of borrowers by the end of March 2019. It is noteworthy that World bank financial inclusion index (FINDEX– 2017) indicated that 80 percent of Indian adults of the age of over 15 years have a bank account. It works out that minimum 80 crores people are connected to the banking system in one form or other but number of people availing credit facility still continues to be poor. Lot of financial literacy efforts are needed to prompt the rural entrepreneurs to approach formal banking system for bank loans. They need to reduce dependence on local lenders who charge exorbitant interest rates and take away the major chunk of their earnings. A sustained financial literacy and persuasive education is needed to divert hinterland towards the organized financial system so that the real benefit of FI can make their life better and more prosperous.

4.11 NSFI 2019-24:

Several countries pursue FI with a view to ensure inclusive economic prosperity. Articulation of National Strategy for Financial Inclusion (NSFI) puts many economies on global map of FI. By mid – 2018, Close to 35 countries including Brazil, China, Indonesia, Peru and Nigeria have already launched their own NFSI and another 25 countries are set to formulate them to expedite systematic implementation of FI. Many countries have modified and updated their NFSI to make them more effective.

In the backdrop of a decade of implementing experience of FI in India and achieving considerable connect of masses with the mainstream financial system, it will be interesting to look at the newly enacted *"National Strategy for Financial Inclusion"* (NSFI) 2019-24 that lays a clear future pathway to accelerate mass connect with the formal financial system. It is a well-articulated document of RBI prepared under the aegis of financial inclusion advisory Committee (FIAC) and is based on inputs from government of India, financial sector regulators and host of other stakeholders, more importantly the financial sector intermediaries who have to implement it.

Future FI strategies are designed to make the financial services available, accessible and affordable in a safe and transparent manner to support inclusive and resilient multi-stakeholder led growth. Further leveraging of BC model, access to livelihood and skill development, financial literacy and education, customer protection and grievance redressal are some of the pillars on which future agenda of FI will be driven. Having set a robust banking and financial infrastructure, the next focus will be on deepening the reach, increasing usage and sustainability of FI so that its synergy could be fully harnessed.

Considerable progress is achieved in reaching milestones in FI in providing access of banking services in terms of branch network, ATMs, POS, BC network, digital kiosks and customer service points etc. Even huge number of new bank accounts was opened after PMJDY scheme was introduced. Simplified asset and liability products were also introduced to make it convenient for people to avail the services. But the challenge remains that customers connected with the banking system are not coming back for business and inoperative accounts are on rise. Either they remain inoperative or even if the customers come back, they do little business. Unless customers borrow and repay loans on regular basis, the real benefit of FI will not reach the target group. The financial literacy efforts are launched but there is a huge missing link

The future success of FI will depend on the ability of the financial system to persuade customers to aggressively use the banking system and increase their entrepreneurial capacity. Having provided wider access to financial services, some of the reasons for shyness of connected customers to use the services can be attributed to high transaction cost, lack of surplus income with people at the bottom of the pyramid, product knowledge, poor financial and digital literacy and lack of trust on financial system. Insufficient documents, distance of service providers and poor quality of services keep away many customers.

Among the future priorities to push FI, simplification of procedures, sharing information about schemes, products and government subsidies and merits of DBT should be the points of thrust. Financial literacy by engaging local people, use of local language and use of BCs to disseminate knowledge will be important. Having established a global leadership in promoting FIs, there is huge potentiality to pump prime efforts to deepen the customer relationship. Unless customers get used to regularly borrow, repay loans, migrate to digital mode, increase transactions and turnover in the accounts, full potentiality of FI cannot accrue to the economy. It will rest on twin pillars. Financial and digital literacy and greater use of banking services by customers can ensure that the end state objective of FI is achieved. Bank's account holders must realize the benefit of banking relationship and how it can add to their well-being and prosperity.

Optimizing FI will be able to rejuvenate the economy and help in accelerating wider growth in hinterland and can bring prosperity to many. The entire stakeholder community should adopt it on a mission mode taking up the responsibility to develop a well-informed and literate society. Educated members of the society should come forward to teach the merits of using financial system, more importantly on savings, borrowing and electronic remittances. FI can therefore be a great differentiator in not only shaping the economy but in deciding the social stature of future generations in the global trajectory.

CHAPTER – 5

CORPORATE GOVERNANCE

The perspectives of corporate governance practices in PSBs are often debated, discussed and their limitations are adequately highlighted. Several experts at various points of time have gone into the issue and made recommendations to upgrade the standard of governance. It is important to highlight its significance, particularly when the state-owned banking structure in India is set to complete close to five decades of yeoman services to the society by disseminating formal banking services to the grass root level economy. The benefits of bank nationalisation are far higher than the weaknesses that has been built into the system perpetuating soft spots of weak governance. During close to five decades, PSBs have witnessed a plethora of transformational phases in its transition to this stage.

Every time, the reason for the deepening challenges stand attributed to the persistent weaknesses in its governance, arising mostly out of its ownership. The government owning over 51 per cent stake in PSBs have been guiding them with different mandates at various points of time calling for change in its stance before they are able to adjust to the earlier stance. Despite the constraints, PSBs have expanded and served the community well. In the last decade, PSBs have upgraded technology to core banking system akin to their private peers and diversified product range to fall in line with the markets and met the aspirations of next generation of young customers. They could have done better if the governance structure is well aligned to its business objectives and goals.

5.1 Tectonic shift in performance of PSBs:

The recent performance indicators of PSBs have shown that they need change in its governance structure. A look at some of their key challenges could reveal the disparities in corporate governance. PSBs have been starkly experiencing several challenges. The unprecedented rise in NPAs, low capital base despite infusion of capital by the government, even net worth is completely eroded in some PSBs. The recent FSR – July 2021 released by RBI pointed out significant threats to PSBs. Erosion in asset quality and depletion in capital adequacy ratio. Even the pipeline stress represented by the data of special mention accounts indicate looming asset quality woes. In fact, after the pandemic, the banks have recovered well due to the timely interventions of RBI. Even the borrowing community could realize the need to maintain their credit history well.

The challenge of rising proportion of stressed assets should not be seen in isolation. When stressed assets are in the range of 2-3 per cent in the banks, they can be considered as a usual phenomenon. But when stressed assets begin to rise at an alarming rate unabated like now, systemic problem can be sensed and board should become more alert to obviate the situation. The credit growth has steeply declined eroding the profitability further. Bank credit year on year (YoY) had declined to 6 per cent from a double digit and is continuing to slip back particularly at a point of time when the economy needs activating flow of credit to the ailing sectors of the economy badly hurt with the pangs of pandemic. Another notable development has been the fact that banks' share in the flow of credit to the commercial sector too is gradually coming down marginalizing the role of banks in reviving the economy. These two major challenges – drop in credit growth and slackness in flow of funds to commercial sector has a cascading impact on the fragile profitability of banks, more importantly of PSBs. These developments some where touches the cord of governance and board control on the growth of the banking business.

Precisely so, RBI brought the issue of corporate governance to the forefront with serial regulatory measures to tackle them with little success for the reason that non-repayment of bank loans did not attract any social stigma. The borrowers, particularly the large corporate over leveraged borrowers whose total stock of stressed assets forms the larger chunk have been evading servicing of loans and largely seek restructuring. Since the slippage of loan account will be large that can substantially change the status of asset quality, banks do accommodate them, effectively postponing the inevitable. It tantamount to throwing good money after bad money but banks are in a fix.

The impact of escalating stressed asset has multifaceted ramifications. Accumulation of stressed assets leads to more human/ resources getting diverted to managing them. This leads to loss of appetite to undertake fresh lending eroding profitability of the bank. Shrinking interest earnings on toxic loans when combined with added non interest earning assets leads to deep cut in net interest margins. Banks will have to continue to pay committed interest on liabilities even when interest earnings on bank loans shrink. Such depressed interest margins will deplete profits leading to inability to quote competitive lending rates. Prolonged truncated profitability will impinge upon the market perception about the bank due to adverse/depleted/negative return on assets and low earnings per share compared to peer banks. It then becomes difficult to access capital needed to meet and maintain Basel III standards. Lack of adequate capital may lead to inability to undertake fresh lending. The long-term impact of high level of stressed assets will ultimately lead to imposition of new prompt corrective action of RBI that will cap growth prospects. So, the intricacies of effectiveness of governance are far and wide and erodes the performance potentiality so gradual that the banks will come to know only when others have done better.

The point of thrust is, any protracted escalation in stressed assets calls for correction in the corporate governance practices. It calls for review of decision support system in banks including lacuna in organisational structure, reporting relations and management of decision flow in the banks. The dire situation of toxic assets in the banking system called for using ordinance way to make banks do what they are supposed to do in normal course of banking. RBI is now empowered to impose penalties for failure to follow its timelines and dictate. While the time will decide the effectiveness of invoking IBC – 2016 by banks for debt resolution, it will definitely receive the attention to speed up debt resolution. The asset quality in banks may improve with borrowers realising that referring them to National Company Law Tribunals (NCLT) may impinge upon their corporate image and their ownership of the entity will be at stake.

5.2 Rising significance of corporate governance in PSBs:

With PSBs accessing capital from the equity market since 1993, the stakeholders including financial analysts, rating agencies, overseas investors and economists have begun to take keen interest in their performance. The movement of the share prices of PSBs on the stock markets is a function of market perceptions. It can also be observed how even large PSBs sometimes invite the impact of market sentiments due to the fact that their governance has not been as professionally driven as is considered desirable by the key stake holders. Though the 70 per cent of market share of banking business considered to be with PSBs has been depleting in the last few years, yet a large chunk of stake holders depend on them for banking services and therefore it is all the more important that standard of corporate governance is always maintained at high levels.

Accordingly, the key performance indicators of PSBs in relation to the private sector banks has been a matter of discussion where the deficiencies, if any in the governance of PSBs always come to fore. Thus, the Corporate Governance (CG) practices in PSBs and lack of autonomy to run them on professional lines has been held as some of the limitations in their functioning. Hence, the government and regulators from time to time have been reinforcing the need to strengthen the governance in PSBs. The government and RBI have been prescribing the 'Fit and Proper' test for board members and have been guiding PSBs to operate independently within the defined autonomy. In order to implement best CG practice, it is essential to understand its concept, present practices and emerging developments.

5.3 Evolution of corporate Governance in Banks:

It will be pertinent to put in right perspective by recalling the earliest definition of CG by the Economist and Noble laureate Milton Friedman. According to him, *CG is to conduct the business in accordance with owner or shareholders' desires, which generally will be to make as much money as possible, while conforming to the basic rules of the society embodied in law and local customs.*

Some more established definitions state that *"CG involves a set of relationships between a company's management, its board, its shareholders and other stakeholders and also the structure through which objectives of the company are set, and the means of attaining those objectives and monitoring performance are determined"*

According to Shri Kumar Mangalam Birla "fundamental objective of CG is the 'enhancement of the long-term shareholder value while at the same time protecting the interests of other stakeholders."

According to Mr. Narayan Murthy, *"Corporate governance is about ethical conduct in business. Ethics is concerned with the code of values and principles that enables a person to choose between right and wrong, and therefore, select from alternative courses of action. Further, ethical dilemmas arise from conflicting interests of the parties involved. In this regard, managers make decisions based on a set of principles influenced by the values, context and culture of the organization. Ethical leadership is good for business as the organization is seen to conduct its business in line with the expectations of all stakeholders"*. It is quite clear that CG is all about the conduct of the top management and their ethical standards.

5.4 The Role of CG:

The spirit of these definitions clearly brings to fore the significant role of CG. If the CG is implemented in totality in banks, it will have impact on the overall health of the banking system reflected in the form of rise in business levels, profitability ratios, dividends paid, market capitalization, earnings per share, net worth, and book value of the shares and so on. The expression of interest of foreign banks to expand operations in India, their strategic move to join collaborations, joint ventures, tie ups, correspondent relations etc with the Indian financial entities are also a reflection of soundness of stable governance policies. Adoption of CG practices in banks has begun to reflect changes in the style of governance and their growth pattern. It also plays the role of a barometer of the ethical and value systems of the PSBs.

More emphasis is laid globally on evolving best practices in CG. Good governance is the sine-quo-none of running organisations to enhance their prospects of growth. The standard of governance of companies has also come to be known as the pulse of advancement of civilization. A set of well-run PSBs in a country can contribute to the enhancement of stake holder value that goes to enrich the society. Hence it is essential that the principles of CG and its regulatory system needs to be reinforced to keep up a productive corporate culture. There have been glaring instances of failure of key companies across the globe, more particularly in the last few years exposing the vulnerability of corporate sector to failures in governance. Such failure of companies has multiple ramifications. Beginning with the identity of the company, all the stake holders and even the society at large are forced to experience irreparable loss.

CG as a school of thought is globally practiced as an ethical, board driven policy prescription that can put banks on a sustained growth trajectory having potentiality to contribute substantially to the society. Presence of a large number of such successful banks builds up a productive environment forging a constructive alliance with the economic development of the country. Hence establishment of a high standard of CG is necessary for consistency in economic development. But many times, certain banks are unable to effectively disseminate its principles to the top management team leading to their failure. Such failed institutions are detrimental to the stakeholders and welfare of the society.

Globalised economies seeking to maximise stakeholder values many times build up a tendency to fall prey to look for short term gains leading to breakdown of systemic controls and many times resulting in the closure of the banks. The demise of the corporate/banks/PSBs begins with the break down in adhering to the ethical values, sacrificing good governance and succumbing of the management to the temptation to make large non existing profits for earning lump sum bonus and higher remunerations.

Even though such possibilities of earning higher remuneration and bonus do not exist in the ecosystem of the PSBs, there could be expectations for non-financial gains. In the sustainable interest of the organisation, effectiveness of checks and balances in protecting the value system and ethical standards of the organisation assumes more importance. More so in PSBs where the leadership changes fast due to retirements and transfer of key persons on promotions or change of assignments. Short tenure of leadership causes uncertainty and vision of leaders cannot be pursued to bring betterment to PSBs.

5.5 Global developments of CG:

Even though different countries follow different standards of CG but globally every country ensures that public organisations should be able to do justice to their functioning for ensuring larger welfare of the community for which they work. Hence, CG mechanisms differ as between different countries. The Governance mechanism in each country is shaped by its political, economic and social history as also by its legal framework. The governance practices adopted in any country reflect national ethos and value systems adopted in that country over a long period of time. For most of the countries the corporate form of organisation did not evolve and emerge through a natural business process. It has been an alien concept transplanted from another soil.

Hence different countries have assimilated it in their own way. In view of this, a pertinent question arises as to whether it is possible to have a set of universally accepted CG standards. In the beginning most of the countries found the company to be merely a convenient form of organisation that enabled entrepreneurs to raise money from a large number of investors for funding their growing business or new ventures especially if they are large. It is a process of setting up a large organisation by pooling resources from a large number of stakeholders. At the same time ensuring that such funds are appropriately utilised for the larger interest of the organisation to do good. The entire policy framework should work towards it.

5.6 Basel Committee's revised Principles of CG:

It will be contextual to refer the Basel Committee's revised principles on corporate governance evolved as part of BIS Committee's 2010 document 'Principles for enhancing Corporate Governance' specifically, the revised principles:

- Strengthen the guidance on risk governance, including the risk management roles played by business units, risk management teams, and internal audit and control functions (the three lines of defense) and the importance of a sound risk culture to drive risk management within a bank;

- Expand the guidance on the role of the board of directors in overseeing the implementation of effective risk management systems;

- Emphasize the importance of the board's collective competence as well as the obligation of individual board members to dedicate sufficient time to their mandates and to remain current on developments in banking;

- Provide guidance for bank supervisors in evaluating the processes used by banks to select board members and senior management; and

- Recognize that compensation systems form a key component of the governance and incentive structure through which the board and senior management of a bank convey acceptable risk-taking behavior and reinforce the bank's operating and risk culture.

With regulators and banks increasingly adopting best practices culture disseminated by BIS, the CG structure need to be aligned to the principles of CG enunciated by BIS. Such approach will improve the governance structure and in turn the welfare of stakeholders. It can be observed that failure to adhere to such principles of set CG norms may, in the long run be detrimental to the sustainability of banks, more particularly the PSBs in the present context.

Several large global economies have been experiencing the ramifications of some of the well-publicised instances of failure of large corporate entities due to slackness in implementing CG putting the stakeholders/society at risk. Instances of failure of well-functioning commercial organisations, including banks is a big threat to the civilised society which needs to be curbed with appropriate policy reforms. With the advancement of science of management, the governance should logically get fine-tuned to sustainably operate in the emerging globalised world to do better to the society.

CG across the globe is omnipotent to create a culture of sustainable growth. Hence every promising organisation which has a vision imbibes best practices in CG to provide sustainability and healthy growth. The challenge is to groom the management to balance between temptations to flout ethical standards in exchange for short term gains. Such temptations step by step can build up into weaknesses which have the potentiality to perish the organisations built strongly over a period of time by great leaders. Hence, the acid test for the Board team is to build a management stream that can strengthen the fence of moral and ethical values of the organisation.

The world has witnessed during the global financial crisis in 2008 that the organisations are vulnerable to high risk in an upbeat economic environment. The incidence of failure of institutions increased during the period further reinforcing the need to strengthen the process of dissemination of steady principles of CG so as to protect the companies/banks from failing. Some of the major instances of failure of CG in leading organisations and their consequences could be summarised as under:

1. The Bank of Credit and Commercial International: Failed in 1991 basically on account of breach of US laws involved in money laundering, illegal remittance and greed to earn more money through remittances that led ultimately to closure of the bank.

2. Barings Bank: An employee in Singapore, Nick Leeson, traded futures, signed off on his own accounts and became increasingly indebted. The London directors were subsequently disqualified, as being unfit to run a banking company on account of their failure to keep a track on the conduct of the dealer which jeopardized the interest of the bank.

3. Bear Stearns: Banking Company that failed in March 2008. Bearn Stearns invested in the sub-prime mortgage market from 2003 after the US government had begun to deregulate consumer protection and derivative trading. The business collapsed as more people began to be unable to meet mortgage obligations. After a stock price high of $172 a share, it was bought by JP Morgan for $2 a share on 16 March 2008, with a $29bn loan facility guaranteed by the US Federal Reserve.

4. Lehman Brothers: Failed in Sept 2008 that led to the spiraling of global financial crisis leading lot of investors to erode their net worth. Lehman Brothers' financial strategy from 2003 was to invest heavily in mortgage debt, in markets which were being deregulated from consumer protection by the US government. Losses mounted, and Lehman Brothers was forced to file for Chapter 11 bankruptcy after the US government refused to extend a loan. The collapse triggered a global financial market meltdown. Barclays, Nomura and Bain Capital purchased the assets which were not indebted.

In all the global instances of failure of banks, there has been a simmering lack of governance and failure of internal checks, systemic controls and checks and balances that speaks high about the gaps in implementing CG.

5.7 Why CG is more important for PSBs:

PSBs having wide network of branches and having large market share has to have multiplicity of roles and responsibilities in carrying out its financial intermediation process. It deals in large chunk of public savings and channelizes into the productive sectors of the economy. Its role is vital for the flow of funds to commercial sector and hence the efficiency with which the funds are channelized holds the life line of the economy. In a bank led economy the transmission of monetary policy of RBI has to be done in the most effective way. Hence, the importance of the top management and board in steering its operations to ensure that the economy keeps growing.

While deliberating on the subject, Dr. D. Subba Rao, former Governor, Reserve Bank of India has observed that *"Banks are different from other corporates in important respects, and that makes corporate governance of banks not only different but also more critical. Banks lubricate the wheels of the real economy, are the conduits of monetary policy transmission and constitute the economy's payment and settlement system. By the very nature of their business, banks are highly leveraged. They accept large amounts of uncollateralized public funds as deposits in a fiduciary capacity and further leverage those funds through credit creation. The presence of a large and dispersed base of depositors in the stakeholders group sets banks apart from other corporates".*

Taking cue from the statement, it can be observed that CG holds much more significance for PSBs as they are not mere commercial entities, their role is much beyond. PSBs represent public trust reposed in the state-owned entities and catalyst of transmission of monetary policy so that the economy grows at desired pace. CG has a sensitive role where the ethics and values bear larger significance in driving banks.

5.8 Learning from the experience:

Learning from the past corporate fiascos will be the best fit to develop more effective systems and procedures to strengthen CG practices in PSBs. It will be in the larger interest of the community to strengthen the CG culture to lend more stability and prosperity to the people at large. Looking at what exactly led to the weaknesses in PSBs in implementing the principles of corporate governance is a unique and innovative way of going into the process of diagnosis. That will help in mapping the fallacies in administering the corporate governance system so as to find better solutions to avert such weaknesses in future. It is quite obvious that looking to the various groups of banks such as New Generation Private banks, Old Generation Private banks, Foreign Banks and PSBs, the simmering weaknesses could be brought out clearly. As the majority stake (over 51 %) in PSBs is held by the government, the onus of their overall governance vests not only with the regulator but also with the Department of Financial services (DFS) as key stakeholder.

The full time Directors on the board of PSBs are now the Managing Directors and Executive Directors supported by a team of eminent Board members, having expert knowledge in various fields. The Non-Executive part time board members comprise of Chairman, one senior representative from RBI and one from Government of India, Ministry of Finance. One Chartered Accountant nominee, three government nominees well versed in banking and finance area. Besides two board members representing workmen and officers of the banks, three share holder Directors adorn the board of typical PSB. The number of shareholder Directors will depend on the public holding of shares. One shareholder Director for every 16 per cent of shareholding by public. Hence, PSBs can have maximum 3 share holder Directors because the public holds up to a maximum of 49 per cent stake and over 51 % share held by the Government of India. In many PSBs government holds much beyond the threshold limit of 51 per cent. Foreign shareholding can go up to 20 per cent of shares in PSBs and 74 per cent for private banks. The board of PSBs is sufficiently broad based and run based on structured meetings of board and sub committees.

Thus, CG is a systematic means to enhance the stake holder value imbibing best practices in conducting growth-oriented business. In a globalised environment, development of work ethos, forging high standards of integrity, creating unique organisational culture embedding value system are important for the long-term sustainability and community welfare. When the globalisation unfolds new opportunities, ring fencing organisational ethos is challenging. It is at this particular juncture that corporate sector is exposed to the risk of making unsustainable quick money. The principles of good governance may get set aside making room for higher risk taking.

The compensation system, incentivising risk appetite, temptation of increasing value of Employee Stock Ownership Plan (ESOP) and host of many temptations opens the organisation to breach their ethical standards and moving to a commercial mode of 'Compete or perish'. As a result, some of the high performing organisations/banks themselves have collapsed due to fallacies in implementing principles of CG. Learning from others mistakes is a sign of wisdom. Hence it is necessary to identify some of the classical cases of corporate failures that caused havoc to the community. While the stakeholder's value had sunk, the more damage is done to the commercial and social fabric of the countries. Unemployment, poverty and drop in the GDP growth that led to untold sufferings to the community which could have been avoided.

The collapse of well performing company/weakness developed in PSBs should not be seen in isolation, it has wider ramification that triggers social mistrust and damages the reputation of the well-functioning financial system. The study will diagnose the gaps that facilitated breaching of CG. Shall take a cue from the case studies and map the failures so that future framework of CG policies can make them strong to insulate against the vulnerabilities. It is therefore necessary to understand innovative and path breaking perspectives of CG and help the policy makers to plan appropriate steps to avoid collapse of large institutions to eventually do good to the society.

5.9 Constraints of the PSBs in implementing CG:

With the opening up of the economy and calibrated implementation of banking sector reforms in terms of recommendations of the Narasimham committee – I and II, there has been a quantitative leap in banking business. Competition arising out of entry of new generation private sector banks led to building up of some systemic pressure on PSBs to improve their quality of customer service and in adopting state of the art technology but much desires to be done on governance front. The guidance of the Ministry of Finance on one side and regulatory dispensation of RBI on the other side have to work in tandem to improve the implementation process of CG in banks. The micro prudential norms for effective monitoring of CG practices in the field level will be equally necessary to ensure its implementation both in letter and spirit.

One of the fallouts of dual control of PSBs and likely interference in the operational and credit decision process of PSBs might have contributed to asset quality woes of present scale and dimension and consequent consistent drop in profitability. Concerned with such large-scale surge in NPAs, lowering capital base, inability of some banks to increase credit due to low capital adequacy ratio, RBI set up several high-level committees to go into the inadequacies of CG practices. Among the prominent, the Committee having been led by Dr. P. J. Nayak is important and its recommendations are under implementation at different stages. While discussing some of the peculiar constraints of the PSBs, the committee states that the:

"Governance difficulties in public sector banks arise from several externally imposed constraints. These include dual regulation, by the Finance Ministry in addition to RBI; board constitution, wherein it is difficult to categorise any director as independent; significant and widening compensation differences with private sector banks, leading to the erosion of specialist skills; external

vigilance enforcement though the CVC and CBI; and limited applicability of the RTI Act.

A level playing field with the private sector banks is lacking. If the Government stake in PSBs is brought to less than 50 per cent, all these constraints can be addressed. This would be a beneficial trade-off for the Government because it would continue to be the dominant shareholder and, without its control in banks diminishing, it would create the conditions for its banks to compete more successfully."

Taking cue from the learned committee, it can be inferred that PSBs suffer from pressures from various sources that impacts the quality of decision support system and judgement, more particularly in lending operations that determines the asset quality, profitability, capital adequacy ratio and general agility of the banks. The autonomy, independence and professional approach in promotions, placements and micro management of PSBs also in some way or other are impacted that leads to quality concerns. The system of selection and nomination of independent Board members on the boards of PSBs are always subjected to arbitrariness and bereft of professional approach that impact the quality of board. The sitting fee for board members is too meagre to attract real talent for the kind of responsibility and accountability cast upon the independent directors under the Companies act 2013.

5.10 Some of the key Recommendations of the Nayak Committee on CG:

- Given poor asset quality and low productivity, either privatize PSU banks or transform governance structure to make them efficient.
- Reduce government stake in PSU banks to less than 50 percent. Remove dual structure of both Finance Ministry and RBI regulating PSU banks.
- Give all regulatory authority to RBI.
- Improve quality of PSU bank board discussions; focus on key

areas like business strategy, financial reports, risk, and compliance.

- The government should transfer its stake in PSU banks to a holding company termed Bank Investment Company (BIC).
- Government should reduce its stake in BIC to under 50 percent and appoint a professional management for BIC.
- For better accountability, BIC should be governed by The Companies Act 2013, and not the Bank Nationalisation Acts of 1970 and 1980.
- Ownership functions to be transferred by BIC to the bank boards.
- Appointments of directors, CEO to be the responsibility of bank boards.
- Have uniform bank licensing regime across all broad-based banks, and niche licenses for banks with more narrowly defined businesses.
- Allow mutual funds, pension funds, PE funds to hold 20 percent in private sector banks, without having to take RBI approval.
- Allow promoter investors to hold up to 25 percent in private sector banks, against the 15 percent ceiling currently.
- Ensure a minimum five-year tenure for bank Chairmen and a minimum three-year tenure for Executive Directors.
- Private equity funds, including sovereign wealth funds, be permitted to take a controlling stake of up to 40 per cent in distressed banks.
- Allow voting rights in proportion to the stake held.
- Bank officers guilty of ever-greening loans (offering new loans to repay old ones) should be penalized financially.

5.11 Developments in revising governance in PSBs:

Even the discussions in first of its kind 'Gyan Sangam – 2015' a conclave of top leaders of banks held under the guidance of honourable Prime

Minister and Finance Minister led to launch of a seven point bank reform package –'Indradhanush'. While its implementation was a work in progress, a second round of 'Gyan Sangam 2.0' in 2016 opened up further discussions and harped on the imminent need for consolidation among PSBs. But such an idea is always met with implementation challenges that slows down the process.

- But then, it was implemented fast with the merger of all five associate banks of SBI (of the seven, two were already merged) with SBI, the mandarins of bank reforms were then determined to move on for another two rounds of consolidation to improve the efficiency. The inevitable reasons for some of the PSBs to have reached the brink of consolidation include among many: (i) fast deterioration of asset quality, (ii) exacerbation of asset quality woes due to Asset Quality Review (AQR) launched to assess the correct state of asset quality, (iii) additional provisions were made against new stock of bad debts pushing most PSBs into loss during FY16-17, (iv) diminishing Provision Coverage Ratio of banks and (v) mounting capital needs of PSBs to be able to continue to lend and to prepare to comply with Basel –III standards as and when it was mandated by RBI.

- Looking to the state of PSBs, perhaps as an early warning signal before consolidation, RBI revised the Prompt Corrective Action (PCA) matrix from April 1, 2017 and imposed the new format of PCA on certain weak PSBs to increase their operational efficiency and to strengthen them.

Thus, PSBs have been well sensitised about the significance of imbibing the best CG practices in their operations. RBI, Ministry of Finance and Banking industry at large have come together to collaborate and implement CG by insulating the loose ends. Based upon the guidance of Dr. P. J. Nayak Committee, several changes have been proposed, beginning with the Union Budget FY16 that were intended to infuse confidence to strengthen the CG system in PSBs. The separation of the positions of Chairman and Managing Directors leading to appointment of

MD & CEO and decision to appoint a Non-Executive Part Time chairman in the PSBs can bring a seminal change in the conduct of the banks. Chairman and Board having an exclusive domain to articulate the vision of the bank to drive the growth and to share the mind of the board members for larger purpose while the MD can oversee the operational aspects of the bank. The rationale might be to ensure that the vision is not impaired by operational constraints of day to day working which can be addressed by line management.

In the same way, the proposed setting up of BIC will in due course be able to bring the kind of independence to PSBs supported by the best of the talent in the industry. The formation of Banks Board Bureau (BBB) now working will be able to induct right talent at the top management leadership. The challenge of PSBs to meet the rising capital needs under Basel III standards can be met, provided the investors are assured of their professional autonomy and independence. A separate BIC with independence can explore more sources to get capital for PSBs looking much beyond the limited budgetary allocations of the government. Lack of sufficient capital may restrict the potentiality of the PSBs to lend to industry and commerce that may jeopardise the growth potentiality of the economy. Hence, way forward, implementation of code of CG can put the PSBs on a better growth trajectory making them more capable to harness the potentiality of vibrant economy. The intended seminal transformation in PSBs will be able to accelerate the pace of financial inclusion that can further augment lendable resources for the banks.

It can also help Dr. Nachiket Mor committee to realise its objectives to reach out to each adult with a bank account and basic banking services of loans and remittances. A constructive CG practice in PSBs can bring best minds to lead the organisations that can connect them to the international banking system on a more robust scale. Moreover, eminent intellectuals and proven industry professionals identified as Chairman of PSBs can think through and bring best practices to lead them. Consolidation in the PSB space can also bring seminal change to transform them into smart entities capable to serve the young India where the demographic dividend can be tapped.

The improvement in the governance of PSBs that is now gaining significance can bring positive change in the way they are run. More professional and performance orientation is set to occupy more space in their functioning. Dissemination of best CG principles to the grass root level to sync the mind of top management with line management will be a modern way of managing new generation PSBs. Way forward, CG has to be an inclusive effort to harness the emerging business potentiality. PSBs will meet a challenge to communicate their mind with the line management.

5.12 Emerging changes:

Based on the experience of banking sector developments in the recent years causing far reaching collateral damage to the financial sector, RBI realized the gaps in governance norms and brought out a *"Discussion paper on Governance in Commercial Banks in India"* (DPG). It also constituted an *'Internal Working Group'* to review extant ownership guidelines and corporate structure for Indian private sector banks. Earlier during August 2019, RBI notified a revised manner, procedure and criteria for determining the 'fit and proper' status of a person to be eligible to be elected as director on the Board of PSBs. These reinforcing steps are intended to strengthen CG framework for developing more robust and sustainable banking and financial system.

The near collapse of Yes Bank, continuing struggle of Punjab and Maharashtra Co-operative Bank (PMC Bank) still under moratorium, cases of conflict of interest in ICICI bank, steep hike in NPAs, more significantly in PSBs and instances of nexus between banks and large corporate borrowers exposes the weaknesses of banks in implementing the code of CG. RBI raised the permissible limit of withdrawal of deposits from PMC Bank to Rs.1 lac while extending the moratorium period for another three months. It is only recently that RBI had accorded "in-principle" approval to one Centrum Financial Services Ltd (CFSL) to set up a small finance bank (SFB), which will take over the beleaguered PMC Bank soon.

The stakeholders of these entities experienced loss of wealth at various points of time when stock markets went through turbulence due to adverse developments. In many instances, the regulatory oversight and measures of scrutiny by RBI was unable to precisely unearth, fix non-compliance and mold the attitude of bank leadership towards CG well in time to prevent the damage. RBI and Securities and Exchange Board of India (SEBI) have been working together to bring best standards of governance but the response and its effectiveness from industry has not been encouraging.

The DPG brings out many new dimensions to strengthen CG and if implemented on full scale can insulate the banks against the vulnerabilities commonly seen in the last few years. Some key aspects of DPG can highlight the impending shift in CG practices in commercial banks in India in near future.

5.13 Separating the three lines of defense:

The DPG reflects the growing concern of RBI about the lack of effectiveness of boards to oversee among others, the functionality of the three lines of defence – (i) the first line of defence vests with the business units assuming, managing business risks that is responsible for revenue generation. It includes identifying, assessing, reporting such exposures considering the bank's risk appetite, its policies, procedures and controls. The way the line management executes its responsibilities shall reflect the bank's existing risk culture. The board shall promote a strong culture of adhering to limits and managing risk exposures. The finance function, even though being part of the first line of defence shall have sufficient authority, stature, independence, resources and access to the board.

(ii) The second line of defence includes an independent and effective risk management function and compliance function. The risk management function complements the first line of defence through its monitoring and reporting responsibilities and checks deviations from laid down norms. Among other things, it is responsible for overseeing the bank's risk-taking activities, assessing risks and issues independently from the first line of defence. The function shall promote importance of business of line managers i.e. those having revenue-generating responsibilities, in identifying and assessing risks critically rather than relying only on surveillance conducted by the risk management function.

The Chief Risk officer (CRO) and Chief compliance officer (CCO) shall play an anchoring role as second line of defence to mitigate risks faced by the first line of defence.

(iii) Finally the third line of defence consists of an independent internal audit function, as well as an independent vigilance function. An internal audit function, among other things provides independent review together with objective assurance on effectiveness of the bank's first and second lines of defence. Internal auditors must be competent, appropriately trained and not involved in developing, implementing or operating the first or second line of defence. The separation must be clear to overcome the issue of conflict of interest. As for the vigilance function, its main objective is to assist the board to achieve its goal by ensuring that all transactions are carried out as per systems, procedures while minimizing the scope of malpractices/misconduct and misuse of funds.

Early detection of control gaps can enable quick action and intervention. The Head of Internal Audit (HIA) and Chief Internal Vigilance (CIV) are also the key functionaries identified to safeguard the third line of defence reporting to their respective subcommittees of the board. In the new governance architecture, CRO, CCO, HIA and CIV are accorded the highest independence keeping them away from the control of WTDs and their removal, if any should be made public as part of foot note of balance sheet by assigning suitable reasons. Department of supervision of RBI should also be kept informed. The overlapping roles between revenue generating arms and control functions are eliminated in the structure separating them with arm's length distance. The controls built in DPG are well tested and if implemented in the same spirit can make a difference to the governance strategy.

5.14 Board structure:

The size of board of bank can now range between a minimum of 6 directors and not exceeding 15 directors depending upon the size, complexity and needs of the bank that should meet once in 60 days or six times in a year. The frequency is increased from four to six to enable faster decision-making. The responsibility of non-Executive directors (NEDs) is made more inclusive with their participation in board meetings and also in different dedicated committees/sub-committees. The continuous tenure of MD & CEO will now be restricted to 10 years for promoter/major shareholder as whole-time director (WTDs). If a WTD is not a promoter/major shareholder, then he can remain in office as MD & CEO continuously for 15 years. However, after a cooling period of three years, they can be assigned the position of WTD subject to an upper age limit of 70 years. Within these limitations, the bank has to submit proposal to RBI for appointment/extension of tenure of MD & CEO at least 6 months prior to completion of tenure. The revised governance norms whenever implemented may unseat present MD & CEOs of some of the lead private banks. It will phase out prolonged single leadership cult presently in practice in some banks protecting the long-term interest of banks.

Concentration of leadership and decision-making process with single person for a prolonged period of time at the top may sometimes prevent development of next line leadership. Finding no avenues to climb to the top of the hierarchy, many competent people may move out of such banks creating vacuum down the line. While this may be a good practice not to allow continuous position as MD & CEO, availability of competent manpower to lead the banks could pose a problem. Building up competencies to man these key leadership positions will require proper attention of mentors and talent hunters. It is only recently that

BBB has taken up the task of mentoring/grooming next level leaders of banking industry, more focused at PSBs. Private banks also should constantly work to tap budding talent and map their competencies.

5.15 Role of Board of Directors:

The DPG bestows obvious overload of expectations from the board with responsibilities ranging from protecting organizational culture, values, managing conflicts of interest, oversight of senior management to setting risk appetite for business growth. The more challenging will be the task of Nomination and Remuneration Committee (NRC) headed by an independent director (ID). Among a host of responsibilities of onboarding directors, its crucial assignment is to evaluate performance effectiveness of the board, board committees, chairman of the board, chairman of committees, board members, WTDs and NEDs, other IDs, senior management and other employees. RBI needs to assure itself that NRC will be able to execute its range of responsibilities doing justice in letter and spirit to ensure that such important processes are not routinized. Looking from a practical perspective, when an ID is to function along with WTDs, other NEDs as a peer, how NRC will be able to discharge the expected functions and stand to the regulatory scrutiny. Keeping in view the sanctity of NRC and its delicate responsibility, RBI may explore involving members of BBB as chairman of NRC to induct external oversight. Leaving it to NED for such important function may vitiate the purpose.

The normal practice of many of the NEDs and IDs of the board is to function in sync with the WTDs to bind as a team and remain collectively responsible. Dissent is normally not encouraged in going organizations as a mark of demonstrating team spirit. Otherwise, major dereliction of CG norms noticed and responsible for ignominy in some banks could not have gone unnoticed until the damage is done. Even whistle blower policy could not serve the intended purpose and top management submissively hushed its voice to tow in line with the assertive leaders at command. A second support will be essential to tackle the role of NRC.

5.16 The future CG reforms:

Even if the new governance is implemented, the test of its efficacy will lie in its monitoring mechanism. The supervisory system of RBI has been constantly on reform mode with risk-based supervision (RBS) replacing the CAMELS model that used to test efficiency of banks in terms of Capital adequacy, Asset quality, Management quality, Earnings, Liquidity, Systems and control. The RBI report is privilege document conveyed only to concerned bank. While globally RBS is considered more sophisticated as a risk centric tool, it is yet to reflect as an improved rigor of supervision to prompt banks to be more risk sensitive.

The applicability of new governance norms is to be implemented in all categories of banks. But looking to the small size and limited competencies of Boards of Regional Rural Banks (RRBs), Small finance banks (SFBs) and payment banks (PBs), they may not be able to implement and function on full scale like other large commercial banks.

Moreover, the Basel Committee on Banking Supervision (BCBS) suggested customization of governance to fit the size and scale of operations. It would be pragmatic to prescribe separate norms for smaller sized banks instead of using 'one size fits all' approach in prescribing standards of governance. Since, appointment of board members in case of PSBs is with DFS, they need to scout for required talent to man critical subcommittees of Risk Management, technology and Audit committee of the board etc. RBI may also persuade government to move towards setting up Non-Operative Financial Holding Company (NOFHC) model for PSBs to eliminate dichotomy of dual regulations.

The CG norms now envisaged should be reinforcing each other in a way to curb the tendency of indifference in implementing them so that changes can be on expected lines. The regulatory norms should go beyond data crunching to measure the riskiness and to levy additional regulatory capital. RBI may have to innovate and devise a separate CG audit framework and groom its representative on the board/head of Risk Management Committee, as a source of regulatory intelligence sharing impressions on how the board and its leadership conducts itself and respects code of CG to protect stakeholder interest. As yet, there is no proposal to withdraw RBI nominee from the board to avoid conflict of interest in terms of recommendations by Dr. P. J. Nayak in his 'Report of the Committee to Review Governance of the Boards of Banks in India' (2014).

Though the deposit insurance has been raised to Rs.5 lacs, yet safety and protection of depositor interest continues to be important. As far as the transparency and disclosure standards are concerned, no new information is added in DPG. RBI may even consider disclosure of its adverse observations found during annual inspection as foot notes to the balance sheet if it can prompt banks to do better and can inculcate the culture of sharing information with the stakeholders. Of course, it should be confined to special notes like KYC default and should not be allowed to use for business purpose.

RBI may also have to revisit the compensation to board members to make it sufficiently attractive to give their best. Presently, the sitting fee and other modes of compensations are meagre in relation to the expected span of responsibilities. A committee may go into these aspects to ensure that more time of the board members is available to banks.

RBI and the internal working committee may have to go much beyond prescribing globally acclaimed standards. They should simultaneously work towards building compatible ecosystem for the board and its directors to function in a professional environment and protect the sustainability of banks. The task of RBI is therefore taller than is contemplated. The future of CG will be a blend of recommendations of Dr. P. J. Nayak Committee and excerpts from the discussion paper on governance. Hence, banks will be traversing an interesting journey in implementing corporate governance.

CHAPTER – 6

BANKS BOARD BUREAU

Banks Board Bureau (BBB) had become functional from April 1, 2016 in terms of the 7-pronged bank reform framework –'*Indradhanush*' envisaged as a follow up of deliberations at the Gyan Sangam – I, the policy makers and bankers conclave held at Pune in January 2015. BBB was meant to independently identify the full-time directors on the board of PSBs that was earlier done by DFS in the Ministry of Finance. It is meant to provide the autonomy to the selection process in terms of the new resolve to keep arm's length distance from the management of PSBs. With the expiry of the term of BBB on March 31, 2018, the term was renewed with new members – BBB 2.0.

The newly formed team of BBB 2.0 will benefit from the preparatory work done by its predecessor BBB 1.0, the new dispensation will have a tough task ahead of it. Looking to the operational state of PSBs, BBB 2.0 will have to gear up to support them with enlarged agenda and handiwork. The asset quality woes, post the introduction of asset quality review by RBI in September 2015 have increased and taken an upward trend and employee morale too is sagging. While many of these issues are beyond its mandate, it may need to account for and address them in order to meet its core objective of fixing the governance of PSBs.

After the two-year term of the BBB ended on 31 March 2018, the government reconstituted it with a new team. The BBB 2.0 has been constituted that has the potential to resurrect PSBs and maintain continuity in its policy stances. It reinforces the government's commitment to reform PSBs, particularly at a juncture when many of them are reeling under unprecedented operational stress. Given the challenging mandate, it has to reinvent its strategic role through greater coordination with all stakeholders, especially the DFS. The revamped BBB assumes the responsibility of continuing to stay dominant in the banking space, with PSBs needing rejuvenation and moral support.

6.1 Genesis and Mandate

The BBB—an autonomous body—was intended to eventually transition into a BIC in line with the recommendations of the Committee to Review Governance of Boards of Banks in India headed by Dr. P J Nayak, set up by RBI in 2014. Mr. Nayak was former head of Axis Bank. The BIC, whenever formed, will hold the government's stake in PSBs and function as an independent special purpose vehicle that would provide the banks greater autonomy.

When the BBB began functioning in its initial form from 1 April 2016, the state of PSBs was much better though asset quality woes had engulfed the system. Banking sector reforms were reinforced when the government launched a set of measures, collectively titled Mission – Indradhanush, after deliberations at the first Gyan Sangam, a meeting of the top leaders of banks that was conducted under the aegis of government and regulatory authorities in January 2015. Since then, the identification, selection, and nurturing of quality leadership for PSBs, as well as the continuity of said leadership, has been under greater focus, with primary responsibility for these tasks being entrusted to the BBB. Similarly, on the recommendation of the Dr. P J Nayak Committee, the position of chairperson was separated from that of managing director and chief executive officer (MD and CEO).

Eminent professionals were inducted for the post of non-executive chairperson, akin to the practice in private banks. A few private sector professionals were also inducted at the level of the MD and CEO in some large PSBs to add external talent to the pool of leadership. The idea was to provide the chairperson a longer tenure to pursue a long-term vision for the bank, while the MD and CEO, a full-time bank executive, could demit office on superannuation as per the service conditions. Such move had the potential to remove the limitations of the MD and CEO's short-term residual service while enabling the non-executive chairperson to steer the bank to realize its long-term growth aspirations.

The recommendations were also designed to improve governance by identifying the right talent for top management positions that come with full-time board seats (chairperson, MD and CEO, and Executive director). Succession planning for leadership roles, and the enforcement of codes of conduct and ethics were also a large part of the mandate. In the realm of business issues, coordinated action to mitigate asset quality woes, though not mandated, also stood out as an important and relevant task. The task of developing differentiated strategies for raising capital through innovative financial methods and instruments is a work in progress.

The limited tenure of two years, perhaps, proved inadequate for the first BBB to accomplish its ambitious goals and put PSBs on the desired growth trajectory while carving out a transition plan to move from government shareholding to a bank-holding company. But it has provided the contours of a road map in its compendium of recommendations that can form the basis to take the process forward (Rai 2018). More importantly, the draft Governance, Reward and Accountability Framework (GRAF), designed to mitigate the dangers of high-risk-taking during good times and risk aversion during bad times, can provoke further thinking that will help adapt and improve it.

6.2 Key Tasks of BBB 2.0

The BBB 2.0 has the distinct advantage of having a clear-cut goal due to the preparatory work that has been done in the past, though the challenges of PSBs have become aggravated and are more daunting now. It may need a different approach or a strategic shift in its stance. But, its biggest limitation will be the need to devise appropriate strategies to win the confidence of the DFS, its biggest stakeholder. The newly constituted BBB 2.0 has to achieve full empowerment through better coordination and relationship-building to guide PSBs towards the goal. The task is made trickier by the fact that PSBs are already required to work under several regulators, each with a different mindset, and, at the same time, cater to the increased expectations of customers.

The BBB 2.0 may find PSBs in a weakened operational state from how the first BBB would have found PSBs. Guiding PSBs through such a weak state with the same level of empowerment could be difficult. Therefore, collaboration with the DFS for speedy structural changes and further strengthening—as well as serious introspection on the mandate— may be desired. This will require winning the confidence of mandarins on banking reforms. Therefore, it will be pertinent to discuss the current state of some of the PSBs and design well-calibrated remedial measures to resuscitate them, even though that may not be part of the current mandate.

6.3 Operational State of PSBs – Prompt Corrective Action:

In order to improve the performance of banks that have been identified to be weak and restore their operational efficiency, the RBI introduced the new PCA format with built-in rectification measures, effective from financial year (FY) 2018–19. The new format of performance evaluation of banks using various parameters and then classifies them into three risk thresholds. Each level denotes a degree of weakness ranging from risk threshold I (less risky) to risk threshold III (very risky). Among others, PCA measures key parameters: asset quality, net non-performing assets (NNPAs), capital adequacy ratio and leverage ratio. NNPAs breaching the 6% level or capital adequacy ratio getting close to the minimum threshold of 10.25% (benchmark at that time now 10.875 until Basel III norms of 11.5 percent is fully implemented) would be clear indicators of weakness. It also tracks concurrent negative rate of return on assets (ROA) ranging from two to four consecutive years. This results in banks posting losses after turning RoA negative.

Based on such metrics, the RBI has imposed PCA on 11 out of 21 PSBs at that time in 2017. The guidance of the central bank and the re-prioritization of their business activities may hasten their revival. Such remedial measures, already imposed by the RBI, can be a good starting point for the BBB 2.0 to understand the operational state of PSBs. Many more PSBs may become subject to RBI surveillance under PCA as and when the performance of banks fit so into the revised PCA framework. The PCA also clearly specified the consequences of the three risk thresholds and the action needed at each stage. So, a forward vision can be articulated depending on the progress in reviving PSBs. The remaining PSBs can test their performance parameters and improve upon them in time to avert the imposition of PCA.

6.4 Asset quality:

Asset quality has always been under focus, but it has been deteriorating rapidly ever since an AQR was undertaken by the RBI in September 2015 to reduce the divergence between the banks' classification of NPAs and the central bank's assessment. As a result, NPA levels zoomed to a historic high. In order to provide an exit route to failed entities and speed up debt resolution, the IBC – 2016 was enacted along with implementing regulatory regime by setting up of the Insolvency and Bankruptcy Board of India (IBBI). All stakeholders are now engaged in coordinated action to resolve debt and improve asset quality. Taking into consideration the stressed assets in the special mention account, SMA-2 (with money overdue beyond 61 days), stressed assets had reached a new height after the relevant data was developed. Henceforth, banks could monitor the credit even when it was overdue 30 days and such information can provide the right kind of surveillance on the quality of credit portfolio.

PSBs hold 90% of such stressed assets. The state of asset quality will have far-reaching implications on the business efficiency of PSBs. Hence, the BBB 2.0 has to pitch in to coordinate the debt resolution process even though it is not part of the mandate. The revival of PSBs will rest, in large part, on how asset quality management gets streamlined.

6.5 Simplified debt resolution system:

In order to simplify the debt resolution process, the RBI has introduced a new set of guidelines, effective on 1 March 2018, for the resolution of stressed assets worth Rs.2,000 crore or more. The new stressed asset resolution framework may increase asset quality woes in the short run, but a stringent resolution process will be required in the long run. Having invoked the IBC, many PSBs are working in tandem with the RBI, the IBBI, debt resolution professionals, and committees of creditors to hasten debt resolution. But many large stressed assets are entangled in prolonged litigation, which is stretching timelines. A lot of legal issues connected to the bidding process were yet to be sorted out. Foremost among these are the two amendments made to the IBC and the issue of special dispensation for stressed micro, small, and medium enterprises.

6.6 Implications of PNB fraud:

The infamous Punjab National Bank (PNB) fraud, followed by a series of loan-related embezzlements, has highlighted the need to reinforce risk governance practices and to improve the effectiveness of systemic controls. The gaping holes that currently exist in operational risk management can jeopardize the sustainability of banks. With their fragile systemic controls and high susceptibility to frauds, PSBs will take a long time to win back public confidence. PNB is struggling with the intricacies of the fraud and RBI has granted the bank the special dispensation of one year to make provision for the losses. Restoring normalcy will be a tedious journey.

Meanwhile, PSBs were losing market share despite the fact that they continue to be the backbone of financial intermediation, especially in terms of their outreach to the hinterland. The revival of the economy, which is gradually limping back to normalcy after demonetization and the implementation of the goods and services tax, could be debilitated if the role of PSBs is allowed to diminish further. Therefore, the sagging morale of PSB employees needs to be revived in order to enable the banks' resurgence.

6.7 Private Banks

At a time when private sector banks were standing out as examples of best practices in corporate governance, the recent imbroglios at ICICI Bank and Axis Bank have flagged possible conflicts of interest in their conduct. They have added new dimensions to the weaknesses in the corporate governance of leading private banks. The ICICI Bank is classified by the RBI as a Domestic Systemically Important Bank (D – SIB), which makes the recent revelations a matter of great concern. In this context, the observations of Standard & Poor's about the impact of weaknesses in the governance process on risk management need to be factored in.

In view of the weak operational state of PSBs, the new BBB cannot isolate these issues even though they are not listed in the mandate. Without getting involved in mitigating the risks of inherent weaknesses, it will be difficult to nurture and improve the effectiveness of the apex leadership. It has also to take up the task of appointing independent directors to the boards of PSBs to make them strong and effective. After appointing them, training them and conditioning their skill sets to meet emerging challenges will be essential.

Going by the experience of the first BBB, the bureau could face another formidable challenge in asserting its anchoring position in driving the future improvement of PSBs. The DFS may be persuaded to fully support the BBB in transforming PSBs to derive the maximum potential benefit from the eminent people on the team. Even revising or modifying the mandate, which was flagged earlier, may be necessary to tackle the current spate of challenges.

Its immediate task will be to soothe the nerves of PSBs, which are caught between the pincers of prolonged debt resolution processes and the implications of gaping holes in their operational risk management. Maintaining the equilibrium between constantly evolving guidelines and the possibility of their implementation at the ground level requires a deep dive into the operational state of PSBs, failing which it may turn out to be another set of good intentions of key stakeholders without the desirable outcome. On the whole, a challenging task awaits the new BBB, where seeking government support, application of foresight, and adapting a flexible approach in grooming board functionaries of PSBs will be necessary to achieve its objectives.

CHAPTER – 7

REVISED PCA FRAMEWORK

RBI initiated the scheme of Prompt Corrective Action (PCA) in 2002 to discipline banks when they report poor and risky financial performance. PCA is a policy action guideline (first in May 2014 and revised effective from April 1, 2017) if a commercial bank's financial condition worsens below certain performance benchmark mark. The PCA framework is a set of guidelines for banks that are weak in terms of identified performance indicators including poor asset quality, insufficient capital and poor profitability with tendency to accumulate losses.

PCA is an early intervention package or resolution guideline by the RBI when a bank turns weak in terms of its performance metrics. In early 2018, there were 12 banks under PCA framework, implying that their financial conditions were weak. Out of these, 11 were PSBs. Later, the government injected capital into the PSBs besides taking several steps to improve their performance. As a result, as on March 9, 2019, there were only six banks (all PSBs) under the PCA framework.

7.1 Trigger points of PCA17

The PCA framework specifies the **trigger points** or the level in which the RBI will intervene with corrective action. This trigger points are expressed in terms of parameters for the banks. The trigger points are – (i) capital to risk weighted assets ratio (CRAR), (ii) net non-performing assets (NNPA), and (iii) return on assets (RoA) and (iv) Leverage ratio – assets size to core capital – Tier – I capital ratio. This means that when a particular bank is reporting the low level of CRAR, high level of NNPA or abysmally low/negative Return on Assets (profit), the RBI will impose PCA framework on such banks prompting them to adopt certain restrictive measures. The scheme was revised in April 2017. Under the Revised PCA framework, apart from the capital, asset quality and profitability, leverage ratio was also to be monitored additionally.

The parameters that invite corrective action from the central bank are – level of CRAR, NPAs, and RoA along with leverage ratio. When these parameters reach the set trigger points for a bank (like CRAR of 9%, 6%, 3%), the RBI will initiate certain structured and discretionary actions for the bank. As per the revised framework by the RBI, in April 2017, capital, asset quality and profitability continue to be the key areas for monitoring. Along with this, leverage of banks also will be monitored.

Thus, based upon the performance parameters of banks during FY17 when banks faced steep hike in NPAs due to AQR of RBI that also led to deterioration of CRAR. It brought a combined negative impact on banks. It is ostensibly intended to improve the robustness of the banking system to align with international standards, keeping Basel III challenges in view.

Compared to PCA – 2002, the new framework PCA-2017 (PCA17) is more granular, stringent and well defined. It was made transparent and is without any arbitrariness. Keeping in view the status of a bank in terms of its NNPAs, Ratio of Tier – I capital to risk weighted assets, ROA and Tier – I leverage ratios – the percentage of the capital measure to the exposure measure as defined in RBI guidelines on leverage ratio.

But the entire narrative of PCA17 converges into a single point of performance reflecting upon the status of asset quality that has a cascading impact on the capital and other aspects of health of the bank causing concern. It is akin to the nervous system that transcends the whole bank. Deterioration of asset quality diminishes profits reducing ROA, erodes capital. All the four parameters are closely intertwined with asset quality. That precisely is the reason RBI makes it clear that it will invoke PCA17 if any if all/some of the performance parameter falls below the defined standards. But the follow up action after invocation of PCA17 will be wide ranging to be applied at its own discretion.

Hence, PCA17 is perhaps a script to forge a set of penal actions for nonconformance to the serial asset quality improvement norms that were rolled out by RBI in a planned sequence. It should be seen as a continuing effort of RBI to transform and strengthen banks. It can be recalled that since 2014, RBI has been gradually upgrading the system of sending early warning signs to banks to provide an opportunity to correct their business mix.

Beginning with data collection of pipeline stress under Special Mention Accounts (SMA –0, I, & II). Formation of Joint Lender Forum (JLF) to hasten joint recovery action in consortium accounts that was subsequently given up as it was not working to the desired extent. Recognizing wilful default as a disqualification in social perspectives, reporting of information on loan accounts under Central Repository of Information on Large Credit (CRILC) and many similar actions.

But never in the past, RBI had prescribed consequences of non-implementation of these measures with the spirit with which it was intended. These were followed by a more serious exercise of AQR that brought to fore the actual magnitude of asset quality. Hitherto asset quality could be shielded by banks under restructuring schemes. Later, restructuring forbearance was withdrawn by RBI sometime in early 2015.

Earlier, RBI also armed banks with debt resolution methods such as Strategic Debt Restructuring (SDR), allowing 5/25 Scheme to enable banks to lend for longer tenor, Scheme for sustainable Structuring of Stressed Assets (S4A) and liberalized S4A but there was no significant impact on asset quality. Instead, the spree of fresh slippage of loans continued more than the amount recovered by banks adding to the pile. If the trend is allowed to continue the CAR of some banks may fall below the threshold level of 3.625 per cent that can have far reaching impact on de-stabilizing such banks.

7.2 Early warning system:

Though PCA17 is set to be made operational from April 2017 based on the performance of 31/3/2017, its classification in the three modes of Threshold-1, 2 & 3 is an effective barometer to put banks on guard. A bank in T1 can reinvigorate its operations so that it does not slip into T2. Similarly banks in T2 should work towards up-gradation to T1 and not allowing degradation. The labelling of banks on the basis of pronounced riskiness in terms of Threshold models can allow sufficient room for banks to change for better. It acts as an early warning tool where they need to act fast to arrest slippage of performance. The board of directors should be able to gauze the signages very early to ensure and direct the banks towards health growth.

Depending upon the threshold risk assessed by RBI, the actions can follow in a host of areas that can restore the health of the bank. The remedial actions of RBI can range from Strategic intervention, special supervisory interaction, changing governance pattern, including change of management, better management to mitigate credit and market risk, HR dimensions by way of putting restrictions in sourcing manpower and payment of compensation, Profitability and operations related aspects. The degree of actions will depend on the degree of riskiness of the bank as perceived by the regulator.

The well thought out PCA17 can be an effective tool to identify the target bank and plan penal action to put it back on track. Since all banks are under the supervisory surveillance of RBI, they should be guided and risk governance should be toned so as not to invite a state where the RBI will be required to activate PCA. But the systemic control is good to put the banks on healthy track. Therefore, while the framework is well designed, it is better if a window of one year or more is provided to the banks or its implementation can be synchronized with Basel III norms. The improved framework of PCA17 can lead to better governance but sudden action may be counterproductive. A reasonable time with prescriptive action plan can be a better way to mend the banks.

Therefore, banks may be provided sufficient latitude to introspect and upgrade their 'Threshold Risk levels' within defined time lines. The residual banks unable to make visible improvements can be put under such stringent restrictions/nursing. Far reaching measures like superseding bank's board, change of management, restrictions in payment of compensation or sitting fee to board members and such other measures will expose the banks to public mistrust which will be difficult to win back even if course correction takes place.

Sudden up gradation of PCA prerequisites from current year may jeopardize the bank's ability to measure up to the new standards. The effort to align bank's capital to Basel III standards is essential but needs to be done taking the ability of the banks to cope with the new standards. Sudden gush may destabilize the process of transformation of banks. The stress in the banking sector exacerbated after the onset of pandemic in multiple ways.

7.3 RBI invoked PCA17

Way back in 2018 when RBI brought 11 banks under PCA, including the big state-owned bank – Bank of India, the restoration of health of banks began. It was formidable challenge to nurse these banks step by step to ensure that they start functioning normally. Their restrictive functioning under PCA could have impacted the flow of funds to commercial sector impinging upon the growth prospects of the economy. PSBs with prolonged weak governance structure is also known to suffer from short term leadership, lack of long-term vision and business objectives unlike its private peers. Bank of India (BOI) joining the other midsized PSBs operating under PCA framework was a stern warning to many other banks.

It was high time for banks to look at their own parameters and avert imposition of PCA. It is a pronounced regulatory tool to acknowledge that the bank is weak and needs to ramp up its performance parameters before it is too late. The team at these banks should accept the challenge to revamp its functioning to improve the identified parameters to exit

PCA status in a planned time span. The immediate job was well cut because they needed to stay focused on improving critical parameters while maintaining normal banking operations.

7.4 More focused monitoring:

PCA is known to be a global systemic control imposed on the banks that have shown early signs of weaknesses in critical areas – Capital, Asset quality and profitability. PCA will impose closer tracking of – Capital to Risk weighted Assets (CRAR), Common Equity Tier (CET)-I, Net NPA Ratios and Return on Assets (ROA) by regulator. In its prioritization, RBI will be more focused on monitoring banks that are placed under PCA. More frequent exchange of information and closer interactions between these banks and regulators with a mind to overcome the weaknesses quickly.

The concern was, if the performance of these banks is not checked at that stage, they may further slip to create systemic risk for the financial system. RBI was candid that the PCA would not in any way disrupt normal banking operations, but it will goad the banks to use more pointed strategies to quickly show improvements in the designated areas. Though it is just an early warning to the management of the banks and may not impact customer related perspectives, but it will call for internal reprioritization in pursuing various lines of activities.

7.5 PCA – a transparent framework:

Imposing PCA by RBI should not be surprising to banks. The revised PCA framework from April 2017 brought full transparency about the three levels of risk thresholds. It also explains the limitations, if any that commensurate with the risk thresholds. Banks can therefore review their own performance matrix and identify their own risk thresholds. They can even plan to avert PCA with a proactive approach.

Bank of India, one of the large banks cannot be oblivious of the fact. The board and top management that review the performance from time to time must be aware of the oncoming risks. The onset of AQR of RBI meant to clean up the balance sheets of banks has highlighted the asset quality woes of banks. Since then, every bank knows its status and the incremental slippages that accumulated NPAs. The impediments in enforcing recovery of NPAs led to enactment of Insolvency and Bankruptcy Code – 2016 followed by its recent amendment to make it more rigorous. The alignment of performance with PCA framework is well in the knowledge of banks.

7.6 Impact of asset quality:

The whole framework of PCA spins around asset quality. Higher NPAs led to more provisions and allocation of more resources on NPA management that lead to poor off take of fresh credit. Embroiled in rising NPAs, many PSBs have stopped fresh lending that led to loss of revenue, cross selling opportunities, fee income, non-fund-based business and ultimately the customer base. Reduction of interest income due to steep slippage of assets and truncated loan base further eroded profitability of banks. It led to lowering of RoA.

Moreover, risk-based supervision of RBI captures the state of asset quality and adverse loan exposure standards, if any that could have impacted capital adequacy. A deep dive into reasons for invoking PCA can explain that deterioration of asset quality is the crux of weakness that permeated the whole internal ecosystem of bank. It ultimately led to sinking of other key parameters forcing regulator to impose PCA. Perhaps an effective systemic control on asset quality including quality of credit origination could have averted imposition of PCA.

7.7 Key strategies:

While the normal prudence in business operations is necessary, the shutting down some of the non-viable ATMs where the hits are too low, below the breakeven point as proposed by BOI could reduce costs. Such strategies have to be viewed from the reputation risk and visibility angle. Other strategies could be (i) Quick sale of NPAs to ARCs, preferably mass sale, if possible. Faster sale of NPAs could have multiplying impact on the capital base as well by reduction of risk weighted assets, trim future provisioning and can shore up capital adequacy. (ii) Going for massive schematic one time settlement (OTS) of Mid/Small size NPAs could, despite haircut can add to the improvement. (iii) Central monitoring of NPAs of Rs.One crore and above to pay more attention for decisions and revival/restructuring/recovery (iv) Continued thrust on incremental lending to appropriate sectors carrying lower risk weights depending upon exposure levels. It will help retain visibility in market and add to interest income. (v) Having set up back offices for many functions, banks should quickly downsize branches in terms of people and expand the outreach of products that go well in the local geography with focus on making them more profitable. (vi) Fine tune turnaround time and trim paper needs to be borrower friendly (vii) Fix turnaround time for internal decision-making processes. (viii) Create a team of Turnaround Leaders (TLs) to execute strategies and monitor implementation from a single point by using technology channels (ix) Closure and merger/relocation of chronic loss-making/unviable branches in a phased manner (x) Improving fee-based services on a mission mode to supplement the income streams. (xi) The board and top management have to remain positive and seek constructive participation of line management to avert further loss of team confidence. It is time to set right direction and handhold execution teams.

BOI and other banks under PCA need not therefore be diffident but have to be aggressive with clear strategies to reverse it. Hence for PCA led banks, it is both a bane and a boon. Bane because of its classification as a relatively weak bank. It can be a boon because it can create an opportunity to quickly turnaround and emerge as a front runner.

CHAPTER – 8

MERGER OF PSBS

The merger of PSBs have taken place by reducing the total number of PSBs from 27 to 12 by April 1, 2020 beginning with completion of merger of all associate banks of SBI merging with SBI by April 1, 2017. Next Vijaya Bank and Dena Bank were merged with Bank of Baroda from April 1, 2019. Then Oriental Bank of Commerce (OBC) and United Bank of India (UBI) merged with Punjab National Bank (PNB), Syndicate bank with Canara Bank, Allahabad Bank with Indian Bank and finally Andhra Bank and Corporate Bank with Union Bank of India with effect from April 1, 2020. This chapter discusses the implications and how the process of mergers has taken place. Going back into introspection, it can be recalled that the proposed amalgamation of Vijaya Bank (VB) and Dena Bank (DB) with Bank of Baroda (BOB) was initially mooted by the government as the first phase of mergers among nationalised banks. The experience of merging Associate Banks of SBI with SBI is different. Its culture and working system may be having some similarities but not so when it comes to each nationalised bank, an altogether, they are different entities with own culture and value systems. Merger among the nationalised banks shall invite more daunting challenges, at the same time having greater opportunity for synergy.

After the individual boards of the three banks – Bank of Baroda, Dena Bank and Vijaya Bank have approved the proposal that it had moved to the government for approval. In order to implement the strategy of merger, some of them formed internal committees to prepare the blueprint for operationalizing the process. Many had to engage external consultants to put through the mergers. It was a historic initiative to revamp PSBs pending since the banking sector reforms were initiated in 1991. This strategic move should be the beginning of transformation of PSBs into smart, big and agile entities to compete with private peers.

Understandably, going into the purpose, the consolidation was not confined to resolve lingering bad loan crisis alone. It had a bigger purpose to make the banking sector more robust and capable to (i) increase lending appetite (ii) conserve capital and (iii) improve risk management capabilities (iv) attain economies of scale in augmenting business growth. Such stronger and bigger PSBs like SBI can support the growing economy.

Yet, the merger was always contentious and debatable policy that can inevitably cause short-term pains with prospects of long-term gains provided the merger process was seamlessly executed with firm but fine balancing of stakeholder interests. The interest of bank employees' unions of various affiliations was to be protected and their competencies had to be brought together to coexist for the growth of the new entity.

The common mindset was never to disturb the apple cart even if synergy in consolidation was clearly visible. Procrastination in taking such strategic actions by successive leadership in the past led to prolonged delay in consolidation despite wide consensus of experts on the idea. In the midst of deteriorating asset quality, many of the weak PSBs were gasping for breath. At such critical juncture, strategic solutions like consolidation in PSB space could not be further postponed. It was time for leadership to initiate such tectonic shift in policies despite diverse public opinions and widespread resentment, in the long-term interest. Any change will witness resistance as these banks were comfortable in the existing ecosystem.

8.1 Broad purpose of merger of PSBs:

PSBs have been operating in buyer's market in the post reform era in the last over two and half decades amid intense competition. The entry of new generation private banks, differentiated banks and increased collaboration with fintech companies, non-banks and insurance companies has led to massive diversification with inherent risks. The technological innovations and greater connect with nonbank financial services has brought new challenges which needed stronger risk appetite and larger asset size. Compared to international banks, the asset size of Indian banks is low. Even after merger, SBI might still be ranking only among top 50 global banks, somewhere around 45. According to the Economic Survey – 2020, an economy of our size should ideally have 5-6 banks in the top 100 global banks. But our banks are low in asset size and have not explored the lending opportunities fully.

Moreover, the changed operating environment demanded new strategies to cope with challenges of maintaining quality and ease of tackling capital adequacy issues, more importantly, to improve operational efficiency to compete with new peers. Perhaps the right time had arrived to think differently and execute reformation of banks. Doing new age banking with archaic mindset was not viable in the long run. When PSBs were at such cross roads, there is an urgent to think beyond socio-political implications of consolidation in the larger interest of strengthening the banking system.

The idea of consolidation of PSBs originated from some of unimplemented recommendations of First Narasimham Committee on the Financial System (CFS 1991). Consolidation among PSBs was also reiterated and emphasized in its second committee on Banking Sector reforms (BSR 1998). It can be recalled that Narasimham Committee had proposed substantial reduction in number of PSBs. Ideally the banking structure should comprise of 3-4 large banks with international reach which can take on larger exposure and possess the competency to operate amid cross boarder business ecosystem. 8-10 national banks followed by a set of local banks and rural banks. Merger of PSBs was also recommended in the report of the working group on restructuring of weak banks led by Shri M. S. Verma, former Chairman SBI (1999).

With State Bank of India standing tall as a behemoth with total assets of Rs. 34.55 trillion (in March 2018) at premier position in the industry followed by HDFC bank at a far distance with asset size of Rs. 10.64 crores. Now the new amalgamated entity (NAE) in PSB space – Bank of Baroda, Vijaya bank and Dena Bank will be the third rank in terms of asset size with Rs.10.19 trillion (March 2019). These mega banks can be followed up by a couple of bigger PSBs coming together with impressive size and wider geographical reach to connect with not only domestic but with global banking system. In view of expert opinions and proven benefits of consolidation stemming from SBI group consolidation, identification of the three PSBs for amalgamation was taken up to make a beginning. This could perhaps be the first leg as a conscious strategy to test success.

8.2 Strength of NAE:

The NAE formed with the assets of three PSBs (BOB, VB and DB) will be stronger and resilient to expand business. The NAE would have better business muscle with deposits and advances at Rs.14.82 trillion. The combined network of the three banks put together will be 9489 branches that can provide wider representation with better customer connect as a strong synergy. The combined Net NPAs will be down to 5.7 per cent much better than aggregate net NPAs of PSB sector struggling with high levels at 12.13 per cent. PCR will improve to 67.5 per cent much better than 63.7 per cent of PSB sector average. The total number of employees will be 85675, a strong force capable to offer, may be improved services eventually to satisfy the expanded customer base. But managing challenges of combining them will be critical to optimize synergy of the three PSBs. Well-articulated and transparent human resources policy without any bias will be able to infuse confidence in the combined entity after merger.

Other strengths will relate to consolidation of capital base. The total Tier – I combined capital shall be 9.3 per cent inching up its capital adequacy ratio (CAR) to 12.26 per cent. Effectively some of the accumulated high net NPAs of DB at 11.04 per cent can be absorbed due to comparatively low net NPAs in other two banks pegged at VB (4.1 per cent) and BOB (5.4 per cent). The transition has to be seamless as the technology platform used by them is uniform – Finacle of Infosys. The weakest link in the value chain is DB working under restricted conditions of prompt corrective action (PCA) of RBI. But the other two are capable to handhold it to form a strong new merged entity.

8.3 Human resource challenge:

In any strategic shift of such magnitude, the challenges ought to be daunting. The biggest factor in implementing the proposed amalgamation will be to reorient human resources of the three banks to integrate them into a cohesive team to take the NAE forward overcoming emotional impact of losing its parental corporate brand image with which the employees have been associated and recognized in the society for decades. People with diverse age profile and independent mindsets used to follow different risk appetite in their parent banks. They have to collaborate together to deliver better value in the NAE creating innovative opportunities to meet their career aspirations. Despite best explanations, the society considers that merged entity was not able to do good business and hence had to merge with another big bank. The employees of acquiring bank are considered better in social circles. It will take time for the differences to sink.

Therefore, the cultural integration and bringing together a coherence among key policies, technology alignment, trimming down organizational structure, redefining lines of business, work flows, systems and processes and reorganizing systemic controls will have to be planned meticulously. The human resources at all levels will have to be geared up to execute the amalgamation process with alacrity and professional stance. An acceptable brand image is to be developed for the NAE. In order to ensure execution of amalgamation process, lot of combined team efforts will be needed. How the leadership is able to accomplish it will decide the future shape of NAE.

8.4 An acceptable identity to NAE:

More critical aspect than managing human resources will be to provide an impressive identity to NAE. Quite often the terms 'merger' and 'amalgamation' are used interchangeably. But in the current context 'amalgamation' is proposed and not 'merger'. Experts point out that merger refers to a corporate restructuring activity of two or more companies into a single company whereby the identities of some of the companies get dissolved. But amalgamation is a wider concept. Under accounting standards, in case of amalgamation, there is not only pooling of assets and liabilities but also involves swapping of shares based on market valuation. PSBs are governed under 'Banking companies (acquisition and transfer of undertakings) Act 1970'.

Therefore, the roll out of amalgamation process required approval of amalgamation by Board of Directors of the concerned PSBs separately. Each bank board should approve the amalgamation process. Based on their resolutions, it was moved to cabinet ministers and both houses of parliament. Only when the amalgamation scheme receives approvals from all concerned, it will be ready for execution. In the meantime, the banks can collaborate together to shape up operationalization of NAE.

In the whole rigor of such approvals, the moot point of keen interest to all will be about the brand identity (name) of NAE. It will be an emotional and sensitive issue. Every PSB in merger process was unique with its own reputation and brand image built over a century. But it will be to use the brand image of at least one of the banks to maintain continuity. Destruction of brand value of all the three mighty PSBs will tantamount to raging them to ground. It will take another hundred years to build it. Therefore, a serious introspection and consensus was needed to go with one of them. It was not possible to jumble up the names just to maintain identity but getting a new name could be easy but then reinventing brand name will be difficult. It required lot of investment in publicity and image makeover globally.

In the given circumstances, even if debated independently without any bias on the track record, continuation of NAE with brand identity of *'Bank of Baroda'* emerges as a consensus and logical name in the larger interest. The reach and depth of image of BOB built in the past brought about a wide international reputation, which should not be withered away. Further, based on the past experience of 22 bank mergers witnessed since 1990 (post reform era), the name of the combined entity was never changed for popularity and assuaging the emotional feelings of stakeholders.

If brand name of 'Bank of Baroda' the premier bank is not retained as name of NAE, the whole purpose of transforming it into robust large size PSB will turn out to be nobody's business. Like State Bank of India, Bank of Baroda was allowed to take care of the two other PSBs so that the bigger PSB owns the responsibility to take amalgamation process to its logical end.

A different name to the NAE just to temporarily appease a section of people will have neither a recognition nor ownership from any of the three PSBs except a psychological feeling of winning a war, which is already lost. Thrust of new identity just to satisfy PSBs involved in amalgamation, as top-down command from North block will tantamount to accepting defeat before the war begins. In order to have stiff accountability for execution on the larger of PSBs, it will be necessary and non-negotiable imperative to retain the identity of the premier bank. If required, a well-calibrated voluntary retirement scheme can also be mooted to reduce the staff strength. It can weed out dissatisfied manpower and eventually reduce intermediation cost. The same pattern of retaining the name of stronger entity continued in the subsequent mergers.

8.5 Operationalization of amalgamation:

As the plan announced by the government, once amalgamation was approved, the NAE was formed and made functional from April 1, 2019 in terms of predetermined time lines led by the teamwork of the three banks. Background work would call for redrafting of many of the policies, drawing up standard operating procedures and deciding stages of workflows to integrate back-office operations for more efficient customer service. It will call for mapping skill sets and talent of every class of employees of all three banks to enable better deployment of manpower and assigning responsibilities to lead profit centers of NAE. Managing human aspects of amalgamation was very critical to improve the outcome. Closing down operational units must be decided purely on business considerations and mutual reciprocation. Setting up different management teams to work on diverse integration projects will have to be backed with faster decision support system.

The NAE can have better risk appetite that serves the very purpose for which amalgamation was initiated. The end state of amalgamation was to ensure that better profitability numbers in future should be able to erase past accumulated losses. It needed a well-calibrated identity neutral approach to trim down redundant flab.

If the real benefit of amalgamation in PSB space is to be derived, certain much-awaited reinforcing bank reforms will have to be quickly implemented, rather simultaneously. It has to begin with added rigor in regulating the top echelons of bank's leadership akin to private peers. Strengthening board governance by introducing new criteria for selection, training and rigorous performance review of IDs that is glaringly missing. Empowering RBI to approve or change the board members including full time directors depending upon the supervisory outcome. Developing sensitivity towards long-term quality consciousness and improved compliance standards can be enforced only if the regulators are fully empowered to do so even with PSBs. That precisely is the reason that RBI is seeking powers to oversee the board structure of PSBs which is currently not in its purview. This limits its ability to oversee compliance in totality.

Induction of quality IDs with domain expertise can well be assigned to BBB set up for the purpose. It will also be necessary to consider removing dual regulation of PSBs by hastening setting up of BIC in line with the recommendations of Dr. P.J. Nayak Committee meant to review governance of boards of banks in India.

The process of phasing out government ownership from 51 per cent to 33 per cent can also be thought through. Hence the success of merger among PSBs will depend much on the ability to manage the aftermath with supporting changes. Using mergers as a standalone initiative without enough reinforcements will weaken the purpose of amalgamation returning inefficiency. The synergy of the bold bank reforms will have to be fully derived to infuse renewed optimism among PSBs. It will need inclusive ownership of all stakeholders in pursuing mergers so that such large and strong PSBs can be strategic players in global banking space.

8.6 Second phase of amalgamation

After the successful merger of Vijaya Bank, Dena Bank with Bank of Baroda, the dawn of the new fiscal year 2020-21 for banking industry brings many more challenges in near term and ample opportunities for growth in the long run. In the midst of fight against the unprecedented global pandemic, going ahead with the consolidation of 10 Public Sector Banks (PSBs) into four large entities will go into history ultimately implementing one of the key pending recommendation of Narasimham Committee – I (1991-92).

Phasing out flab in the organizational structure, optimizing branch network, better deployment of talent and more importantly acquiring robust risk management and lending capabilities are some of the intended merits in the long term. The newly formed 12 strong and smart PSBs should eventually be able to compete with new generation peers and should be able to raise the bar of performance in the inclusive journey of banking industry.

8.7 New pecking order of PSBs:

Based on the business data of March 2019, SBI, the banking behemoth will lead the pack with business of Rs. 52.05 trillion, PNB will be the second big PSB after merger of Oriental Bank of Commerce (OBC) and United bank of India (UBI) with it reaching business level of Rs. 17.94 trillion leaving behind Bank of Baroda at third position with its business at Rs 16.13 trillion.

Canara Bank will stand at fourth position commanding a business of Rs. 15.2 trillion. Union bank, Andhra Bank and Corporation Bank together will reach a size of Rs. 14.59 trillion. Indian bank and Allahabad bank will make another smart PSB with business standing at Rs. 8.05 trillion. Post-merger, these business figures are likely to be different quarter after quarter, once the newly formed bigger and smarter banks shapes up and crystallization of business takes place. The consolidation is expected to attain better economies of scale with better operational efficiency. It will take considerable time for the new entities to command the patronage that they once enjoyed.

Coming to the strengths of the outgoing PSBs, the shareholders of merging PSBs will get shares of PSB with which they are merged as per merger ratios approved by their bank's boards and government. Since it is a strategic consolidation process initiated to trim down the number of PSBs and to focus more on making them big and strong, the merger of any underlying PSB, as a consequence, does not necessarily reflect upon their operational efficiency. For example, the shareholders of OBC will get 1150 shares of Punjab National Bank (PNB) with which it is merged in lieu of its 1000 shares whereas UBI shareholders will get only 121 shares of PNB in lieu of 1000 shares. These share swap ratios clearly reflect their intrinsic strengths and hard work they did during the period they were operating under PCA of RBI. OBC recouped so well after it was placed under PCA that it surpassed PNB, its acquirer. A phenomenal performance, indeed.

8.8 Continuity of customer service:

In order to maintain minimum disruption in service to customers, the technical integration of digital operating platform is important to ensure that the customers of merged banks are able to operate their accounts in the newly formed bigger PSBs with greater ease and convenience. While lot of homework must have been done prior to merger to ensure interoperability of bank accounts of customers, still the interruptions will have to be handled with a collaborative support of merging banks and their vendors.

The ongoing lockdown and tendency of low foot falls will provide enough time for the new entities to initiate business process reengineering so that operational procedures are synchronized with the merging entity. The support of customers will be needed in near term to approach parent branch for non-routine transactions. The digital outfits of any bank will be able to provide basic routine services; more so when interchange charges of ATM usage has now been temporarily dispensed with. A quick capacity building and understanding each other's operational nuances is necessary to ensure that the initial pain points causing customer discomfort are minimized.

8.9 Harmony in human relations:

The leadership at all levels of the newly formed PSBs will have the tough challenge to convince by their action and treatment of employees of merging PSBs with care and concern. Behavioral aspects will be important to maintain good harmony in various spans of management hierarchy. Over a period of time, the differences among employees may sink. Rightfully so, many PSBs went for hectic and speedy internal promotions of their people after announcement of consolidation plan to protect their own interest. There will be not much to offer for the new management except creating a friendly unbiased working environment and better subordinate – superior relationships.

Similarly, trimming down organizational structure and rationalization of branch network will be an inevitable outcome of consolidation where sensitivity in dealing with human relations will be explicable in positioning and deployment in unified responsibilities. Many PSBs follow a 3 – tier structure – Branch, controlling office and corporate office whereas others still have 4-tier structure with geographical area control structure as an add on. Taking an unbiased view, the new PSB has to adopt a single policy in the best interest without upholding merging bank's superiority. Same collaborative view should be taken in merging and closing of multiple branches in the same location. Customer concentration and convenience of outreach should be the driving point in rationalizing the branch network.

The new PSB regime can prove worthiness and stand to the test of efficiency provided it removes the divide between merged entity and merging entity as fast as possible. Though all banks work in same regulatory frame, the procedural and cultural divide is vast. Even documentation and vetting of proposals for various activities could be different. It is a big challenge to bring them at par and quickly dissipate the differences in near term.

The challenge will be to tackle soft parts of merger dealing with mind integration than brining physical infrastructure together. If human aspects are dealt properly, the merits of consolidation can be harnessed eventually in terms of improved asset quality, capital adequacy, lending appetite and systemic controls. The historic move of consolidation can be fruitful only if the newly formed PSBs in collaboration with regulators and government can improve the effectiveness of corporate governance.

CHAPTER – 9

PRIVATIZATION OF PUBLIC SECTOR BANKS

After merger of PSBs, the next phase is evidently privatisation. The case for privatisation is gaining ground as a follow up policy to mergers. It can be affirmed that PSBs have progressively improved their competitiveness adoption of technology and new business process reengineering in line with the consumer needs. The turnaround time of various services could be fine-tuned with anytime and anywhere banking spreading fast on digital mode. PSBs have geared up fast to offer products and services to customers with comparable standards of efficiency. The branch interiors have been revamped to suit digital ecosystem. They demonstrated resilience and adaptability to change but could not attain sustainable pace of growth in line with the potentiality. These limitations led to merger among PSBs with privatisation as another strategic move to make them more vibrant and relevant to a growth economy.

The speed and appetite to grab market share has slowed down after the private peers and diversified banking and non-bank entities started competing in a big way. The imprint of legacy issues and challenges of transformation continued to impinge upon their operational efficiency. Their fragility compared to private banks broadly stems from (i) low capital base, (ii) high NPAs (iii) poor quality of standard assets vulnerable to further slippage, (iv) large volume of low value business due to mass banking (v) low profitability with some PSBs carrying protracted negative return on assets (ROA) (vi) low market capitalization and tepid investor sentiments.

It is a good case to analyse why the progressive reforms, enhanced competition with entry of new banks, continuous capital support, upgraded regulations and watchful lens of government could not bring the desired change in the working culture and governance in PSBs. They now remain better but could not gain the strength and operational efficiency sufficient to attract capital from markets and stand on their own as independent commercial entities.

Based on the government experience of relentlessly providing capital to PSBs, the Economic Survey and Union Budget – 2020-21 have rightly voiced concern and decided to pause capital infusion, knowing well that they cannot undertake fresh lending without capital support. Instead of providing capital support and losing it to loan losses, PSBs will now be nurtured to augment capital directly from equity markets.

Unless the reasons are identified, even future strategies may not put them back on the desired track. Large-scale consolidation of PSBs can create larger entities with better risk appetite opening up scope to shrink branch network but it may not be the panacea against their inherent weaknesses. A case for privatisation is another imminent policy shaping up the future of banking.

9.1 Impact of capital infusion:

Despite massive doses of capital infusion by the government beginning 1992 and pump priming it with recapitalization bonds during 2018-20, PSBs are still struggling to maintain minimum 11.5 percent of CRAR in terms of Basel – III framework. The Basel III standards are set to be fully implemented soon with the impact of pandemic receding fast and normalcy in making. In some weak PSBs, the ownership of government has breached 90 percent mark from the ideal level of 51 percent. Due to such weak capital base, PSBs are unable to compete in fresh lending with their private peers. Their decisive role in lending to productive and micro sectors of the economy is fast diminishing with capital adequacy ratio hitting the wall with no scope for government to infuse. The only option for PSBs is to raise capital from the market which will be possible only if the fundamentals are improved. Some of the weak PSBs are now in a catch 22 situation. Neither the performance fundamentals can improve to attract capital from market and without capital the performance parameters cannot be improved. The newly opened small finance banks and other intermediaries are fast overtaking PSBs in fresh lending by demolishing past bastions. The only solution in the given situation seems to be to privatise so that capital can be infused by private entrepreneurs and the ecosystem can be driven towards a private ownership.

9.2 Hint at privatization:

Partly to obviate the situation, large-scale mergers and consolidation in PSB space was mooted as part of ongoing bank reforms so that investors may evince interest on bigger banks with larger risk appetite. Strengthening performance indicators to attract capital will need inclusive and sustained efforts from all stakeholders. The recent budget proposal to divest even minority stake held by the government in IDBI Bank hints at likely move towards privatization, way ahead. It is possible as IDBI Bank Ltd is a public financial institution governed by Companies' act 2013 whereas the government of India (GoI) regulates PSBs under the Banking Companies (Acquisition and Transfer of Undertakings) Act, 1970; the Bank Nationalization Act, 1980, and the State Bank of India Act, 1955. Privatisation of PSBs seems to be on way to solve the perennial need for them to hold sufficient capital. While privatisation as a solution to remove some of the weaknesses of PSBs could be explored but it is necessary to find the reasons for the stark difference in the working of two sets of banks in India – PSBs and Private sector banks. Understanding the precise reasons will help in root cause analysis so that together with privatisation, other grass root level inadequacies are addressed to ensure that the bigger purpose of making them more efficient and active can be served.

9.3 Impact of bank reforms

It can be recollected that based on the recommendations of Narasimham Committee – I (1991) and Narasimham Committee – II (1998), several bank reform measures were introduced to enable PSBs to function and compete on commercial lines while continuing their predominant role to pursue social banking with extensive outreach. Despite the limitations of dual regulatory regime of RBI and Ministry of Finance represented by DFS, PSBs have struggled hard to move closer to compete with private banks including the new generation banks entered after liberalization of banking sector. The quality and sustainability of PSBs improved with adoption of international prudential standards set by the BCBS from time to time.

PSBs successfully adopted income recognition and asset classification (IRAC) norms and made provisions against bad and doubtful debts and even against standard assets. They incorporated Internal Capital adequacy Assessment Policy (ICAAP) in line with capital adequacy framework prescribed by Basel committee from time to time. Adopted advanced technology based on core banking system to provide 'anywhere and anytime' banking services. At the same time, deregulation of interest rates, reduction in cash reserve ratio (CRR) and statutory liquidity ratio (SLR) and flexibility in managing liquidity enabled them to improve efficiency. Integrated risk management policies helped them to apprehend and mitigate risks.

Improvement in the look and feel of some of the high-end branches in metro and urban areas increased use of alternate digital channels and improved quality of customer services. Diversification of products, bank assurance offerings and digital kiosks improved their visibility. Engaging consultants for reorganization, business process reengineering to harness technology, moving towards lateral recruitment of specialists, introduction of fast-track promotions, issue of ESOPs, payment of incentives to select top notch performers were some of the areas of changes adopted under the autonomy that enabled PSBs to improve their overall operational efficiency. Banking sector reforms have thus improved resilience to put up with the challenges and brought them closer to private banks in terms of providing customer services. The government deepened further reforms to improve the robustness of banking system.

9.4 Next generation reforms:

With intent to further strengthen bank reforms; government convened a mind meet – Gyan Sangam – I in January 2015. Its deliberations culminated into a seven-pronged strategy – *'Indradhanush'* that was rolled out in August 2015. In nutshell, it led to (i) separation of position of Chairman and Managing Director (CMD) in PSBs into (a) non-executive Chairman and (b) a full-time position of Managing Director and Chief Executive Officer (MD & CEO). (ii) formed a separate entity – Banks Board Bureau (BBB) in April 2016 to independently identify talent to fit the positions of full-time directors – MD & CEOs/Executive Directors (EDs) for PSBs. (iii) Capitalization – Rs. 70000 crores to be infused in next 4 years at that time. (iv) De-stressing – tackling bad and doubtful debts. Hastening enactment of Insolvency and Bankruptcy Code (IBC) – 2016 and formation of Insolvency and Bankruptcy Board of India (IBBI) could be considered part of it. (v) Empowerment – assuring no government interference with freedom to hire people (vi) framework of accountability – fixing key performance areas (vii) governance reforms.

Similarly, another meeting of policy makers known as 'manthan' was held in November 2017 to discuss about infusing large-scale capital of Rs. 2.1 trillion through recapitalization bonds when NPAs went up after the asset quality review of RBI. It led to introduction of another reform agenda under *'Enhanced Access to Service excellence (EASE)'* a quantitative performance measure designed in collaboration with Boston consulting group (BCG) to measure efficiency and smart service levels of PSBs. These new generation reforms have added a performance orientation based on quantitative business outcome.

9.5 Missing gaps:

Based on these sets of reforms, PSBs have significantly improved overall efficiency. But certain limitations in autonomy and corporate governance were the missing links that escaped the regulatory scrutiny. Imbalance in the corporate governance practices systematically brought down the performance of PSBs. While reforms were pushing up performance a few notches up in certain parameters but the missing gaps were bringing them down by a few notches more in some other parameters dragging them down in the end state.

Too much focus on managing asset quality led to growing indifference towards fresh lending and business growth. The credit risk appetite was not built sufficiently to harness full potentiality of business. The market share of PSBs dropped from 70 percent in 2010 to 64 percent by March 2021 and the downward tilt is on. The PCA imposed on some of the PSBs had debilitating impact. Though both the group of banks operated within the same macroeconomic, legal, regulatory and business environment, their efficiency levels were ostensibly different due to different operating pressures and prioritization of business segments.

9.6 Divide in performance culture:

In evaluating performance orientation, private banks are found to be totally profit driven whereas PSBs had to focus more on social banking and financial inclusion to increase customer connect. Thus, one pursues profitability; the other is unable to work on augmenting profitability due to different performance obligations cast on them by their key stakeholders.

As a result, private banks focus on *'commercial banking'* whereas PSBs follow *'Social banking'* that sometimes proves to be a drag on the operational efficiency. It also creates a bias in the market. Collateral free loan seekers approaches PSBs increasing the operational costs whereas better credit worthy people seek services of private banks. The divide is obvious. Creamy layer of entrepreneurs whose wallet share is substantial are fast shifting the patronage from PSBs to private banks, though the trend is coming down now due to the transparent policy of state-owned banks.

9.7 Compensation for social costs:

Financial intermediaries can be used for promoting inclusive banking for social well-being. But the only need is to compute 'social costs' of financial inclusion and extensive outreach and reimburse such overheads to bank that deliver social banking services without any bias. It is understandable that no service can be provided free in a competitive world with end state objective of commercial sustainability. A protracted negligence in compensating 'social costs' has been one of the contributing factors pushing PSBs into a state of despondency.

In the journey of modern banking, private banks enjoy full autonomy to work based on 'quality, size' and intrinsic 'profitability of businesses'. They have choice to select customers whom they would like to serve. On the other hand, PSBs have no choice to choose customers. Customers that walk into bank branches have to be accepted even for opening a no frill account without any compensation for social costs. Such fine lines of difference in their role is not drawn up by any statute but have formed automatically with the implied understanding of all stakeholders.

Even the expectations of stakeholders have such demarcations in mind. Customers expect subsidized services from PSBs whereas they are prepared to follow queue protocol and pay service charges to private banks. Such tendency to undermine services of state-owned banks further increases the divide sucking out profitability and operational efficiency.

9.8 Performance management System:

In the same realm, the performance management system has been institutionalized differently. The basis of measurement of performance and benchmark of efficiency are differently aligned. It is difficult to provide incentives for better performance and disincentives for poor performance in PSBs. The stark difference in human resource management is obvious. PSBs hire employees for 'lifetime' whereas private banks employ them so long as they are found useful to the organization. Issue of 'pink slips' for non-performance is common in private banks whereas PSBs have to pay wages that are agreed at industry level irrespective of internal costs and profitability. This has embedded work cultural divide. When implied mandate of performance, remuneration, perquisites and assessment practices are different, expecting similarity in efficiency levels is not possible.

9.9 Weak governance:

This does not imply that governance in private banks is perfect. There are aberrations in corporate governance that surprises stakeholders when conflict of interest becomes public. But in PSBs, the gaps in corporate governance are structural 'ab initio' functioning under dual regulation. The lines of businesses are directed by the stakeholders depriving functional independence to choose commercial viability. The performance of different groups of banks in implementing PMJDY, and PMMY, loans to MSME units, agriculture sector and to small and marginal borrowers starkly brings out the difference in the inclination to serve the masses in hinterland.

Ever since nationalization of banks in 1969/1980, the efficiency levels of PSBs are determined not by profit alone but by the extent of reach and fulfilment of socio-economic goals. If PSBs are designed to serve a different purpose, calling for parity with private banks may not be tenable.

9.10 Solutions and future agenda:

As a way forward, while keeping journey of bank reforms intact, it will be necessary to remove constraints of PSBs which are well in the knowledge of stakeholders (i) remove structural differences in governance of PSBs to bring parity in efficiency levels to attract private capital. (ii) Performance management system and compensation policy has to be fine-tuned to attract larger commitments from employees. (iii) creating an ecosystem is necessary where non- performing employees have fear of losing job to encourage performance. Not opting for promotion and immobility of employees, one size fits all compensation policy has wrecked the working culture. (iv)Granting full autonomy to PSBs by reducing the government stake from 51 percent to 33 percent in terms of the recommendations of Narasimham committee – II (1998). (v) Hasten setting up of Bank Investment Company (BIC) as a holding company as recommended by the *'Report of the committee to review governance of boards of banks in India (2014)'* (Chairman: P.J. Nayak). Such a move could reduce the ambiguity arising from dual regulation and ownership bias. (vi) Merging a weak bank with strong banks in term of recommendations of the *'Report of the working group on restructuring weak public sector banks (1999)'* (Chairman: M.S. Verma) can be a possible solution. Even merging a PSB with a private bank could also be considered if synergy is evident from the hybrid format. (vii) Consider reimbursing 'social costs' of banking as price for connecting people with the formal financial system that can plough back into exchequer in the form of improved tax collections on the incremental increase in wealth. (viii) Desist from imposing performance obligations that are not commercially viable or compensate the overheads. The choice of lines of business should be left to individual banks.

The tinge of privatization in the form of reduced government stake should be able to grant full autonomy to PSBs to function independently at their choice. If the banking system is to actually play the expected role in shaping aspirational India, segregation of social costs and divesting stake in PSBs need to be considered as a next reform measure after consolidation, lest we should be struggling again. The commitment to put banks on such strong footing without bias need to be demonstrated with appropriate change in their working system even if they are privatized. As a follow up of announcement made in union budget 2021-22, the privatisation of PSBs is being pursued.

9.11 Privatization move of PSBs:

Though Niti Aayog reportedly submitted the names of four Public Sector Banks (PSBs) – Central Bank of India (CBI), Indian overseas Bank (IOB), Bank of India and Bank of Maharashtra among others to the core group of secretaries for picking up two of them for privatization, CBI and IOB are touted as probable banks with indications of uptick in their stock price sentiments.

These banks were under private ownership until their nationalisation in 1969 and their privatisation now mark a strategic shift. It indicates the maturity of the society where the need for state owned banks is still relevant but not mandatory. Since some of the newly formed private banks set up in post-reform era have done comparatively better even in hinterland, exploring privatization and complete commercial autonomy can help these entities grow to their potentiality and relieve the government from the obligation to provide recurring capital assistance. Though the privatisation of PSBs may not happen during this fiscal but going forward, it may fructify in the coming fiscal 2022-23 but latest status indicates that Bank of Maharashtra and Central Bank of India are the top probable two PSBs on the radar of privatisation. They have been favoured for privatisation, though the Indian Overseas Bank (IOB) has also found suitable for the exercise either this year or possibly later.

As a follow up measure, the government is all set to roll out the bank privatisation process of PSBs. Starting with the IDBI Bank's strategic divestment, it had begun consulting RBI to draw out a security clearance framework for screening potential bidders of PSBs. For this the Department of Investment and Public Asset Management (DIPAM) will be putting in place the framework which would ensure that potential buyers will meet the fit and proper criteria of the RBI. In doing so, DIPAM is planning to bring the central bank on board to vet candidates in the first step itself. According to DIPAM the bank privatisation process would be different from the sale of any other PSU, and more restrictions and measures will have to be put in place.

The PSB privatization framework would ensure that the privatisation process would go forward only when suitable candidates show interest in acquiring the lender. This will further ensure that the process does not fall through at a later stage if the bidders fail to meet the RBI's criteria. RBI considers several factors to determine whether a candidate is fit and proper to be a shareholder director of the bank. This includes applicant's integrity, reputation, track record in financial matters, tax laws compliance, ongoing proceedings of serious disciplinary or criminal nature and financial misconduct among others. Central Bank of India and IOB have also been reportedly considered for privatisation.

To begin with, the government is looking to sell 45.48% of its shareholding in IDBI Bank to transfer the management control to the new buyer. By assessing the market appetite and in consultation with the transaction advisor and RBI, the government and RBI will together to determine the quantum of the stake dilution. KPMG India has been appointed by the government as the transaction advisor for the IDBI bank sale.

9.12 State of target PSBs:

But both the PSBs identified for privatisation are on weak trail with RBI placing CBI under PCA in June 2017 due to high ratio of NPAs and negative return on assets. IOB is under PCA since 2015. But Bank of Maharashtra is on a better footing in terms of its fundamentals. Recently government infused capital of Rs. 4800 crores in CBI and Rs. 4100 crores in IOB allocated during 2020-21 to shore up their capital adequacy ratio (CAR). As a result, government stake reached 86.4 percent in CBI and 95.84 percent in IOB. The improved CAR may help them to exit from the PCA restrictions.

Despite nursing under PCA regulations for considerable period, they still continue to be plagued by high NPAs, capital constraints and low credit growth. Some of the NPAs of these banks may get transferred to NARC – bad bank for improving CAR as and when it gets operationalized.

Though the challenge for the acquirer would be to overcome the inherent weaknesses to mend their operational efficiency but the greater mileage will be the access to low-cost resources and wider presence in hinterland, a unique value proposition. It takes decades of hard work to shape that way. Besides the intrinsic operational weaknesses, PSBs in general have legacy problems like age profile, skill sets and digital capabilities, more so when quality of human resources works as a competitive differentiator.

9.13 Preparing for privatization:

The government having assured that interest of employees will be taken care, these banks may logically offer a voluntary retirement scheme (VRS) to its employees to reduce the flab and to make space for the new owner to induct fresh lateral talent. But VRS many times may become counterproductive with flight of talent. Reports indicate that enterprising employees of these banks are on prowl for new jobs. It is therefore critical to think through to fit right conditionality of VRS to avoid such pitfalls.

It should be open to only employees of say above the age of 45-50 years. Employees promoted in the last 3 years may also be made ineligible. Compensation should not be linked to residual service in which juniors will stand to benefit. It should also be made essential to settle the staff loans so that recent entrants may not leave the organisation. VRS offer amid privatization will have better response due to psychological apprehensions of working under private ownership. Once the ownership changes, the rules of the game will however change. Performers will stay and non-performers shall be phased out trimming the manpower in next 2-3 years.

As far as pension liabilities are concerned, the acquiror has two options. (i) One time settlement on the lines of pension commutation system (ii) hive-off and form a pension trust adding on to its existing corpus to service the pensions so long as the liability persist. Since employees joining after 2004 are covered by New Pension Scheme

(NPS) and are not part of pension, the need for pension payment may eventually get phased out.

The proposed privatization move has to be approved by core group of secretaries. It then goes to Alternative Mechanism (AM) led by finance minister before it gets a final Cabinet nod. Amendments to the Banking companies (Acquisition and Transfer of Undertakings) Act, 1970 will be needed to privatise PSBs and they need to be brought under companies Act 2013. Once the ground is made ready for privatisation to take off, the next challenge is to find a competent buyer.

The stakeholders of existing large banks may consider acquiring these PSBs, retain them as wholly owned subsidiaries with independent identity until they attain better operational efficiency. They can eventually merge with acquirer bank. It is always challenging to create a policy template for privatization first time but it can work as a set standard for future.

One of the objectives of privatization is to create big banks. Unless privatized PSBs are merged with existing large private banks, they cannot ultimately attain the kind of scale and size to develop higher risk appetite. Hence, privatization is an uphill task needing to tackle multiple challenges and exploring new ideas but it can pave way for developing more sustainable and strong banking system benefitting all stakeholders. The government ultimately aiming at creating 4-5 large banks of SBI size to be in the international league so that they have formidable role in financial intermediation to fund growth prospects, post pandemic. Recently, honourable Finance Minister desired that India should have about 20 banks of SBI size which will take considerable time. As it is, even more bank of size of SBI will need huge efforts and rejig of banks. Hence privatization should be followed by large scale merger to create big banks with sufficient capital base and credit risk appetite.

CHAPTER – 10

DIGITAL TRANSFORMATION

The acceleration of digital penetration that began with demonetization but slowed down later has again come back at a greater speed and efficiency after the onset of the pandemic. Like several other sectors, banking sector too is battered with the Covid induced stress and is using several strategies to assist its borrows using the leverage provide by RBI. In this milieu, digital thrust has assumed critical role after the onset of pandemic. Technology has been widely applied to tackle some of the challenges in more ways. The exacerbated asset quality woes, shrinking capital base, call to restructure stressed assets are some of the key challenges in near term where monitoring through digital mode becomes essential.

Granting increased loans to ailing units to quicken revival is another immediate priority. Amid these critical near-term adversities, some long-term opportunities are in the horizon. The pick-up in the pace of digital infrastructure, diversification of digital products combined with the shift in the attitude of customers clearly indicates future potentiality of digital transformation which is set to work as a key differentiator.

Instead of banks persuading customers to use the digital mode, it is the customers who have begun to proactively seek digitally driven banking products/services. Such an attitudinal shift of customer preferences can be transformative to tow the banking system to a more efficient digital trajectory akin to international best practices. It is the opportune time for banks to recognize the merit in the impending change and put appropriate systems in place to fully tap the synergy of digital infrastructure. The long-term sustainability of banks will depend upon their ability to mine opportunities of digital transformation for better operational efficiency and profitability.

10.1 Opportunity in making:

Going beyond working in the long term for societal change to develop digital life style, bank's key end state objective is to improve (i) operational efficiency and (ii) reduce the intermediation costs. Implementing right digital governance can help enhance stakeholder value. But due to natural resistance to change, Indian banking system could not effectively get anywhere closer to these long-term objectives. It would have taken years of efforts for banks to forge an alliance with customers to persuade them to use digital banking utilities. But one of the unintended consequences of the pandemic is the sudden shift in the appetite of the society to increasingly adopt digital mode to stay physically away from banking touch points. The bank employees, hitherto shy of using technology for day-to-day activities have suddenly discovered its power and they picked up flair that can go a long way in taking digitization forward.

Thus, the opportunity for banks is to strike the right chord to ensure that such Covid induced tilt towards digital channels becomes customer's perpetual life style. The steady digital transformation sweeping across the globe when seen together with the development of digital capabilities in Indian financial markets will be convincing that it is the right opportunity to transform the society into a digital savvy so as to make financial intermediation more cost efficient, safe, secured and user friendly. Looking to the intense use of digital mode by customers and bank's offerings online, RBI has been rightly emphasizing the need for greater focus on cyber security to create an appropriate safety net for users.

10.2 Global trends in digital transformation:

Digital financial services have globally expanded fast due to the ongoing telecom revolution and surge in smartphones. It has led to an explosion in data demand, while the accompanying growth of mobile applications has seen a range of disruptive players creating intense competition. Proliferation of information, communication and telecommunication (ICT) applications in delivering banking and financial services are fast shaping up digital transformation. Neo banks – following virtual business model – branchless banks have made an entry and reached 45 globally by 2019. While crypto currencies are making way using blockchain technology, even digital currencies are making way in some of the economies including China and South Korea. Others may follow the trend to digitize the economy and gradually move towards less cash society. RBI is also contemplating to go for digital currency.

The fusion of synergy of banks, non-banks spearheaded by entry of fintech entities have converged into digital transformation that brings more convenience to users. The ICT led speed in the cross-border payment and settlement systems followed by accelerated capital flows highlighted the need for improving digital transformation. Amid the rising shift towards digital mode, the pandemic has further forced users to adopt technology to stay away from physical presence at the outlets. Even handling of currency is feared as a source of spread of virus that further activated digital means for settling financial transactions.

Due to such Covid induced rapid digital banking growth, digital payments volumes could see a CAGR of 23.8 percent set to reach US $ 15 trillion by 2025 rising from a level of US $ 3.7 trillion in 2019 that is estimated to have reached US $ 5 trillion by now. E-commerce platforms are among the best-funded ASEAN businesses and according to a study by Google and Temasek, e-commerce is projected to grow exponentially in ASEAN region, from US$5.5 billion in 2015 to US$88 billion by 2025.

In the journey of digital transformation, adding an innovative dimension, cloud service providers offer a wide range of services. They include supplying storage space, computing power, creating developer platforms, providing software and web applications etc. Outsourcing activities and processes by using such services can be an efficient way to improve the operational efficiency. It allows financial entities to save costs and resources, use synergies, optimize processes and gain access to specialist knowledge in furthering digital penetration.

In the journey of digital transformation, payments through mobile applications occupy 42 percent of total global spending by consumers. It is noteworthy that the way data is consumed in 2020 had a tectonic shift. As Covid19 pandemic swept the planet, almost all aspects of life – right from work place to working out shifted online and people moved to digital world of apps.

According to recent report by Hotsuite – a social media management platform, almost 65 percent of the world's eligible population now logs into at least one social media platform with 376 million new users since last year. It works out to 12 new digital users per second. Going by the viewership – Face book – 2.6 billion, whats app and You tube each has 2 billion while Instagram has 1.08 billion. The trend shows the potential uptick due to Covid19. Number of digital banking users are estimated at 3 billion by 2021 that may scale up further due to the pandemic.

New contactless payment channels, using voice, wearable technology and even sound waves, have emerged to further improve customer experience by eliminating the need to reach out for physical debit/ credit cards. Virtual cards are making a fast entry and soon there may not be a need to hold a physical plastic card. Even alexa of google is able to provide information on financial services if security features are loaded into it and protective measures are well taken care.

With machines performing human-like tasks, AI has the capability to bring enormous transformation in the payment sector lowering operational costs. Currently, AI enabled chat bots assist customers in opening or closing accounts, transferring funds and solving doubts 24x7. Use of robotics and AI has reduced human intervention in the sector. Growing affluence, rapid urbanization, and expanding education, are propelling strong demand for financial services. Flowing from these global experiences, domestic financial services are bracing to provide digital experience.

10.3 Domestic Digital infrastructure:

Regulators and banks have strategically expanded digital infrastructure more significantly during the last decade 2010-2020 to create a digitally enabled banking ecosystem to move in line with the global trends. It enabled banks to reach out to users far and wide to an extent that was not possible through stand-alone 'brick and mortar' branch banking model pursued for decades. Banks have collaborated well to provide universal access to banking services *'round the clock, round the globe'* forging a tectonic shift from traditional branch led banking to bank led banking thus making a branch customer, a bank customer enabling access from any touch point of the bank. Moreover, government and regulators have been developing steady ecosystem for digitization after enactment of *'Payments and Settlement Systems Act–2007'* eventually leading to greater interoperability, connectivity even among different service providers.

Besides interoperability and seamless connectivity, banks have added numerous technologies and shaped products and services to meet the changing aspirations of new age customers. The convenience of portability through digital wallets/mobile/app-based banking has enabled *'banking on go'* for tech savvy users. Smart phones are shaping up as mini bank branches enabling many forms of services, more importantly the transfer of funds. The per capita, per annum digital transactions have gone up from 10.73 in 2017 to 22 in 2019 fuelled by UPI interface. The post covid data is still to crystallize but trends of increase are clear. Amid the lockdown in July, India had the highest percentage of people spending more time on social media after Philippines.

In the backdrop of such digital innovations, alternate delivery channels could be developed fast. The number of ATMs has increased from 75645 in April 2011 to 210478 by June 2020. The number of POS terminals have increased from 5,95,958 in April 2011 to 50,39,359 in June 2020. The number of debit cards have begun to increase after National Payment Corporation of India (NPCI) was set up in 2008 reaching 845 million by June 2020. The business correspondents (BC) points have been set up in villages as part of banking outreach. The handheld POS devices driven by solar system/solar chargeable cells is good mode in remote villages where disruption of electricity is a regular phenomenon.

Differentiated banks have made an entry to provide affordable banking services, more particularly to the people at the bottom of the pyramid in hinterland. Ten SFBs and seven payment banks have been set up to push digital banking. Among them, India Post Payment Bank (IPPB) – a large payment bank with synergy of close to 1,50,000 post office outlets can take the electronic banking to masses in a big way. Payment banks cannot lend and can presently accept deposits of up to Rs. 100,000. The limit is raised to Rs. 2 lakhs by RBI.

With Cooperative banks coming under the regulatory ambit of RBI, these set of banks can also play a constructive role in spreading digital banking culture in hinterland. E-KYC and Video KYC has come handy to comply with regulatory dispensation. Keeping the outreach capability of cooperative banks, the window is opened for them to be converted into small finance bank to take greater part in providing digitally driven banking. These developments indicate possibility for banks to gauge the depth of reach of digital mode. According to the World Bank's Findex – 2017 (financial inclusion index), 80 percent of Indian bankable population (above 15 years of age) have a bank account and a debit card is provided to most of them thus taking digital banking to masses.

Faster round the clock – on all week days, the availability of remittances through NEFT/RTGS and instant retail payments through digital wallets enabled many micro transactions to go on electronic mode. UPI has added huge capability to settle remittance transactions. Expansion of electronic banking services enables – money transfer & payments, access to finance, payment of insurance premium, mutual fund savings, other forms of savings & investment. While banks were building internal digital capabilities to compete with each other, fintech revolution added another dimension to pump prime digital transformation.

10.4 Increasing Fintech role:

Financial Technology companies popularly known as Fintech companies branching out into activities broadly related to (i) Payments (ii) lending (iii) insurance and (iv) Wealth management. Fintech entities have made their foray as start-ups are engaged in providing financial services in a virtual mode and initially entered the payments and remittance space and gradually diversified into peer-to-peer lending, crowd-funding, trade finance, insurance, account aggregation and wealth management. Through collaboration with FinTech players, several banks are diversifying into a hybrid model where mobile wallet services broadened the scope of customer convenience.

Banks are not only facing competition from Fintech companies but also from large technology companies (BigTechs) that are entering into financial services industry in a big way. Building upon the advantages of data-network activities, some BigTechs are venturing into payments, money management, insurance and lending activities that can potentially eat into the market share of banks.

It is estimated that there are over 1300 fintech entities. Recognizing the importance of fintechs in driving the growth of digital lending, RBI has taken initiative to create a 'regulatory sandbox' to promote innovations besides fostering cooperation with Fintech hubs from Singapore, UK, China etc. Thus the wave of Fintech presented an opportunity to inject new dynamism and new growth in financial services.

10.5 Digital lending:

It is estimated that around 19 start-ups in the Peer-to-Peer (P2P) marketplace segment have been funded by overseas investors and venture capitalists. Fintech lending Companies such as *Faircent, Loanframe, Neogrowth, Lendingkart* leverage digital data footprints and technology targeting the middle class, millennial & MSME entrepreneurs. As compared to traditional banks and non-bank lending institutions, they are able to dispense quick loans at lower cost with minimal paperwork to the satisfaction of borrowers.

Even now the entry barriers are high in lending segment, as losses tend to be high in such operations. Recently RBI has begun to regulate P2P lending and regulated these companies as a NBFC. Hunting for credit has always been the biggest challenge for millions of small businesses and micro entrepreneurs. They run from pillar to post to get finance for working capital or any other financing requirements. Digital access to loans if made available seamlessly can help build enterprise in India. Since it may not be viable for commercial banks to go for low-ticket micro credit, they can collaborate with fintech intermediaries to create a mutually amenable and sustainable business model. Keeping these emerging needs, rightly, RBI has opened up co-origination model of lending for banks and NBFCs. If explores, it could be a win win value proposition for them and it can go a long way in dispensing credit to needy sectors of the economy using digital platform.

10.6 Challenges in digital transformation:

While the spread of digital banking is benefiting millions of customers and stakeholders, there are several challenges from the bank's perspectives. Initial investment in building digital infrastructure is high and pay back opportunities are low in near term. The impact of the pandemic has added a new thrust on digital banking. Increased number of users hitherto hesitating to try digital delivery modes has suddenly found merit in adopting electronic mode. Such shift in customer preference towards digital banking should be fully harnessed to intensify digital transformation for long-term efficiency and profitability. But before articulating strategies to act in time, following key challenges must be kept in view.

(i) Obsolescence of Technology:

Depreciation is steep and obsolescence is fast. Despite competent manpower in banks, management of technology is highly vendor centric with risks of rising costs. Cost sensitive customers are not prepared to pay for the cost of higher investment in acquiring the digital infrastructure and banks cannot levy charges on many services due to regulatory and government mandate. Recovering costs of technology is tough, at least in the short term. It also calls for frequent up-gradation of hardware and software that eats into the profitability of banks.

(ii) Cyber Security:

Breach of cyber security standards, digital frauds and attempts of miscreants to trap innocent customers to compromise their identity credentials to siphon funds from accounts always pose constant threat. Many customers operate digital platforms – ATMs, Internet banking and mobile banking and digital wallets without enough digital literacy that may tend to become victims of such fraudulent people. Banks have to strengthen cyber security and have engaged ethical hackers to test the vulnerability of their firewalls from time to time so that they remain well protected from the cyber-attacks. The efforts of banks and rising investment in providing cyber security can improve the confidence of customers that will further boost up user base. But banks will have to scout for newer opportunity to offset the increased costs in providing cyber security – an inevitable necessity.

(iii) Imparting Digital Literacy:

Though RBI in coordination with banks launches massive financial and digital literacy campaigns but operating knowledge on safety is yet to penetrate deep into the rural customer base that fall easy prey to such sly attempts. RBI also uses print and electronic media to sensitize public about the risks in digital banking and alerts them but the efforts are not reaching the target group in sufficient measure. Digital literacy has to be now a part of school curriculum as life cannot be separated from digital usage and everyone should have minimum knowledge on how to use the electronic devices and remain protected from the cyber-attacks. Once the cyber-crime perpetrator is aware about the customers and their familiarity with the use of digital platforms, they may not venture into it. It has to go a long way in all stakeholders coming together to enhance societal knowledge in using digital utilities, a formidable part of modern life.

(iv) Competition:

Banks encounter stiff competition in providing digital banking services with fintech companies, differentiated banks and non-banking companies compelling faster value addition to the technology platform and use of robots and state of the art technology based on AI. All these add to the costs without enough compensation. In the short run banks are offering digital services more like add on services with a hope that increase in business will eventually cover the enhanced costs.

(v) Customer protection:

In order to create a compatible digital banking ecosystem, RBI prescribed progressively higher customer protection measures. It is made mandatory for banks to compensate customers as part of policy, if they report the fraudulent transaction within prescribed time lines. But banks may not be in a position to compensate if customers have compromised their credentials with the fraudsters. Banks are also required to appoint an internal ombudsman separately for attending complaints related to digital transactions for speedy redressal of grievances. Institutionalized support system is being developed to protect customers against cyber-crimes.

(vi) Inactive debit cards:

Though digitally active customer base is on rise; still inactive and inoperative debit cards are high. 20 percent of debit cards were found inoperative when debit cards had to be migrated from magnetic strip to chip-based debit cards to prevent their vulnerability to frauds. Having spent money on providing debit cards, deepening of relationship is possible only when there is use of debit cards and migration of customers take place from manual operations to digital mode. Another formidable challenge is not only to provide debit cards but to make customers use it in digital outlets instead of visiting bank branches for routine transactions. The digital kiosks are now equipped with cash acceptance machines and cheque deposit machines, pass book printers etc to ensure that routine needs of customers could be met at these outlets.

10.7 Covid induced digital thrust:

Building upon the policy of 'Digital India' mission launched by the government in 2015, there has been intense thrust on digitization across sectors. Banks already under technology mode got further impetus to draw synergy from other interdependent agencies to accelerate digital transformation in financial sector. The post demonetization of high value currency in November 2016 accelerated digital banking volumes.

RBI, NPCI, government and banks have worked closely to create an active digital ecosystem by imparting public education on the merits of digital mode and its ability to cut leakage in subsidy transfers and enabling quick money transfers. While the digital journey was in progress, the catastrophic attack of coronavirus ravaged not only the life style of people but pushed the economy to abyss in the near term. Banking and finance, considered the most essential services continued even during lockdown to prevent the spread of life-threatening virus that can lead to Covid19.

The digital banking mode – Internet and mobile banking, is suddenly discovered as a rescue tool for users. Customers reluctant to come to bank for fear of contracting virus stayed home and operated banking through digital devices. Even micro financial transactions for buying essential medicines and grocery went digital. Once, a customer is used to digital experience, it is rare for them to revert to manual mode. It is not like transactions. When digitization happened, the transactions went digital and the moment physical cash replenished, the people had the comfort of dealing in cash. Contrary to that tendency, the digital mode is experienced as quick, reliable, accurate and anywhere access that makes digital banking an unstoppable mode provided the customer is aligned to it. Soon the volumes of electronic transactions soared to dizzy heights. The only issue to be addressed is the cyber security issues that need to be addressed to provide protection to customers. It became a priority for regulators and banks all other intermediaries.

Most of the banking work began to get into digital mode. Remote access of monitoring data, use of video conferencing, even interviews, review meetings, press conference, analyst meets, inauguration of new services, conferences and back-office operations and many more activities have moved to digital platform cutting huge costs. In the process, the human resources have gained immense experience in handling technology in executing their responsibilities. These practices are expected to stay with the banking system.

Quickly, even the ministry of corporate affairs permitted holding online board meetings and even statutory annual general meetings (AGMs) began to go virtual. There are reports that even a large number of shareholders are able to virtually attend the AGMs. Webinars and online interface had become a way of saving time and costs. This new found economic way of doing work remotely is expected to be sustained to take the digital transformation to a new trajectory to improve the operational efficiency and profitability. The business strategies to be articulated in future must factor the share on ongoing digital transformation to add value to the business proposition.

10.8 Strategies to pursue digital transformation

Thus, in the realm of capacity building, technology is a great enabler with its exponential power to handle business of millions of customers, under multiple lines of activities with high precision, efficiency and accuracy. Such qualitative capacity is not possible on manual mode. Going by such logic, adoption of latest banking technology should create immense space to multiply business volumes. The exponential scale of business should provide significant improvement in profitability to eventually add value to the stakeholders. But harnessing technology requires multipronged business strategies, implementation and monitoring to convert strategies into outcome.

When it comes to pursuing digital transformation as means for growth, the related strategies must be of long term well aligned to the emerging scope of digitization keeping Fintech revolution, Covid19 impact and demographic shift as strategic differentiators. As a result, banks should rely on multiple steps and strategies to embrace technological innovation; ranging from investing in FinTech companies and funding their own FinTech subsidiaries and to collaborate with Fintech companies. Banks and non-banks are partnering to offer the combination of trust and innovation to the Indian consumers. This "best of both worlds" approach has resulted in tremendous growth in the number of digital payment outlets that is expected to continue. These strategies can effectively ensure that banks retain market share, as customers increasingly value more efficient and cost-effective services and retention of customers is made possible. Among many deep-rooted long-term strategies, most pertinent of them are discussed.

(i) Widening and deepening relationship:

Making use of the evolving digital ecosystem and tech savvy new generation employees, changing customer profile, the next task must be to work out methods to tap the full potentiality of newly connected customer base that is established through the financial inclusion done so far. Widening customer base should be a continuing effort but mining the business worthiness of existing customers will hold the key to growth. It is necessary to set up a distinct vertical to deepen customer connect on both asset/liability side. Set benchmark for monitoring beginning with per capita deposit/loans and digital transactions. If debit card/internet banking and mobile banking account remains unused for 2 quarters, the system should be able to flag it for digital follow up with passive customers. Number of products used by each customer also needs to be kept on radar. Intensifying customer engagement with banks should be high on the agenda of banks in long term.

Innovations such as paperless *'Only digital savings accounts'* with no cheque book, passbook, account statements etc can be introduced for students for retail payments with relaxed criteria and higher interest rate. No footfalls at the branch from these Gen-Y and Gen-Z customers and hence transaction cost will be low.

Virtual meetings can be held with high value customers selectively on rotation to understand their needs and aspirations and action taken reports on suggestions must be followed up. Even after so much of digital push, it is estimated that there are only 100 million digital users in the banking system that has potentiality to add 500-600 million in next decade. If it is so, the value addition due to digital transformation can be a game changer with potentiality to go up by 5-6 times of existing level of digital transactions. Work to widen and deepen customer relationship should be a continuing strategy.

(ii) Optimization of Operational efficiency:

Having built strong digital infrastructure making huge investment, the strategy should be to ensure that it eventually works as a money guzzler for bank. The hardware and software customized for banks should work at its optimum efficiency. Managing vendors is a tough task. Vendors often run the outsourced services with inexperienced and inadequate manpower to save their costs and often delay post sale service of digital equipment and software. The service level agreements must be enforced verbatim to ensure that all the ATMs and systems work well to provide confidence to the customers.

Any deviation in turnaround time (TAT) in attending to bank call by vendors must be pursued and followed up seriously. The instances of deviations must be mapped and suitable penalties are to be imposed. The collateral damage to the reputation due to non-maintenance of digital outfits is immeasurable. Any lacklustre approach in enforcing discipline in managing technology eats away the fragile profitability and can demean the reputation. Measurement and monitoring of operational efficiency should be the continuing strategy.

(iii) Sensitizing human resources:

In service industry, competency of manpower can be a competitive differentiator. Grooming employees to handle technology should be another important strategy. Continuous training of human resources in managing and using technology should be an integral strategy. Identification of people with better appetite to use technology should be identified as digital transformation agents with suitable rewards and incentives. They need to be trained so that they can sensitize other staff members as to how to handle minor glitches in technology. They should not only use technology wherever it can be used but inspire others to use it to spread the culture of digital applications at workspace.

Human resources should be sensitized to learn the nuances of AI and machine learning (ML) tools to improve efficiency. Barometers of IT sensitization should be set. Institutionalization of systems audit by peers and interdepartmental audits should be introduced. The need of IT experts in day today banking operations should be done away with and employees in the department should be made capable to handle minor maintenance problems. Cost of training of human resources should be considered as an investment in capacity building and not as expenditure. The long-term benefits of digital orientation and application friendliness should be kept in view.

(iv) Financial and Digital literacy:

Using the large network of branches and lead bank in the area, massive financial and digital literacy campaigns should be launched. RBI has developed multilingual financial and digital literacy literature. Banks should also develop small in-house video stories on how to use digital delivery channels and screen them in village Panchayats/schools/public places. This can be outsourced to a good and well-spread NGO active in the hinterland. A cadre of bank volunteers can be developed with the enrolment of working employees or retired employees.

These people can volunteer to spread financial and digital literacy on how to operate accounts, how to borrow and repay the bank loans. The importance of role of banks in promoting enterprise should be highlighted. Tie up is also possible with schools/colleges/NGOs in the area to reach out to masses. Bank people can hold street talk on developing healthy banking habits and ensuring safe digital operations.

RBI has taken lot of initiatives to sensitize people on banking and cyber security. Banks can use it as a plank to take it forward. Even NABARD/RRBs/BCs should be tapped to continue public education efforts. Financial and digitally literate customers are safe customers of bank, who in turn can be persuaded to spread digital culture in their area. Each one can teach one and take banking to masses. Well informed customer base could be the right source to widen digital banking outreach.

(v) Customer protection:

If digital infrastructure is maintained well, customers will find it easy to operate with minimum chances of complaints. But if there are complaints, bank should put firm strategies as embedded customer management policy to ensure timely resolution. RBI has mandated appointment of separate 'Internal Ombudsman' (IO) for digital transactions. IO should be the catalyst for growth by putting well organized time driven redressal systems to boost customer confidence. Banks should imbibe best practices in dealing with customer complaints on unauthorized digital transactions.

RBI, as part of customer protection measures, has set limited liability of customers in un-authorized Electronic Payment Transactions in banks and also in PPI issued by authorized non-banks. It has set a time schedule within which the customers should bring unauthorized transactions to the notice of banks/designated non-banks for taking suitable action and reimbursing proven wrongful debits. Zero tolerance policy towards delay in attending customer complaints should be pursued with well-entrenched response time lines. As long-term strategy, customer service grading and auditing should be introduced as a systemic control and managerial intervention must be ensured to correct inconsistencies.

Digital transformation will certainly be the future of banking and financial sector. Covid induced digital thrust can be used as an opportunity to put the banking system on robust digital trajectory to (i) widen customer base for exponential business growth (ii) deepen customer relationship (iii) enhance digital experience with improved quality of customer service (iv) increase operational efficiency visible to customers (v) cut transaction cost by shifting mass of customer transactions to digital mode (vi) create better value chain for stakeholders (vii) adopt global standards in digital transformation (viii) develop 'ease of doing business' with the help of improved technology in banks to enhance efficiency (ix) add to the profit potentiality in the long run (x) create a competitive differentiator.

NPCI the first and only umbrella entity to operate retail payment and settlement system, has earned many applauds for itself and the country in its stellar journey so far. The RBI has recently issued invitation and can consider to grant license for more NUE to be interoperable with the NPCI, to create competition, foster innovation, broaden and deepen digital payments, accelerate financial inclusion and mitigate single point failure. The entire payment system is dependent on NPCI, a huge operational risk for the system. Given the huge opportunity, one would expect significant interest from new players with deep pockets. SBI was contemplating to apply for a license to create competition to NPCI. Many more may come forward to set up digital payment and settlement infrastructure. This will create a more buoyant digital payment infrastructure with competitive efficiency, providing an alternative.

Besides such structural changes, digital transformation will call for coordinated action at all levels to innovate a different digitally abled bank. Initiatives undertaken by the Government, RBI and the banking industry have led to a radical shift towards ubiquitous digitization, which has provided an impetus to adopt state of the art technology. There is a unique confluence of several positives like demographic dividend, 'Jan dhan, adhaar and mobile (JAM) trinity', etc., that would further support rapid digitization of financial services in India. Along with making inroads into their traditional business turf, banks are diversifying into newer areas such as insurance, asset management, custodial services and investment related advisory services.

This is the opportune time when banks can put systems in place to fuel digital transformation to make the digitalization improve the profitability and stakeholder value of the banks. The Covid19 induced digital tilt of customers should be used as a springboard to catapult banks to a new high speed digital trajectory that begins to add sustainable rewards. The front-runners in the league of tapping digital transformation can be the real winners to stay ahead.

CHAPTER – 11

DIGITAL LITERACY

Digital Literacy is the ability of individuals and communities to understand and use digital technologies for meaningful actions within life situations. With the increasing entry of digitalization in everyday life and activities, it is necessary to make our community fully equipped with knowledge to use the technology devices and join in the mainstream of development. Buoyed by the pandemic, the digital footprints in financial intermediation have deepened and its exponential rise with clear potentiality in future. The demographic dividend of young India with average age at 29 years is opening up vast opportunities for accelerated digitisation. The digital banking channels are fast reaching out to rural areas with Business Correspondents (BCs) and retail grocery outlets equipped with Point of Sales (POS). With internet and mobile connectivity stretching far and wide, the rural business community too has come to understand the merits of accepting digital means to settle even micro financial transactions.

According to recent RBI data of July 2021 number of ATMs are 2,13,433, POS terminals are 46.08 lakhs, debit cards have reached 90.6 crores while credit cards are at 6.34 crores. The number of basic savings bank deposit accounts (BSBDA) has reached 64.92 crores by March 2021, of which 43.41 crores of bank accounts are contributed by the Prime Minister's PMJDY. PMJDY is now made into open-ended scheme with focus shifted from covering 'families' to 'individuals. This will accelerate opening of new accounts and issue of debit cards further adding to the scope of digital banking.

11.1 More digitization:

On the recommendation of Dr. Nachiket Mor 'Committee on Comprehensive Financial Services for Small Businesses and Low-Income Households', several differentiated banks were rolled out. More significant is the setting up of payment banks. The 'India Post Payment Bank (IPPB)' holds more potentiality due to its deeper reach in interior hinterland with post office outlets close to 155000. The payment banks can play a greater role in digital payment space as they are not allowed to lend. In addition to banks, close to 1000 fintech companies are fast collaborating with banks and have floated diversified types of prepaid payment instruments to increase scope for using digital mode for small value transactions. The neo banks – virtual banks are entering financial intermediation market.

Several banks and card issuing organizations have provided 'payment gateways' for customer convenience to enable quick online payments. The Internet and mobile banking transactions are generally supported by dual authentication based on one time password (OTP) routed through registered mobile number. With development of such huge digital banking infrastructure, the number of user base is set to increase manifold. Along with spurt in digital bank users, the systems are getting exposed to cyber threats. The digital mode is convenient and accessible any time but unless the user is conscious about the operational risks, it becomes difficult to ensure customer protection.

11.2 RBI initiatives:

Looking to the potentiality of digital banking, RBI has now further liberalized interoperability among entities using PPIs and Digital Wallets (DWs). The holders of PPIs can now transfer funds from one PPI to another and also to a bank. Even account portability methods among banks are being worked out to expand scope of digitization of banking. With number of internet user base rising from 500 million in June 2018 to 730 million by 2020 and smart mobile phone base increasing from

339 million to 402 million during the corresponding period, there will be exponential rise in digital transactions.

Despite expanding scope of digital banking, large number of potential customers is still shy and apprehensive in using digital and online services. Compared to the debit cards issued by banks, the ATM hits are far from satisfactory. In order to allay their fears, there is an urgent need to focus on customer education. Rightly so, RBI has recently started a new campaign of using electronic/print media using prime shows in televisions to spread the messages on financial and digital literacy investing huge funds. It is in the public interest to sensitize bank customers. It is in addition to financial literacy and credit counselling Cells (FLCCs) operating in rural bank branches and some of the block level centres are actively collaborating in the task of spreading financial and digital literacy. Financial literacy efforts are continuing for several years but digital literacy is a recent phenomenon. More efforts are needed to disseminate digital literacy among masses.

11.3 Government initiatives:

Among many initiatives to expand digital education, government introduced a digital literacy mission known as 'Digital Saksharta Abhiyan (DISHA) or National Digital Literacy Mission (NDLM). It has been formulated to impart IT training to 52.5 lakh persons, including Anganwadi and ASHA workers and authorized Public distribution outlet dealers in all the States/UTs across the country so that the non-IT literate citizens are trained to become IT literate so as to enable them to actively and effectively participate in the democratic and developmental process and also enhance their livelihood.

The target group of participants will be trained under the programme in two phases. In the first phase, 10 lakh beneficiaries will be trained under the scheme. Out of this, 6.3 lakh beneficiaries will be trained on Level 1 and 2.7 lakh beneficiaries will be trained on Level 2. Nine lakh beneficiaries will be eligible for training fee support from the government. The rest 100,000 beneficiaries will be trained by the industry and civil society partners. Under Phase II, 42.5 lakh persons will be trained, which also includes Anganwadi and ASHA workers and authorized ration dealers.

As part of implementation of NDLM, the National Institute of Electronics and Information Technology (NIELIT), a government outfit in Ajmer is conducting courses under National Digital Literacy Mission (NDLM) as part of Prime Minister's vision of "Digital India". They impart training to one in every eligible household in selected Blocks in each State/ UT of the country. They will be imparted computer skills. The objective is to impart basic ICT skills relevant to the need of the trainees, which would enable the citizens to use IT and related applications and participate actively in the democratic process and further enhance opportunities for their livelihood. The persons shall be able to access information, knowledge and skill through the use of digital devices. The training inputs are calibrated in two levels – Appreciation of digital literacy (level -1) and Basics of digital literacy (Level 2). Level -1 will make a person IT literate so that he/she can operate digital devices, like mobile phones, tablets, laptops etc to get their work done. The level 2 is of a higher standard to equip participants with IT skills to effectively access the various e-governance services being offered to the citizen by the government and other agencies. The beneficiaries will in turn be able to impart IT literacy to the community as trainers and extend the reach of digital literacy to masses in phases.

11.4 Customer protection:

The strategic move of RBI for customer protection is laudable and explains its increasing importance. It must be understood that conducting responsible banking is the onus of customers too. In the melee of catching up digital banking convenience by new set of users, vulnerability to cyber-attacks is on rise. Fraudsters are always on the look out to find the weaknesses both from bank and customer angle. Stealing identity and pilfering digital money is possible in many ways unless the customer is cautious and joins banks and regulators in safeguarding digital banking space.

Therefore, it is expedient to sensitize bank customers to preserve the sanctity of passwords, login id, Card Verification Value (CVV) and One Time Password (OTPs) meant to ensure safety of customers access to bank accounts through digital mode. As part of enforcing customer protection measures, RBI directed banks to make good the loss on account of unauthorized digital transactions if the customer reports it to banks within 3 working days, provided the customer has not compromised the identity credentials. There is limited liability to the customers if reported between 4-7 days. If the wrongful transactions are reported after 7 days, banks can deal with it in terms of board approved policy. Subscribing to SMS services of banks can bring wrongful transactions to the notice of customers quickly. It is necessary to teach people how to protect their digital accounts. How frequently the password to be changed. How well the password can be calibrated to make it difficult for intruder to guess and hit. If digital is the pathway for future, imparting digital literacy is the only way to equip our customers with its knowhow.

In our quest towards digital banking to reduce cost of operations and improve efficiency, every stakeholder will have to join in effectively sanitizing digital banking space. Every business entity, institutes, schools, colleges, corporate houses and social activists will have to put up banners, broadcast messages educating public on how to safely use the digital banking mode. A sustained and collective commitment of every responsible stakeholder will be necessary to educate the public. At this phase, digital banking is not an option. Digitization is part of development in every walk of life and therefore digital literacy should be comprehensive to transform the lifestyle of people into a digital friendly regime. Augmenting resources to bring digital literacy to the centre stage can only make our digital financial intermediation safe and fraud proof.

The stakeholders have been working hard to ensure that compatible ecosystem is built to educate people. As larger part of RBI policy to promote digital inclusion, making online remittances through NEFT/RTGS in savings bank accounts free from January 2020 was indeed significant. It was also now made available on 24/7 basis facilitating quick fund transfer round the clock. RBI vision for digital payments and settlement system – 2019-2021 released in May 2019 clearly intended to *"empower every Indian with access to a bouquet of e-payment options that are safe, secure, convenient, quick and affordable".*

In the same realm, the "Report of the high-level committee on deepening of digital payments (Chairman: Mr. Nandan Nilekani)" envisaged a tenfold increase in digital payments in the next three years. RBI reinforces easing digital payment foothold with several continuing collaborative measures that can evolve a robust and seamless payment ecosystem. Enhancing access to financial touch points and reducing cost of access has been the twin drivers of digital inclusion. The recent growth in digital banking infrastructure could foster cultural shift in the intensity of use of electronic mode of payments and settlement, more encouraging is its adoption even in hinterland with the active use of BCs.

11.5 Spurt in digital infrastructure:

Moving beyond setting up full-fledged bank branches, banks started to expand base of alternate electronic delivery channels at a much faster pace, more importantly well after mobile connectivity, mobile network, internet services were made accessible and affordable to people at the bottom of the pyramid. As a result, the number of POS terminals, number of ATMs, debit card and credit issued increased at a greater pace to make a difference.

Close to 1200 fintech companies collaborate with banks to increase digital outreach in different forms. 45 wallet players, 50 UPI – based payments service providers and 142 banks on the UPI platform are actively collaborating with each other to deliver services to customers.

Such digital spread extends to telecom companies, e-commerce entities and banks and even Internet companies and messaging applications. If their services are to reach the target group, familiarity in using them is necessary. Hence, digital literacy is an essential thrust point.

As a result of proliferation of financial sector touch points, the scope for financial inclusion (FI) through digital penetration increased significantly. The number of BSBD accounts quickly increased due to roll out of PMJDY scheme adding mass of new customers. But the formidable challenge is the increased inoperative bank accounts that limit merits of FI. World Bank estimates indicate that 47 percent of such bank accounts are inoperative and 23 percent of PMJDY accounts remain dormant. The gap in imparting financial and digital literacy is evident.

11.6 Stretching digital payment mode:

Small Finance Banks and Payment Banks have also been set up to improve outreach and to pursue FI intended to benefit people at the bottom of the pyramid comprising mainly migrant labour, village workforce, low-income households, small businesses and other unorganized sector entities. Disseminating digital banking culture to the grass root level is a gigantic task.

The scope for setting up new SFBs has also been increased with its licenses now available 'on tap' and cooperative banks and Payment Banks can also apply for conversion into SFBs with certain relaxations. Non-Bank peer-to-peer lenders (NBFC – P2P) and introduction of new type of prepaid payment instruments (PPIs) will go a long way in deepening FI through further digital penetration.

The merchant discount rates (MDR) – the charges that merchants have to pay to banks on transactions done on debit/Credit was waived off while presenting the union budget 2019-20. Companies with a turnover of Rs.50 crores or more are mandated to provide free facility of payment through Rupay debit card and UPI QR code to customers from January 2020 and tax of 2 percent will be levied on entities drawing cash of over Rs.1 crore during a year. In view of recent efforts, digital payment volumes have seen considerable growth.

11.7 Global Microscope – 2019

It is noteworthy that Global Microscope – 2019, a report on the *'enabling environment for financial inclusion and the expansion of digital financial services'* released by Economic Intelligence Unit (EIU) ranked India well ahead of its peers among 55 countries studied in the report. It assessed regulatory and policy environment in its approach towards digital inclusion though it did not measure FI outcomes. The progress in five domains considered by the report were related to (i) Government and Policy Support, (ii) Stability and Integrity (iii) Products and outlets (iv) consumer protection and (v) infrastructure.

While increases in countries' scores across the index provide evidence of more favourable environments for financial and digital inclusion around the world, Colombia, Peru and Uruguay maintained their rankings at the top. Among the BRICS economies, the ranking of India is considerably ahead. Brazil 9, Russia 19, India 5, China 11 and South Africa at 13. It affirms that India is steadfast in pursuing FI through digital thrust for which infrastructure is getting built and policies are made inclusion friendly.

While the global recognition of India's policy thrust for pursuing FI through digital approach is encouraging, tackling inoperative accounts and deepening FI efforts by public education on digital use to realize its actual potentiality to contribute to economic well-being of the society remains a formidable challenge.

In order to make FI work to ensure that the benefits of inclusion reach the intended target group of the society, seminal changes need to be introduced in the spread of financial and digital literacy and credit counselling. While many stakeholders have been doing sporadic work but are not well coordinated to optimize its effectiveness.

Inadequate institutional efforts to disseminate financial awareness among the grass root level are keeping even financially connected masses (those having bank accounts and debit cards) away from the formal financial system. Adequately equipping and empowering institutions engaged in disseminating comprehensive digital literacy programs will be essential to unleash the potentiality of the huge financial and digital infrastructure built and designed to sub serve FI.

These formal/informal institutions should be able to coordinate among themselves to galvanize services of informal local bodies, social agencies and non-government organizations (NGOs). Such local work force may be formed into voluntary change agents with some structure of incentives to unleash their full potentiality. BCs in villages can be an integral part of such change agents to create social awareness and to highlight benefits in using the formal financial system. Over a period of time, such institutions should be able to phase out informal money lenders who charge usurious interest rates and make people perpetually indebted flogging them into debt trap. The missing link in FI is now obviously the lack of financial and digital knowledge of massive user base.

It is the right time to accelerate literacy campaigns particularly when digital culture is spreading fast with introduction of GST, Fast Tags and other online utilities of daily use. Right synchronization of comprehensive literacy efforts with the evolving payment and settlement ecosystem should be able to take India close to the end state objectives of FI by 2030, by when sustainable goals of UN are to achieved. In order for the digital banking to thrive, a concerted efforts to boost digital and financial literacy will be essential.

CHAPTER – 12

CHANGING LENDING APPETITE OF BANKS

In response to the economic distress, banks were unable to aggressively lend. In an unprecedented economic crisis, addressing collateral damage of the pandemic on banking sector, like many other sectors is a complex and prolonged collaborative process. When the whole borrower community was in the grip of crisis, banks have to reach out to them so that they survive and be able to repay the loans. But the problems of banks exacerbated with the potential deterioration in asset quality. In the Covid induced disarray, banks found the potential surge in NPA and its impact on fragile capital base scary. During disruptions of this magnitude when deterioration in asset quality poses a systemic threat, sustained policy interventions are needed to build an ecosystem suitable for banks to lend. Dissemination of bank credit is indispensable to bail out distressed borrowers and to revive the economy. Even before banks needed the intervention of the central bank, it had come out with policy support. Lower interest rates, reduced cash reserve ratio, ample liquidity and relaxed prudential norms to enable banks to restructure the loans, that the borrowers were unable to service. Moratorium on loan repayments were initially permitted for 3 months that was extended by another 3 months keeping in view the gravity of impact of the pandemic on the borrowing community.

The inevitable fear of spike in NPAs after the end of moratorium on loan repayments, additional provision against rising NPAs, diminishing profitability and other adversities added to the already low risk appetite of banks leading to subdued credit growth. As a result, even the trailing low credit growth at 6.1 percent on 27th March 2020 further fell to 5.5 percent by 28th August 2020 inviting the attention of regulators. Correspondingly, the outstanding bank credit went down by a notch from Rs.103.2 trillion on March 27, 2020 to Rs102.11 trillion by August 28, 2020.

Looking to decelerating credit flows, RBI observed that banks are not gearing up well to respond to the crisis and are unable to rejuvenate credit flow despite abundant liquidity and accommodative monetary policy stance. Moreover, banks continued to park excess liquidity with RBI under reverse repo route even when its interest rate was brought down to 3.35 percent to encourage banks to lend. The lacklustre response to sector specific Targeted Long Term Repo Operation (TLTRO) 2.0 conducted by RBI has also indicated protective approach of banks. Thus, RBI considered that such debilitating risk aversion of banks could be eventually self-defeating and banks have to play a more defining role using the synergy of stakeholder support.

While usual measures of monitoring and follow up for recovery of loans should continue but from a pragmatic angle, overall reduction in NPAs at this point of time may not look likely as most of the borrowers are in distress and liquidity starved. But comfort can be drawn from the past NPA behaviour to exude confidence to tackle the asset quality woes as and when normalcy restores. Every time, NPAs of banks spiked, they came down subsequently and the same trend is expected now.

12.1 Historical movement of NPAs:

The rise and fall of NPAs are not only linked to macroeconomic disruptions but also to policy shifts. Gross NPAs peaked to a new high of 23.2 percent in 1993 when asset classification norms were implemented under banking sector reforms. In the next decade it came down to 7.26 percent by 2003-04 and to 3.83 percent by 2013-14.

Again, when AQR was introduced by RBI in Sept 2015 (a policy shift) and withdrew forbearance of restructuring of loans, gross NPAs began to rise to reach a peak of 11.18 percent by 2017-18 that began to descent to 9.3 percent in 2018-19. The long-term swings in NPAs are therefore a function of policy and macroeconomic shifts and implications in the change in external environment.

12.2 Covid induced asset quality woes:

Just before the onset of the pandemic, NPAs of banks began to show early signs of improvement falling from 9.3 percent in March 2019 to 9 percent by March 2020. But the situation changed after pandemic mauled the economy. RBI in its recent FSR – June 2020 estimated that NPAs are likely to inch up to 14.7 percent by March 2021 in severe stress conditions and to 12.5 percent in base line scenario.

But looking to the lingering crisis, banks should gear up to handle NPAs of a level going even beyond the RBI estimates in severed stress conditions. Hence, near term expectations to cap NPAs in distress situations is difficult to realize and banks while continuing to improve their capacity to lend should be prepared for a long haul in managing asset quality. Realizing the extraordinariness of the Covid induced distress; banks have to live with higher NPAs for next two years or so. But the inevitable asset quality woes should not be allowed to overwhelm the functioning of banks.

12.3 Challenges for banks to lend:

Among many enablers, liquidity and capital adequacy are immediate near-term drivers to activate lending. In response to the ongoing pandemic, RBI while bringing down the policy rates had infused enough liquidity using many innovative windows and assured to pump more as and when needed to keep up the momentum of revival. Again, basing on FSR – June 2020 data, the CRAR of banking system was 14.6 percent in March 2020 and expected to go down by 133 basis points in base line scenario to reach 13.3 percent and may even nosedive to 11.8 percent in severe stress by March 2021.

As part of relaxations in prudential norms, the last tranche of implementation of Basel – III framework was postponed from March 2020 to September 30, 2020. It effectively sets the benchmark of minimum capital conservation buffer (CCB) at 1.875 percent of risk-weighted assets against the requirement of 2.5 percent taking minimum CRAR to 10.875 percent (minimum CAR of 9 percent plus CCB of 1.875). After the end of moratorium, the default in loan account will increase the risk weighted assets forcing banks to reach closer to the minimum benchmark of CRAR and will be neck and neck in maintaining CRAR. Many individual banks may even breach the levels. Hence any aggressive lending approach of banks may lead to breach of CRAR compliance inviting regulatory action.

Moreover, RBI has already imposed 10 percent additional provision on restructured loans under its scheme of 'Resolution Framework for COVID-19-related Stress'. However, the extent of hiving off the Covid induced stress of borrowers will broadly depend upon the applicability of the loan restructuring scheme keeping in view the five broad parameters related to leverage, liquidity and debt serviceability identified by the RBI appointed Kamath panel for the 26 sectors of the economy. The committee will however be vetting exposure of loans of more than Rs. 1500 crores. Rating agency ICRA estimates that loans of banks and non-banks close to Rs.10 trillion may become eligible for restructuring. According to the brokerage firm Jefferies, 60 percent of loans under moratorium may be eligible for restructuring, rest may potentially add to the NPA pile. Hence banks could be hesitating to lend with fear that NPAs in making will eat into the fragile capital base. It will also depend upon the interpretation of restructuring scheme to cover the target group of beneficiary borrowers. It must be borne in mind that excluding many of them from the scheme will not only mar their credit history but may also obliterate revival of the economy to that extent. Banks should take a positive posture in interpreting the guidance of RBI based on Kamath Committee recommendations.

12.4 Policy to pump prime credit flow:

Though slowdown in the flow of credit growth has never been a panacea to improve asset quality, creation of a compatible collaborative credit positive ecosystem will be essential. It is the critical need to lend to revive the economy more importantly to entrepreneurs at the bottom of the pyramid that supports large section of population to survive in hinterland. Recognizing the extraordinariness of the global calamity, Basel Committee released its guidance in April 2020 for facilitating central banks to suitably respond to the Covid-19 outbreak. Going by its spirit, RBI permitted zero risk weight against loans extended under Emergency Credit Line Guarantee (ECLG) scheme and excluded moratorium period in classifying assets as NPAs. Basel Committee extended time lines for implementation of Basel – III framework till January 2023.

In the given circumstances, government and RBI will have to consider policy support going beyond past trends to enable banks to lend. Looking to the fragile capital base, government was rightly considered to infuse capital in PSBs to the tune of Rs.20,000 crores through recapitalization bonds without burdening the exchequer. But more action was needed to relax prudential guidelines to enable the banking system to cope with the disruption caused by the pandemic.

The mandarins of policy could explore to more pragmatic relaxations to create a conducive environment for banks to act in time. May be some of the relaxations in prudential norms will be needed to make them work for enhancing the flow of credit to commercial sector. Specific relief measures tailored for MSME sector will help the worst suffering sector to fight out the crisis and revive. Additional provision of 10 percent prescribed by RBI on restructured portfolio will add to the burden. All efforts and support measures will have to be MSME centric so that banks are in a better position to help them out.

12.5 Bank level action:

Since it was difficult to extend loans during Covid times based on past loan policies, banks needed to frame separate 'Covid loan policy' for a period of say one year only to extend loans to *existing standard borrowers'* whose credit history is already with banks. A set of Covid loan schemes may be introduced for existing borrowers for providing quick cash flows to restart the economic activities.

Besides the restructuring schemes mooted by RBI for (i) stressed MSME borrowers up to Rs.25 crores and (ii) other Covid induced stressed loans to be restructured in terms of Kamath Committee recommendations, bank that can be articulated, yet another 'Covid Restructuring Policy' to explore supporting stressed existing loan accounts on a broader parameter to cover those that are stressed but not falling within the two RBI schemes. Bank can always have its own restructuring policy with the only difference that these may not get the further concessions but if the bank is convinced, they can introduce a separate loan restructuring policy.

Nothing prevents banks from taking a commercial call to restructure loans, if it is convinced about the reasons for stress are genuine and providing more time will enable the entrepreneur to come out of the crisis. The only difference will be (i) such loan account has to be downgraded in terms of prudential norms (ii) provision was to be made as applicable to classification of NPAs. Banks can always identify such loan accounts that merit support in this crisis as a proactive measure and help them to revive and contribute to the economy.

Even if such relief is not granted to borrowers, the loan account, in any case has to be classified as NPA casting its adverse shadow on his credit history. This will then rule out any possibility of revival. Banks should keep a broader vision in mind that a potential performing borrower is more important than holding NPA and triggering action. Recovery measures under Insolvency and Bankruptcy Code (IBC) having been stalled for six months with power to extend up to one year, there is no point adding to the stock of NPAs. It was better to provide space for the entrepreneur to explore revival-taking risk a notch higher than pushing towards closure of the unit. With these covid centric policies, line management in banks should have been fully empowered to lend, restructure and grant temporary enhancement in limits on relaxed criteria but not compromising regulatory compliances. Lack of such proactive initiative to bail out entrepreneurs will only add to the gloom.

Procedural reforms, more digitization of lending, documentation needs may also be mooted to hasten loan processing. Digital online lending windows may be opened accepting loan requests with scanned supporting papers to be verified only at the time of disbursement of loans. As the additional lending is focused on existing borrowers, the credit risk may remain considerably low. Fresh lending to new borrowers may however be allowed based on the rigor of past loan policy.

In a situation when the aggravating pandemic lingers around spreading fear and despair limiting mobility of people due to sporadic local lockdowns even after opening up activities under unlock 4.0, revival of the economy is likely to be delayed. Banks and stakeholders should be prepared for prolonged fight with the pandemic.

As such, banks in collaboration with the regulators and government should be able to tackle the Covid induced stress by accelerating credit growth. Banks should also hive off the Covid induced stress by bringing a greater number of distressed borrowers within the scope of restructuring schemes of RBI or under those to be envisaged by banks at their level. Lack of any such proactive accommodative measures by banks can also be termed as risk aversion. It is not lending alone. Absence of finding ways to reach out to distressed borrowers in critical times is equally important to help speedy revival of the economy. Fearing the inevitable rise in NPA pile, it cannot be the right strategy not to reach out to ailing class of borrowers. Even if some of such rescued borrowers eventually flourish in business, their pay back to banks will be better and stronger business relationship could be built.

Thus, hesitant baby steps in tackling the economic distress may not provide the kind of buoyancy needed at this point of time to rescue the distressed enterprise. If pump priming of bank credit is the need, the policy support and coordinated bank level efforts have to be proportionate to the distress. Unprecedented policy measures will be needed to tackle unprecedented degree of crisis stemming from the pandemic. Lending appetite is a function of quality of lending portfolio. Quality of lending portfolio cannot suddenly surface. It needs to be developed over a period of time with consistent efforts by the banks and they need to collaborate with RBI. When some policy support comes from RBI, banks will have to move a few steps ahead to see that long term interests of sustainable asset quality is well protected.

The government has reached out to banks well in time by introducing the ECLGS of up to Rs.3 trillion that was subsequently increased to Rs.4.5 trillion. Even the criteria of eligibility has been gradually relaxed at various points of time to make more and more entrepreneurs eligible for the government guaranteed loans. Even those who availed the facility at the beginning of the scheme can now avail another 10 percent of their outstanding loan as a second doze of relief. Taking cue from it, banks could also come up with various other supportive measures at bank level to help entrepreneurs to emerge from the crisis.

Lending appetite is not only providing credit but to take a bunch of measures to create an ease of doing business environment. Providing restructuring facility to existing borrowers in distress and creating an ecosystem for better accessibility of loans, simplification of procedures, driving them on digital mode are some of the measures that could combine into reinforcing pillars for credit growth. Capital adequacy and base of NPAs will however remain the basis for the purpose. More innovative supporting efforts can be carved out to bail out the economy. Increasing lending appetite is the collective and continuous work of all stakeholders, at a time when the industry is fighting one of its worst crises.

CHAPTER – 13

ASSET QUALITY MANAGEMENT

The asset quality has been under unprecedented stress as bank borrowers were in distress due to Covid19 induced lockdowns and related disruptions. The homebound labor migration too exacerbated the woes of the borrowing community that forced cut in activities even after phased opening up of the economy. Still the activities could not be resumed on full scale. Some of the business units even had to be closed sine die due to the ongoing pandemic. Its adverse impact will linger on much after the pandemic recedes. They needed extensive support to restore activities. Due to the paucity of demand, some of the units were unable to work in full swing. When the economy was coming to terms with the damage of first wave of the pandemic, the second wave further ravaged many units aggravating the distress and more number of borrowers were unable to service the loans and interest. Some sought rejig of loan repayment terms while others needed immediate cash flows to restart activities. These developments exacerbated the asset quality woes impacting the bank profitability/capital adequacy and badly truncated the fresh credit flow. This chapter is designed to cover the impact of these factors on the asset quality and how it may shape the future of banking.

Asset quality is a broad indicator of multiple factors that builds an ecosystem of banking that supports enterprise in an economy. Management of asset quality is a concern for all stakeholders. The nuances of asset quality management keep changing with changes in social and business ecosystem, economic affluence, litigation literacy and many other dynamic factors. It includes but yet goes much beyond the scope of the lenders. The society, the culture, integrity, credibility of intermediaries that create the value chain of asset quality management in financial system needs transformation.

Each stakeholder has to contribute in totality to ensure that asset quality sustains and is able to create new and better benchmark. If any one of the value creators is failing or performing less than their potentiality over a sustained period of time, the other one fails. But the primary responsibility for the asset quality is of lenders who lends funds accessed from depositors in trust. Lenders have a fiduciary responsibility to protect the interest of depositors who place the funds with trust in the ability of lenders to manage them.

13.1 Credit risk is omnipresent:

Though the 360-degree credit culture that leads to asset quality is built by the society – a range of stakeholders, including the lenders. The simple logic of deposit account holders would be that financial intermediaries should not undertake a business that they cannot manage efficiently. They are right. But one must understand that there is no business without risk. The financial intermediaries assume a lot of risk in managing deposit resources, even the risk of their survival. As stakeholders, depositors who earn interest – that partly include risk premium cannot be isolated completely from the credit risk that they are taking by placing their hard-earned money with the lenders. They need to be mindful that there could be risks of default from the banks as has happened in the past – the ongoing PMC Bank fiasco is a classic example.

By placing deposits with a bank is therefore not completely risk free – absolutely. But the probability of default is rare but even if remotely, it manifests, the depositor should be prepared to absorb the risk. That is why now government has raised the deposit insurance to Rs.5 lakhs and the recent amendment to the Deposit Insurance and Credit Guarantee Corporation (DICGC) Act allow access to deposit insurance funds within 90 days of imposing moratorium. The individual depositor can have access to funds after 90 days, a great relief to depositors in distress.

In order to roll out an agenda to improve the asset quality in the coming years/decades, concerted action is needed by each stakeholder. It is much more important when India is looking to unleash its animal spirit in pushing big growth in GDP in the post pandemic era. While majority of credit management improvements have to come from banks and other lenders, the supportive action should be from regulators, borrowers and society at large.

On the top of all, the much needed continuous improvement in 'ease of doing business' by the government and more importantly how it is made to trickle down to the grass root level entrepreneurs. With the dissemination of financial and digital literacy, a radical social transformation is necessary not to tolerate loan defaulters and even abstaining gradually from dealing with those who intentionally abstain from honouring their loan commitments or opt to diversify funds to unrelated more risky activities. Unless inclusive sustained participation is ensured, asset quality in not an area that could be improved to the desired sustainable level. It is a collaborative action agenda that should be pursued.

13.2 Risk based pricing:

In managing asset quality in the modern banking system moving in the new decade beginning 2020, banks will have to innovate business process reengineering using the early alert system. They should hone skills to assess the credit risk correctly and price the assets (loans) in sync with the underlying risk of counter party linked to the probability of default.

Banks should be in a position to absorb the losses arising out of default of loans by providing enough profitability buffers by right risk adjusted pricing in managing the lending risks. Now, banks will find difficulty in fixing risk-based pricing if the probability of default and credit risk measurement is not correctly calibrated. Going into the basics of asset quality management, we link to the fact that the very purpose of financial intermediation is to mobilize public savings (bank deposits) that can be systematically deployed to fund enterprises (bank loans) that can plough back into the economy as added gross domestic product with its multiplier impact.

This process of obtaining deposits and deploying as loans can go on seamlessly if the borrower pays back loans to enable banks to repay to depositors. The cycle of mobilizing deposits and granting loans can break if the borrower is not repaying the loans with interest in time. It leads to asset liability mismatch for banks. The deposit account holder has to be paid back his money while the loan granted has not yet been recovered causing disruption to the process.

13.3 Surge of NPAs lowers credit growth:

In response to the economic distress, banks are unable to aggressively lend. In an unprecedented economic crisis, addressing collateral damage of the pandemic on banking sector, like many other sectors is a complex and prolonged collaborative process. In the Covid induced disarray, banks found the potential surge in NPAs and its impact on fragile capital base scary. During disruptions of this magnitude when deterioration in asset quality poses a systemic threat, sustained policy interventions are needed to build an ecosystem suitable for banks to lend. Dissemination of bank credit is indispensable to bail out distressed borrowers and to revive the economy.

The inevitable fear of spike in NPAs after the end of moratorium on loan repayments, additional provision against rising NPAs, diminishing profitability and other adversities added to the already low risk appetite of banks leading to subdued credit growth. As a result, even the trailing low credit growth at 6.1 percent on 27th March 2020 further fell to 5.5 percent by 28th August 2020 inviting the attention of regulators. Correspondingly, the outstanding bank credit went down by a notch from Rs.103.2 trillion on March 27, 2020 to Rs102.11 trillion by August

28, 2020. But by July 16, 2021, the non-food bank credit reached Rs.107.92 trillion aided by the disbursements made under government guaranteed loan scheme – Emergency Credit Line Guarantee Scheme (ECLGS) modified four times from its inception till July 2021.

Looking to low appetite of bank credit flows, RBI observed that banks are not gearing up well to respond to the crisis and are unable to rejuvenate credit flow to the desired levels despite abundant liquidity and accommodative monetary policy stance. Moreover, banks continued to park excess liquidity with RBI under reverse repo route even when its interest rate was brought down to 3.35 percent to encourage banks to lend. The lacklustre response to sector specific Targeted Long Term Repo Operation (TLTRO) 2.0 conducted by RBI has also indicated protective approach of banks. Thus, RBI considered that such debilitating risk aversion of banks could be eventually self-defeating and banks have to play a more defining role using the synergy of stakeholder support.

While usual measures of monitoring and follow up for recovery of loans should continue but from a pragmatic angle, overall reduction in NPAs at this point of time may not look likely as most of the borrowers are in distress and liquidity starved. But comfort can be drawn from the past NPA behaviour to exude confidence to tackle the asset quality woes as and when normalcy restores.

13.4 Covid induced asset quality woes:

Just before the onset of the pandemic, NPAs of banks began to show early signs of improvement falling from 11.18 percent in March 2018 to 9.3 percent in March 2019 to 9 percent by March 2020 that has now come down further to 7.48 percent in March 2021. But the situation is changing with exacerbated adversities in the ongoing pandemic causing local lockdowns and fear of new variants of the virus emerging as threats. The devastation caused by the second wave itself had caused immense loss of productivity of various sectors of the economy. With fear of third wave with more virulent forms of virus is threatening the recovery of the economy with its adverse consequences on the asset quality of banks. RBI in its recent Financial Stability Report (FSR) – June 2020 estimated that NPAs are likely to inch up to 14.7 percent by March 2021 in severe stress conditions and to 12.5 percent in base line stress scenario. Again the FSR of July 2021 shows a much better NPA position. The asset quality of banks in March 2020-21 improved to 7.48 percent. Out of this, the GNPAs of PSBs are higher at 9.5 percent and private banks had lower levels at 4.8 percent. It estimates that the asset quality may deteriorate to 9.80 percent by March 2022 in case of base line stress and to 11.22 in case of severe stress.

Looking to the distress of the borrowers due to the Covid19 impact, honorable Supreme Court of India imposed a standstill clause on the classification of loans as NPAs as of August 31,2020 when the moratorium of total six months period ended. It led to a ban on classifying any loan as NPA even if interest and installment was not serviced. The apex court also ordered waiver of compound interest for all borrowers who availed the loan moratorium announced to counter the impact of Covid-19 distress. On March 23, 2021, the standstill clause on NPA classification was lifted and the banks had started classifying loans as per prudential norms.

As an abundant precaution, banks were maintaining record of loan impairment where the default was found and set them apart as proforma NPAs. Internally banks were maintaining the records separately while externally they were considered as standard assets. Accordingly, banks were also making provisions against such potential NPAs. That is the reason that banks could maintain a provision coverage ratio close to 70 percent.

But looking to the lingering crisis, banks should gear up to handle NPAs of a level going even beyond the RBI estimates in severe stress conditions. Hence, near term expectations to cap NPAs in distress situations is difficult to realize and banks while continuing to improve their capacity to lend should be prepared for a long haul in managing asset quality. Realizing the extraordinariness of the Covid induced distress; banks have to live with higher NPAs for few years until the entities are back to normal in the post Covid19 era. But the inevitable asset quality woes should not be allowed to overwhelm the functioning of banks. Banks will have to encounter certain challenges while gearing up in the next decade but it is a good discovery that banks have learnt how to handhold the borrowers in crisis times. So far banks were conversant with lending when the going of the business entities is good. Now the restructuring, lending to weaker units, supporting with second doze of loan has lead banks to work out several supportive methods to stand by the borrowers in times of need.

13.5 Challenges for banks to lend:

Among many enablers, liquidity, capital adequacy and sturdy provision coverage ratios are immediate near-term drivers to activate fresh lending. In response to the ongoing pandemic, RBI while bringing down the policy rates had infused liquidity close to Rs.15.7 trillion using many innovative windows and assured to pump more. Again, basing on FSR – July 2021 data, the capital to risk weighted assets ratio (CRAR) of banking system that was 14.6 percent in March 2020 and is expected to improve to 16 percent much beyond the minimum CRAR of 10.875 percent. Even if the Basel – III norms are fully implemented by October 2021 as is expected, the minimum CRAR will have to reach 11.5 percent. By all standards, banks will be having comfortable CRAR based on which pace of lending can be increased. The challenge for banks will be to maintain liquidity, CRAR and enough provisions.

The challenge of augmenting capital needs deep dive into the components of CAR so as to maintain capital planning in relation to management of asset quality. The risk-weighted assets are the result of quality of assets. Any shift in risk weightages will shift the CRAR. Hence keeping track will be necessary to maintain lending momentum and asset quality status. As part of relaxations in prudential norms, the last tranche of implementation of Basel – III framework was postponed due to pandemic. It effectively sets the benchmark of minimum capital conservation buffer (CCB) at 1.875 percent of risk-weighted assets against the requirement of 2.5 percent taking minimum CRAR to 10.875 percent (minimum CAR of 9 percent plus CCB of 1.875). Now its implementation stands postponed to October 1, 2021.

After the end of moratorium, the default in loan account will increase the risk weighted assets forcing banks to reach closer to the minimum benchmark of CRAR and will be neck and neck in maintaining CRAR. Many individual banks may even breach the levels. Hence any aggressive lending approach of banks may lead to breach of CRAR compliance inviting regulatory action.

Moreover, RBI has already imposed 10 percent additional provision on restructured loans under its scheme of 'Resolution Framework for COVID-19-related Stress'. However, the extent of hiving off the Covid induced stress of borrowers will broadly depend upon the applicability of the loan restructuring scheme keeping in view the five broad parameters related to leverage, liquidity and debt serviceability identified by the RBI appointed Kamath panel for the 26 weak sectors of the economy. The committee will however be vetting exposure of loans of more than Rs. 1500 crores after they are processed by banks and submitted to the committee.

Rating agency ICRA estimated that loans of banks and non-bank close to Rs.10 trillion may become eligible for restructuring. According to the brokerage firm Jefferies, 60 percent of loans under moratorium may be eligible for restructuring, rest may potentially add to the NPA pile, or some of them may get repaid. Hence banks could be hesitating to lend with fear that NPAs in making will eat into fragile capital base.

It will also depend upon the interpretation of restructuring scheme to cover the target group of beneficiary borrowers. It must be borne in mind that excluding many of them from the scheme will not only mar their credit history but may also obliterate revival of the economy to that extent. Banks should take a positive posture in interpreting the guidance of RBI based on Kamath Committee recommendations.

13.6 RBI resolution framework 2.0

Because of the continuing uncertainties created by the resurgence of the COVID-19 pandemic in India in the more devastating second wave, RBI on May 5, 2021, has announced Resolution Framework 2.0 for Resolution of Covid-19 Related Stress of MSME borrower units. With this notification, RBI announced the extension of the facility for restructuring existing loans without a downgrade in the asset classification. Restructuring under the proposed framework may be invoked up to September 30, 2021, and would have to be implemented within 90 days after invocation. It would however attract the usual 10 percent provision to be made by the lenders as buffer, in case these loans turn out to be NPAs.

Restructuring of advances to MSME was introduced in January 2019 to provide relief to stressed MSMEs. Giving due acknowledgment to the importance of MSMEs in the Indian economy and also to create an enabling environment for the MSME sector formally, a one-time restructuring of loans to MSMEs that were in default was permitted without an asset classification downgrade, provided the MSME account was a 'standard asset' as on 1st January 2019. The built up of stock of restructured assets could be a big challenge in the coming years till they are normalized and borrowers are able to repay the loans in usual course of time.

So long as the recovery retains some momentum, credit losses seem to be manageable. A renewed downturn after the second wave and if a third wave erupts can potentially put further pressure on business finances. Corporate balance sheets can be more exposed than at the start of the pandemic because of a substantial increase in borrowing, particularly by even low profitable firms as loans were made available on favourable terms. While ample credit supply helped compensate for rising losses in the early stages of the pandemic and some firms have built sizeable cash reserves, it is unclear whether additional credit would be forthcoming should economic conditions worsen once again?

The adverse effects of rising corporate insolvencies would be magnified through their impact on banks and other financial institutions. Recent stress tests suggest that most banks hold sufficient capital to meet their regulatory requirements even in the face of a severe downturn. However, they also point to a significant hit to capital buffers, which could constrain the supply of credit to healthy firms and dampen business investment. Low bank profitability in an environment of low-for-long interest rates heightens the challenges and could hinder banks' ability to build buffers and raise new capital. Hence, if the pandemic pans out further and deepens its damage, more policy interventions will be needed to protect the asset quality of banks.

13.7 Policy to pump prime credit flow:

Though slowdown in the flow of credit growth has never been a panacea to improve asset quality, creation of a compatible collaborative credit positive ecosystem will be essential. In times of economic distress, renewed fresh loans and supportive bail out loans to existing units will be critical to revive the economy more importantly to entrepreneurs at the bottom of the pyramid that supports large section of population to survive in hinterland and where the livelihood of masses is connected. Recognizing the extraordinariness of the global calamity, Basel Committee released its guidance in April 2020 for facilitating central banks to suitably respond to the Covid-19 outbreak. Going by its spirit, RBI permitted zero risk weight against loans extended under Emergency Credit Line Guarantee (ECLG) scheme and excluded moratorium period in classifying assets as NPAs. Basel Committee extended time lines for implementation of Basel – III framework till January 2023.

In the given circumstances, government and RBI will have to consider policy support going beyond past trends to enable banks to lend. Looking to the fragile capital base, government is rightly considering infusing capital in PSBs for the time being during FY21 to the tune of Rs.20000 crores through recapitalization bonds without burdening the exchequer. But more action is needed to relax prudential guidelines with fixed time lines for their graded restoration to pre-covid level beginning from 2022-23 completing the process by say, March 2025.

Banks should be in a position to make a clear distinction between viable borrower businesses in the long run and learn to support them with any kind of handholding. Survival of good business units will be able to support the banks in the long run. They should not be allowed to sink due to non-availability of support that will drag the future prospects of the bank. Surviving borrowers will be the means to improve the asset quality of the banks and hence bailing out borrowers will be essential. Banks should be able to keep an eye on the track record and capability of revival of the units.

13.8 Bank level action:

Since it is difficult to extend loans during Covid times based on past loan policies, many banks have designed separate 'Covid loan policy/ Covid loan products for a period of say 1-2 year only to extend loans to *'existing standard borrowers'* whose credit history is already with banks. This specific policy should get integrated with bank's loan policy over a period of time after the pandemic recedes. Though new covid specific loan schemes have been worked out but they should be merged into normal loan products as the covid dissipates. They should be calibrated with such features as to normalize the terms even for existing borrowers for providing quick cash flows aligned to the working cycle of requirements of economic activities.

Besides the restructuring schemes mooted by RBI for (i) stressed MSME borrowers up to Rs.25 crores and (ii) other Covid induced stressed loans to be restructured in terms of Kamath Committee recommendations, bank can articulate yet another 'Covid Restructuring Policy' to explore supporting stressed existing loan accounts on a broader parameter to cover those that are stressed but not falling within the two RBI schemes. The initiatives of bank at present will decide the future shape of the distress-hit borrowers. Banks should learn to support with modified loan, recovery and one time settlement of loan policies whenever extraordinary kinds of situation arises. The same old norms cannot serve the changed circumstances.

Nothing prevents banks from taking a commercial call to restructure loans at their level in the long-term interest of asset quality, if it is convinced about the reasons for stress. The only difference will be (i) such loan account has to be downgraded in terms of prudential norms (ii) provision is to be made as applicable to classification of NPAs. Banks can always identify such loan accounts that merit support in this crisis as a proactive measure and help them to revive and contribute to the economy.

Even if such relief is not granted to borrowers, the loan account, in any case has to be classified as NPA casting its adverse shadow on his credit history. Banks should keep a broader vision in mind that a potential performing borrower is more important than holding NPA and triggering action. Wherever the units are viable, the efforts of banks should be to rescue them. Recovery measures under Insolvency and Bankruptcy Code (IBC) having been stalled initially six months and extended to a year with power to extend up to one year. There is no point adding to the stock of NPAs. Better to provide space for the entrepreneur to explore revival-taking risk a notch higher than pushing closure of the unit. With these covid centric policies, line management in banks should be fully empowered to lend, restructure and grant temporary enhancement in limits on relaxed criteria but not compromising regulatory compliances. Lack of such proactive initiative to bail out entrepreneurs will only add to the gloom.

Procedural reforms, more digitization of lending, documentation needs may also be mooted to hasten loan processing. Digital online lending windows is opened up accepting loan requests with scanned supporting papers to be verified only at the time disbursement of loans. As the additional lending is focused on existing borrowers, the credit risk may remain considerably low. Fresh lending to new borrowers may however be allowed based on the rigor of past loan policy.

In a situation when the aggravating pandemic lingers around spreading fear and despair limiting mobility of people due to sporadic local lockdowns even after opening up activities, revival of the economy is likely to be delayed. Banks and stakeholders should be prepared for prolonged fight with the pandemic.

As such banks in collaboration with the regulators and government should be able to tackle the Covid induced stress by accelerating credit growth. Banks should also hive off the Covid induced stress by bringing a greater number of distressed borrowers within the scope of restructuring schemes of RBI or to be given benefit of restructuring within the bank's own schemes. Lack of any such proactive accommodative measures by banks can also be termed as risk aversion. It is not lending alone. But absence of finding ways to reach out to distressed borrowers in critical times is equally important to help speedy revival of the economy. Fearing the inevitable rise in NPA pile to abstain from lending cannot be the right strategy. If the credit remains stagnant, the NPA ratios will look bigger because of base and pace syndrome. Even if some of such rescued borrowers eventually flourish in business, their pay back to banks will be better and stronger business relationships will establish.

Thus, hesitant baby steps in tackling the economic distress may not provide the kind of buoyancy needed in future to continue to rescue the distressed enterprises, way forward as a policy. If pump priming of bank credit is the need, the policy support and coordinated bank level efforts have to be proportionate to the distress. Never before policy interventions were needed so drastically compared to the position now for a better asset quality in future where all stakeholders in the value chain need to intervene.

13.9 Banks can move against guarantors:

In a significant move in the management of asset quality, the apex court upheld the government notification of November 15, 2019 issued under the Insolvency and Bankruptcy Code (IBC) – 2016 authorizing banks to proceed against guarantors for recovery of residual bad loans after recovering the possible amount from the principal borrowers. The honourable Supreme Court held that the initiation of an insolvency resolution from paying up the loan dues to the financial institutions is governed under Section 126 of Indian Contract Act 1872. It provides for a 'guarantee' wherein the creditor reserves the right to begin insolvency proceedings against the personal guarantor if the principal borrower does not repay the full outstanding loan. The guarantor of the loan is under obligation to pay up the difference between loan outstanding and loan recovered from the asset of the principal borrowers.

Even banks have a right to proceed only against guarantor. It can be recalled that in a decided case, 'SBI v. Indexport Registered [(1992) 3 SCC 159: AIR 1992 SC 1740]' the Court held that the decree-holder bank can execute the decree against the guarantor without proceeding against the principal borrower. Section 128 of the contract Act provides that the guarantor's liability is coextensive with that of the principal debtor.

Therefore, the landmark judgment has opened up avenues for banks to invoke IBC against the principle borrower and guarantor either simultaneously or one after the other when the hair cut amount (difference between outstanding loan and recovered loan dues) is known.

According to ICRA, the gross non-performing assets (GNPAs) of banks is estimated at 9.6 – 9.7 percent in March 2021 and may reach 9.9 -10.2 percent by March 2022. Going by these data points, the outstanding GNPAs against outstanding bank credit of Rs. 109.51 trillion as on March 26, 2021 will work out to Rs.10.62 trillion. Though there is no concrete data available on the loans that are guaranteed by a guarantor, it is estimated that banks will be empowered to enforce recovery against corporate loan guarantors in loans of close to Rs.1.8 trillion in 42 large bad loans out of GNPAs of 10.62 trillion.

Since the implementation of banking sector reforms, there has been gradual empowerment of banks to enforce recovery of bad loans.

Beginning with the enactment of 'Securitisation and Reconstruction of Financial Assets and Enforcement of Securities Interest **Act**, (SAERFAESI Act – 2002)' enabling recovery of bad loans without the intervention of the court, formation of Debt Recovery Tribunals (DRT), setting up of *Lok Adalats* under the aegis of DRTs for settlement of loan recovery with mutual consent of borrowers and lenders, formation of Asset Reconstruction Companies (ARCs) for sale of GNPAs and enactment of IBC – 2016.

13.10 Future prospects of asset quality:

Besides the legal, administrative, regulatory, internal institutional level credit policy, monitoring, recovery and debt resolution processes evolving into more effective tools for better asset quality governance, the skills sets of the banks too are improving. The borrowers and guarantors, present and potential are becoming more sensitive towards interest rates, service charges and processing fees – a good sign of a prudent borrower. The increase in number of prudent borrowers increases the prospects of better loan recovery leading to better asset quality management. Such conscious and prudent borrowers would not like to disrupt their business, diversify their funds and land up in protracted litigations. The loan repayment culture is contagious. If the society is developing an orientation towards keeping loan repayment commitment, they will prompt their suppliers, buyers and customers to do the same evolving better overall conducive ecosystem.

When these developments are seen together with the situation after Covid19 catastrophe, the lessons the borrowers would carry will be positive and the developments in credit growth ecosystem is befitting for better lending and loan recovery system. This new ammunition provided by the government and IBBI (Insolvency and Bankruptcy Board of India) will be able to empower banks to resolve the debt recovery issues with more resolute.

It goes a long way in creating a sturdy credit culture and is a clear sign to the borrowing community that there could be ease of borrowing in a growing financial system but it comes with an obligation to keep the sanctity of debt contract, it is equally important. Banks are therefore getting into a better format for asset quality management in the years to come.

CHAPTER – 14

'PROJECT SHASHAKT' – A DEBT RESOLUTION MODEL

There have been lot of developments in the area of debt resolution post the introduction of AQR by RBI. The real focus on debt resolution began with AQR that followed ideas culminating in the formation of a bad bank in India – a historic move. The rising NPAs in banks has been causing anguish and has been hitting glaring headlines more significantly in the last two – three years following AQR with banks disclosing more NPAs and declaring more losses quarter after quarter. It then led to many banks getting into prompt corrective action of RBI. There was an air of disappointment among stakeholders including bank employees over the reluctance of bank borrowers to honour the debt contract. It is necessary for leaders in the banking system to understand the kind of efforts made/committees that worked on debt resolution and how important it is to maintain good quality assets in the banking system. Though not implemented, certain committees have given rise to better recommendations how to deal with various dimensions of asset quality and how they need to be tackled on sustainable basis. It will be interesting to read the saga of such developments. It is necessary to understand that any decision that results in an action has a history and thought process.

According to Financial Stability Report (FSR)- June 2018, the Gross NPAs (GNPAs) have reached 11.6 per cent by March 2018. The forward outlook of RBI further indicates that GNPA may touch 12.2 per cent by March 2019. As a result, finding ways to resolve the bad loans has become most critical dimension of policy discussions among key stakeholders. Since 90 per cent of such GNPAs and stressed assets currently estimated close to Rs. 15 trillion are with PSBs, the government, RBI and banks are working out strategies to resolve the mind-boggling volumes of bad loans.

Looking to the gravity and pace of accumulation of such large volume of NPAs, RBI has been using twin strategies. (i) Prevention of future NPAs in banks by strengthening monitoring and origination of existing credit portfolio (ii) resolution of existing stock of NPAs to de-stress the banks. Several rounds of discussions to create a special purpose vehicle (SPV) to hive off NPAs were mooted but it did not come through. Government, as stakeholder infused large volume of capital through recapitalization bonds. But the action of RBI and government was not enough to tackle the accumulated pool of NPAs. Moreover, the stock of restructured assets began to slip into NPA category adding to the volume of pile.

14.1 Setting up committees to resolve NPAs:

In view of large divergences observed in asset classification and provisioning in the credit portfolio of banks as well as the rising incidence of frauds in the Indian banking system, an Expert Committee has been set by RBI under the chairmanship of Shri Y H Malegam, a former member of the Central Board of Directors of RBI on 20 February 2018. It has a large diversified agenda and its report was awaited that can lay a strong footing for debt resolution.

In the meantime, Finance Ministry, has set up yet another committee of Public Sector Bankers led by Mr. Sunil Mehta, Chairman of PNB and Chairman of Indian Banks Association (IBA) on 8 June, 2018 to quickly find out if setting up a separate state-owned Asset Management Committee (AMC) will be viable and also to draw up an action plan to identify right strategies to resolve the NPA crisis in banks. The committee was given a short period of time of two weeks to come with strategies and action plans.

In the given poor loan repayment culture etched among majority of the borrowing community, it is very difficult to find a 'quick fix' to address bad loan mess. Despite such limitations of time and onerous task, the Sunil Mehta Committee (SMC) brought out a well thought framework of time bound NPA resolution system. The project of NPA resolution has been aptly known as project 'Shashakt'. Since it was accepted by the government and was to be implemented in banks, it will be interesting to look at its implications on the NPA portfolio.

14.2 Highlights of SMC:

Within a short period, SMC has succinctly brought out a comprehensive five-pronged NPA resolution framework – project 'Shashakt'. The key recommendations include dropping the idea of setting up a bad bank. But it advocated the plan to set up a separate Asset Management Company (AMC)/Alternate Investment Fund (AIF) for absorbing large sized NPAs of over Rs.500 crores. The theme of time bound resolution is good but its success will depend on the enforcement rigor. (i) Creation of an intra-bank vertical for template driven resolution of NPAs of up to Rs.50 crores, which needs to be resolved in 90 days. It is to be supported by a steering committee. This is akin to 'One Time Settlement (OTS)' scheme used in banks based on its internal policy. Many banks follow OTS, as a first measure to avert accumulation of NPAs. Effectively NPAs up to Rs.50 crores are now to be handled within the bank with available normal tools of recovery. But creation of a separate vertical for managing NPAs of up to Rs. 50 crores may be a new idea for more focused attention. Its feasibility will depend on the size of such category of NPAs in individual banks. (ii) Inter-creditor Agreements (ICAs) format of resolution of NPAs of Rs.50 crores to Rs500 crores led by consortium leaders which is almost akin to formation of Joint Lender Forum (JLF), subseqeuntly discontinued by RBI. The approval by 66 per cent of lenders and time line of 180 days is new but the cue was perhaps drawn from IBC debt resolution format.

(iii) The resolution of NPAs of over Rs. 500 crores will move to newly formed AMC/AIF.

The most stringent condition prescribed in it is the need for AMCs to redeem the Security Receipts (SRs) issued to banks within 60 days. How recovery by AMC can be enforced to redeem SRs within such short period of time is to be worked out. (iv) It also envisages invocation of IBC – 2016 if other resolution options fail. (v) Creation of asset trading platform for both performing and NPAs is an innovative move. It can be an effective method of price discovery of dud loans depending upon their intrinsic value but will depend on participants in the trading platform and its depth. There is no ready secondary market for performing assets now. It will be good if a market is created through this mode so that early exit from certain loan accounts may be planned even to balance exposure and risk of particular sectors. Banks may also sell good loans at a premium making money, in case of quality assets to balance risks/exposure of portfolio.

14.3 Strategies for resolution of NPAs:

Keeping the recommendations of SMC, a review of present NPA resolution strategies will be needed to find ways and means to fit them in the existing structure of banks. The existing recovery mechanism in banks will have to be upgraded to work on the lines suggested by SMC. In this context, banks will have to continue to (i) mobilize normal recovery process through bank's internal persuasive policies including use of 'One time Settlement (OTS) scheme. Full recovery can also be possible in the case of recently slipped NPAs. Such borrowers will be making every effort to protect the unit/enterprise from withering away. Banks have been making hectic efforts using normal recovery mode. It can be recalled that escalated NPAs led to RBI placing 11 PSBs under its prompt corrective action. It has been concentrating more on recovery of NPAs due to restrictions on lending operations. Some good success is seen in certain banks in recovering and up-gradation of NPAs. The NPAs that have been classified after RBI's AQR may be tackled on priority. Such units might be in a working state. The chronic portion of NPA pool may be the residual part that requires use of resolution process or even it may stretch to the distress level of liquidation. (ii) Revive the borrower units classified as NPAs that are viable and can operate with support from various agencies inviting new investors/ entrepreneurs to corroborate. Even feeble sign of viability of unit must be captured in the larger interest of sustaining employment and aiding economic growth. If units are sold to new investors, the right kind of price discovery is essential for protecting the interest of banks and delinquent borrowers. There should be no distress sale for viable units at deep haircuts as far as realizing intrinsic value of underlying assets is concerned. (iii) Ensure right price discovery of assets of units which are totally unfit for revival to reduce the burden of haircut for banks. Its liquidation should be able to provide justice to borrowers and banks, more so when failure is on account of business downturn.

It may not be possible to fully recover the outstanding NPAs with their realizable value at the end state of the resolution process even if the recoveries through the three methods specified in (i), (ii) and (iii) outlined above are combined with provisions built by banks. It is noteworthy that PSBs have made huge provisions against NPAs in the last three years and built substantial corpus to meet the deficit. Despite rise in the stock of NPAs, the provision coverage ratio (PCR) (in March 2018) of private banks has reached 51 per cent. PCR of PSBs was also estimated at 47.3 per cent much above the 40 per cent threshold needed to invoke IBC.

Therefore, identification of sources of funds to meet the gap between outstanding bad loans and realizable value of underlying assets after absorbing provisions of banks is likely to be the ultimate loss to the banking system. Of course, even provisions made thus far is a loss to the banks failing which they could have added to the profitability and benefited stakeholders. Such gap is to be met by augmenting internal resources.

14.4 Merits of Project Shashakt:

Certain features in the resolution model were unique and innovative. Focus on bank level settlements for NPAs of up to Rs. 50 crores by setting up a dedicated vertical can be pursued by banks on a continuous basis. But there has to be adequate manpower allocation and empowerment to branches to accept haircuts looking to the difficulty in the realization of value of underlying securities. Institutionalising the process of debt resolution with policy support and discretion of line authorities will be essential to make it produce the desired results. More flexibility to bank branches will enable quick resolution. Presently, the OTS Schemes of banks are very conservative and it is difficult to get settlement done. Many of them often fail to materialize. The biggest stumbling block is inability of banks to accept haircuts and to determine the staff accountability if the realisability is short of perceived value of the assets at initial stage.

Ultimately banks get much less recovery at the end of the legal process or through IBC than what was offered under OTS. The time lag is another loss to the banks. Hence OTS need to be made pragmatic. It is better if such settlements are accepted at the initial stage. The uses of external experts to work out resolution plan for loans of over Rs.50 crores and up to Rs.500 crores can also be another checkpoint to avoid easy restructuring of loans. This systemic check by involving external agencies to wet resolution plans is also contained in RBI's revised debt resolution framework.

But keeping in view the procedural intricacies established in the banks, it might be difficult to adhere to the time lines fixed by SMC. Moreover, looking to the experience of ongoing resolution through use of IBC, management of time lines could be a great challenge. But the asset-trading platform if deepened can create exit opportunities even for performing loans. The intention of quick time lines is to retain value of assets and to help borrowers to settle NPAs and get going with their business. The SMC has therefore created a good framework, which can be further fine-tuned during its implementation to make it work better.

14. 5 Challenges in implementation:

Operationalization of the scheme requires lot of homework at bank level to come up with standard operating Procedures (SOPs) with action points and pin pointing granular time lines at each stage of the process. Accountability for delay has to be established as a systemic control. This will need an internal capacity building and training of associated teams to ensure rigidity in compliance. The broader objective is to retain the value of underlying assets and allay the sufferings of hapless small and medium entrepreneurs struck with bad loans. Employment generation and protection of jobs are also inherent in the scheme of resolution. No debt resolution is possible without cooperation of borrower. Therefore, borrower should be aware that once he/she is free from the stigma of delinquency, they should be eligible to avail loan facility again with banking system like normal borrower. They can hope to restart a failed entity to make it better after learning from past failures.

The resolution of debt using this mode should not create bar for future borrowings. There should be some incentive to borrowers to close the NPA account.

Hence, banks have to educate borrowers and impress upon them to respond so that the 'Shashakt' project transcends the whole banking industry to effectively mitigate the bad loan mess. Appropriate board approved policies and instruction manual for operationalization of the SMC recovery template must be institutionalized to enable branches to undertake recovery process. Banks already have multiple verticals for credit monitoring. Creation of separate vertical for handling SMC template for accelerating recovery should be necessary in banks, which do not have robust monitoring mechanism. Or else banks may carve out a designated vertical to handle the related tasks.

14.6 The beginning of implementation of SMC:

After acceptance of SCM report, it is noteworthy that work on its implementation has already started. 56 lenders have come forward for signing ICAs shortly for NPAs of Rs. 50 crores to Rs. 500 crores to be resolved by coordination among lenders. The agreement prohibits dissenting creditors from making an easy exit. 66 per cent of lenders by value have to approve the resolution plan, which will be binding on all lenders. The dissenting member can sell their loans at a discount of 15 per cent of liquidation value to other lenders and exit from the consortium or buy the entire portfolio paying 125 per cent of liquidation value if it finds the whole NPA unit worthy. The resolution plan will be submitted to an overseeing committee comprising of experts from the banking industry. It also has a standstill clause for 180 days baring lenders from taking any legal action against the borrower for recovery of dues except for criminal breach. The lenders have to get the ICAs approved by their boards before signing it.

In the same league, in order to enable banks to set up an independent Asset Management Company/Alternate Investment Fund (AIF) for bad loan resolution, banks are seeking approval from Securities and Exchange board of India (SEBI) to allow AIFs to own more than 51 per cent in listed securities and blanket exemption from takeover code if their acquisitions in resolution process meet certain conditions. AIFs will be majority owned by banks and institutional investors.

Lenders are also seeking RBI approval to treat the risk weights of investments made in these entities as per the rating assigned by rating agencies instead of assigning flat 150 per cent of risk weight as of now. After three years the risk weights will go up to 250 per cent which can be a stumbling block. A higher risk weight will impinge upon the precious capital of the bank and will also mark down the ability of banks to lend. If these norms are eased banks could save Rs.5000 crores and speed up debt resolution. The investment required through AIFs are currently pegged at Rs. 1.3 trillion to meet the needs of debt resolution.

14.7 Steps to prevent future NPAs:

SMC has reinforced measures to prevent build-up of NPAs in future by suggesting robust governance and credit architecture. Lot of concrete efforts has already been initiated to create a permanent framework for stressed asset resolution, which would definitely work towards reducing future NPAs. The new stressed asset resolution framework for stressed assets of Rs. 2000 crores and above is already introduced from 1 March 2018 with provision that if the Resolution Plan (RP) of the bank fails, banks have to invoke Insolvency and Bankruptcy Code (IBC) – 2016 within next 15 days. RBI strengthened early detection of stress with the help of classification of loans under special mention category (with over dues of up to 1-90 days) as a prelude to their slippage into substandard. This will provide enough elbowroom for banks to protect the quality of assets. RBI also introduced enough systemic controls and created need for robust checks and balances with more frequency in reporting under CRILC. RBI is also about to set up Public Credit Registry (PCR) to improve market intelligence on credit history and other comprehensive information to strengthen decision support system. Such a move will prevent borrowers from escaping their obligation to service the loans in time.

Moreover, the regulatory forbearance (facility of lower provision) for restructured loans has also been withdrawn from April 2016, which was enabling banks to go for easy restructuring of loans. Even borrowers have come to understand that repaying bank loans in time will be in the larger interest of the economy. They cannot remain in business without repaying bank dues. Thus, the recent developments will further reduce incidence of default in bank loans.

In a way, it can be said that a robust ecosystem is getting built to create a good repayment culture though at the bottom of the pyramid promises of agriculture loan waivers and such tendencies are causing disruption. In view of these factors, the recommendations of SMC will not only reinforce resolution process but can also go a long way in eventually creating a sensitive credit culture.

14.8 Ways to make SMC successful:

But the limitations of SMC framework have to be well tackled if actual resolution is to be accelerated as per the design. (i) Bank level resolution system has to be well calibrated with transparency in the process with clear 'to do list' for line management. (ii) The policies to protect decision makers in allowing on the spot haircuts based on net present value of money must be put in place. The conservatism and rigidity in stance will impede the process. (iii) Staff engaged in the process will have to be enterprising with good risk appetite. They need to be groomed for the purpose. The performance incentives and reward structure must be firmed up at the board level. (iv) As far as possible, immunity to employees against decisions taken for NPA resolution should be ensured. The internal rules and standards may have to be redefined. (v) The implementation process calls for greater collaborations among banks, regulators, investors, and various external agencies, which may not in normal course, evince any interest in helping banks in NPA resolution. The government has to institutionalize a process to ensure their sensitivity towards the onerous task. (vi) It must be realized that NPAs are no more limited to be the bank problem. It is a systemic menace, which has potentiality to cause immense collateral damage to every stakeholder in the value chain. Hence its resolution must be considered as a joint task.

Therefore, the extent of success of NPA resolution process through SMC framework will, like in earlier dispensations also depends on the responsiveness of connected stakeholders with same degree of seriousness who have their own role to play. If the government, the major stakeholder of PSBs should also keep bank leadership inspired to take up the task without fear and favour to end the menace. The apprehensions and fear has to be overtaken by the ability of leadership to take decisions with a spirit of enterprise. The debt resolution decision making skills needs to be restored to make the format work. Making people 'Shashakt' is equally important to maintain NPA resolution 'Shashakt".

The significance of the recommendations of Mr. Sunil Mehta committee – popularly referred as project – Shashakt provides a series of thoughts and nuances of managing NPAs and more importantly to resolve them at the earliest. It may not find acceptance in the same format but lot of new ideas and thoughts emanating from the report will find way in future committees. The committees work on coordination. The seeds of solutions coming up in various committees in fact might be the work of earlier committees, the origin of which may or may not find link in the recommendations.

Today, if the Bad Bank is formed in India, its origin and thought process can be connected with not only various committees and policy dispensations in India but from across the globe. The formation National Asset Reconstruction Company Ltd, yet another ARC but owned by government is the result of past hard work of many. Until the loan repayment culture improves at the society level and unless everyone realises the significance that honouring loan commitments by one will provide funds for another new entity that can have the potentiality to add country's GDP, it will be very difficult to manage the asset quality of banks. It should be the collective responsibility of the society as to how we wish to shape the enterprises and how responsible borrowing and repaying culture is embedded in the society.

Some laws, some new norms, some decisive people will not be able to resolve the perennial problems of asset quality. The cultural shift and attitudinal change must come from the conscious of the people as a societal values and not from the external force of law. Using laws for debt resolution should be an exception and not against the behaviour of the society. Lot of reforms at the grass root level with financial literacy will be needed to make the change happen. But good beginning is a best starting point for debt resolution. Project Shashakt adds one new chapter in the history of debt resolution.

CHAPTER – 15

INSOLVENCY AND BANKRUPTCY CODE (IBC) – 2016

RBI, way back in February 2018 issued a templated guidance to banks about invocation of various recovery tools within the time lines set in it. Since the discretion for recovery action has not been retained with banks and a óne size fits all' kind of dictum was issued. Many stake holders were irked leading to the matter up to the honourable Supreme Court. After the apex court had squashed the RBI directive of February 12, 2018 on time bound management of NPAs, there was an air of despair among banks and respite to delinquent borrowers. But it was not so. Lenders continue to be well empowered to use available recovery tools to well manage their asset quality.

The spirit of apex court was to ensure equitable justice and had no relation with the right of the lender to recover loans from the borrowers. A loan is a contract between a borrower and a lender entered into with certain terms. Both have to honour its terms. Since the *one size fits all*' order of RBI calling for invocation of Insolvency and Bankruptcy Code (IBC) – 2016 against defaulting borrowers of Rs. 2000 crores and above where resolution does not work out in 180 days could not stand to the test of law and is pronounced as *ultra vires.*' But the verdict does not dilute the powers and discretion of banks to recover the loans. The only difference could be in terms of time lines and choice of banks using the legal tools that fits the individual borrower.

Irked by such RBI straight order, many corporate sector borrowers, particularly of power, shipping and sugar sector, had moved honourable Supreme Court. According to ICRA, the verdict of the apex court may impact debt worth Rs 3.8 lakh crore across 70 large borrowers, of which Rs 2.0 lakh crore is spread across 34 borrowers in power sector. This was the statistics at that time.

15.1 Need for RBI Action:

Lenders were finding it difficult to follow a time schedule in invoking the rights to recover the bank loans. The delinquent borrowers could not repay loans not because they do not want. But there were certain external factors that came in the way of their enterprise. Looking to the persisting default and non-uniform approach of banks in resolving debts, RBI had to issue such guideline. Even protracted divergence in NPA data of banks and RBI has also led to this development. If prudential norms are interpreted in the way in which they are designed, then there can be no scope for divergence of NPA data. Both lenders and RBI should be on one page but due to bank's own way of interpretations, the divergence could be a cause of concern for the central bank.

Beginning with lending profligacy, restructuring of loans to buy time to prevent them from turning into NPAs, tendency of ever greening of loans, attitude to pretend and extend, and growing lender – borrower accommodation and such other desperate short-term measures suppressed asset quality woes. RBI was unable to assess the actual state of asset quality to appropriately address them.

Before going harsh with the circular, RBI calibrated several progressive measures to guide banks to tackle asset quality woes that did not work well. It brought out a *'framework for revitalizing distressed assets in the economy'* in January 2014 mandating certain steps for early detection of incipient sickness. Had set up Central Repository of Information on large Credit (CRILC) on loans of over Rs.50 million. Early identification of default is made essential under 'Special Mention Accounts (SMA)' introduced in September 2002 but was reinforced in

2014. It required banks to identify loan accounts showing early signs of delinquency under SMA0 (default of up to 30 days), SMA1 (31-60 days) and SMA2 (61-90days) to take preventive follow up action. Formation of Joint Lenders Forum (JLF) was made compulsory in loan accounts of Rs. 1000 million and above that are flagged under SMA category to work out a viable corrective action plan (CAP). RBI then suggested use of schemes such as Corporate Debt Restructuring (CDR), Strategic Debt Restructuring (SDR), S4A, 5/25 and so on to help weak but viable enterprises to revive and stem the rot.

But none of them worked to the desired extent. Vexed with such outcome and lingering uncertainty in the state of asset quality, RBI launched AQR in September 2015 to make banks to disclose the correct state of asset quality. As a result, gross NPAs steeply increased from 4.62 percent in March 2015 to 12.1 percent by March 2018.

15.2 Debut of IBC:

Synchronizing with the ongoing efforts of RBI to speed up debt resolution, the government in coordination with other key stakeholders promulgated Insolvency and Bankruptcy Code (IBC) – 2016 and had set up Insolvency and Bankruptcy Board of India (IBBI) to provide an exit route to failed entities and also thereby incorporated an effective legal tool for time bound debt resolution. Even after IBC – 2016 was put in place; banks were still apprehensive in invoking the act.

Ultimately, RBI had to issue directions on February 12, 2018 mandating banks to necessarily invoke IBC if resolution does not work within 180 days of default which had become contentious because once the IBC is invoked, the ownership of delinquent entity passes on to the Committee of Creditors (CoC). But such stern move of RBI was just to help banks in the speedy resolution of stressed assets. Had banks judiciously enforced the regulatory dispensation and acted in time without unduly accommodating borrowers to distort NPA levels, there would not have been a need for such RBI direction.

15.3 Impact of IBC:

Following the RBI fiat, many banks and operational creditors then queued up with various National Company Law Tribunals (NCLTs) to hasten debt resolution. Close to 15000 recovery petitions were filed. But most of them were settled before admission for the fear of losing the ownership of the units. It explains the latent power of IBC where delinquent borrowers on their own chose to pay up the dues before action is initiated.

After distilling such cases, only 1484 cases were ultimately admitted for resolution, of which 586 cases were resolved and closed by the end of December 2018. 63 cases were withdrawn after admission under section 12A of IBC after recent amendment to the act. 898 cases are still undergoing Corporate Insolvency and Resolution Process (CIRP) in various NCLTs. The recovery rate through IBC stands at 48 percent as against 26 percent through other modes of recovery. More significant is the reduction of average recovery time to 300 days in contrast to 4.3 years that it used to take with other recovery tools.

15.4 Status after verdict:

While the government may now use authority under section 35AA of Banking Regulation Act to direct RBI to issue such directions to banks, but lessons from the whole episode puts back the onus of asset quality management on lenders. It will now be up to the individual banks to evaluate each loan default on merits and use recourse to recover loans. Even now banks can restructure the loans if external developments have brought difficulty to the entrepreneur to service the loans. But banks will have to classify such restructured loans as per prudential norms and make suitable provisions. RBI withdrew the forbearance in provisioning and classification on restructured portfolio to bring better transparency in asset quality management. But even then, banks can take a pragmatic view on restructuring of loans on case-to-case basis as a hand holding measure to bail out genuine delinquency in the long-term interest of enterprise. It is only recently that early signs of reduction of

NPAs are visible. The momentum has to be kept up. While waiting for modified RBI guidance, banks will have to continue to aggressively use IBC to protect its sanctity in the war against NPAs.

15.5 IBC Centricity in Banks

With the end of RBI deadline for resolution of stressed assets of Rs.2000 crores and above, banks have moved on to invoke IBC – 2016. According to the estimated data, banks had to move National Company Law Tribunals (NCLTs) against 70 large NPAs to recover close to Rs.3.8 trillion making a provision of 50 per cent. Majority of them belong to power sector. But with a comfortable PCR of private banks standing at 51 per cent and PSBs at 47.1 per cent by March 2018, they may not find it difficult to scale up the required provisions to invoke IBC against the delinquent borrowers.

This brings to focus the more critical role of IBC as savior of banks against the menace of toxic assets. The refusal of Allahabad high court to intervene has upheld the sanctity of policies of central bank. It is a different issue that with the guidance of RBI and in consultation with other stakeholders, a temporary solution could be found in the larger interest of the economy to avert the impasse in power sector. But the writing on the wall is now clear that borrowers cannot get away without honoring bank commitments. It restores the sanctity of debt contract between banks and borrowers. The development is a great respite to PSBs groaning under the weight of 90 percent of stock of toxic assets. It is a strong signal for industry but an equally important guidance that banks need to improve their internal capability to effectively manage IBC centric asset quality management. The competencies need to be widely disseminated, when RBI extends such guidelines to NPAs of below Rs. 2000 crores. In a wider context, government is also set to extend scope of IBC to cover cross boarder insolvency cases to provide comfort to foreign institutional investors.

Another IBC centric development is the ability of banks to recover close to Rs. 50000 crores in 32 cases initially admitted by NCLTs. The average haircut of 44 per cent in these cases was considered better than other forms of recovery. Having already made a provision of 50 per cent against these assets, banks can reverse the excess provisions. The merits of IBC can be further hailed from the reports that about 2100 companies have cleared their outstanding loans working out to Rs.83,000 crores for fear of losing control on their units after government amended IBC-2016 to bar promoters of delinquent companies from bidding. IBC is thus not only meant for speeding up debt resolution but is also emerging as a deterrent for existing borrowers to prevent future default.

15.6 Rising work load at NCLTs:

In order to cope with increased workload, Ministry of Corporate Affairs (MCA) is contemplating to double the existing strength of 11 NCLTs. With potential rise in number of cases and allowing shifting of resolution cases from one NCLT to another for speedy disposal, more bank level preparation was needed to train people to invoke the law. In the midst of increased load on NCLTs and rise in grievances of applicants, presence of a single NCLAT also may not be enough. Keeping these practical difficulties, the expansion of infrastructure of NCLT was to be speeded up. Even then, one of its differentiating features of maintaining time lines in resolution or liquidation prescribed at 180 days at that time with additional grant of 90 days total 270 days is not strictly adhered. Now the time line is increased to 330 days. When a large number of cases are now received under the new dispensation, it was difficult to adhere to the time lines by NCLTs. Even bank level infrastructure to invoke and follow up the IBC cases need lot of preparation.

With rise in traffic, Insolvency and Bankruptcy Board of India (IBBI) increased its surveillance. Its regulation of conduct of Insolvency Resolution Professionals (IRPs), valuers and committee of creditors (CoCs) is under close scrutiny. They are most important anchors in implementing Corporate Insolvency Resolution Process (CIRP). The IRPs have the dual responsibility to manage the operations as a going concern on behalf of the firm while implementing CIRP. CoCs as trustees of the financial creditors have to work in coordination with IRPs to optimizing value chain.

They act as the fulcrum between adjudicating authority and stakeholders –debtors, creditors – financial as well as operational and resolution applicant. With experience of the first and second lot of NPAs referred to NCLTs, the bank employees connected with the task could gain substantial hands-on experience and can be better get equipped to deal with its intricate procedures. Many of the legal litigations and corresponding judgments pronounced by courts/NCLTs/NCLAT in the past can act as a foundation and guidance for strengthening decision support system in speeding up CIRP.

15.7 Bank level competency:

In order to operate in IBC centric ecosystem, banks will have to work towards galvanizing in-house competence to effectively handle CIRP related skill sets and develop appropriate standard operating procedures (SOPs) to streamline working. Banks should evolve a board level policy to create a cadre of professionals well rounded to handle CIRP activity to be part of committee of creditors. It will need a blend of incentives and assured career prospects with long-term mindset. The normal way of assigning job role may not enable human resources to specifically pick nuances of handling stressed asset resolution with specialist mindset, particularly when it is emerging as a technical legal centric function. In one of the recommendations, Sunil Mehta committee too highlighted the need to carve out a separate vertical to deal with stressed assets. As a policy perspective, banks may have to work hard to develop specific talent, groom and retain them. A combination of in-house and lateral entry of professionals will have to be planned to pool legal experts, valuers, engineers, turnaround specialists and operational bankers to build resolution and recovery teams. Business as usual mode in enforcing resolution of stressed assets may not be effective in the emerging IBC centric regime.

15.8 Impact of pandemic on IBC -2016

The catastrophic impact of Covid19 on the economy has put the borrower community under unprecedented stress. Stoppage of activities due to lockdowns, disruption in production, migration of labor caused dip in demand and other adversities had a cascading impact on all activities including banking. Several relief measures were organized with RBI coming up with moratorium on loan repayment and allowing restructuring of loans to provide more time to borrowers to cope with the crisis. As larger part of ongoing mega stimulus package to fight the impact of coronavirus (Covid19) pandemic, the government has stalled invocation of IBC – 2016 for one year to provide more comfort to ailing delinquent entrepreneurs. It can enable, among others the worst affected MSME sector to get adequate time to recoup from the distress.

The minimum threshold to initiate insolvency proceedings against MSMEs has also been raised from Rs 1 lakh to Rs 1 crore to provide relief to micro and small units and prevent such small loan defaults flowing to National Company law Tribunals (NCLTs). It will enable bigger debt resolutions to get priority in settlement. Looking to the magnitude and depth of economic distress from virus scourge and massive disruption in production, the postponement of debt and insolvency proceedings was a fair move to allow them to recoup the lost momentum of productivity and growth. Besides the financial support, policy forbearance to insulate borrowing community from such legal actions can enable them to rejuvenate industrial growth.

15.9 Performance of IBC:

Taking stalling of IBC during pandemic for year as an opportunity, a look at how it contributed to the banks in hastening recovery will be appropriate. Stocktaking can begin by recalling that that IBC – 2016 was effective from December 1, 2016 opening up an opportunity to file bankruptcy petition by failed enterprises/lenders/operational creditors and a quick time bound debt resolution option, more importantly for lenders. The three-year performance data from its since inception, until

December 2019 on the progress of CIRP will be able to resonate the depth in achieving its objectives.

A total of 3312 CIRPs have commenced till December 2019. Out of them, 246 have been closed on appeal or review or settled. 135 have been withdrawn, 780 have ended up in liquidation. 190 companies could be saved with approval of their resolution plans. Remaining 1961 cases are under consideration at various stages of CIRP.

15.10 Larger impact of IBC:

Besides the near-term quantitative impact, improving the loan recovery of banks, IBC has enabled India to substantially scale its tally in the World Bank's 'Ease of doing business index (EoDB)' report 2020. It improved from 100 in 2018 to 77 in 2019 to 63 in 2020 among 190 countries. A driving feature is the contribution of IBC in the form of 'resolving insolvency' factor that went into in assessing EoDB that went up in ranking from 108 in 2019 to 52 in 2020. The strength of insolvency framework stands at 7.5 points in the World Bank's scale of 0–16-point metrics as against the average of 11.9 of OECD countries.

The distressed loan recovery rate of bank's works out to 42.5 percent of the amount involved through IBC-2016 as compared to 14.5% under the Securitization and Reconstruction of Financial Assets and Enforcement of Securities Interest (SARFAESI) Act, 3.5 % from Debt Recovery Tribunals (DRTs) and 5.3 % from lok adalats. The average time taken in resolution works out to 364 days compared to the duration of 4.3 years by use of other laws/tools. The efficacy of the code can be further gauzed from the fact that bank claims worth Rs.3.74 trillion have been settled before admission of application or before formation of Committee of Creditors (CoC) etc.

These data-based facts highlight the significant role of IBC under the efficient regulatory glare of Insolvency and Bankruptcy Board of India (IBBI) that has begun to systematically create a strong network of stakeholders to create robust debt resolution system. It is set to change the credit culture. Such behavioral transformation will have the potentiality to improve the sanctity of debt contract in India.

Moreover, the spate of amendments to improve the overall effectiveness of IBC framework since its enactment and precedence of landmark judicial verdicts are set to make the insolvency resolution process more robust and speedier. Though the new timelines are set at 330 days, it could be made faster provided the skill sets of insolvency resolution professionals (IRPs) and members of CoC could be fine-tuned to take faster and apt decisions.

Due to the faster pace of debt resolution when the velocity and recycling of loan funds and banking resources increase, the pace of economic growth can catch higher growth trajectory. In a bank driven economy, activation and stabilization of debt resolution and bankruptcy process has the potentiality to better position India in the global economy as is evident from the consistent improvement in EoDB ranking.

15.11 Skill sets of stakeholders:

The IBBI and banks should use this window of opportunity of one year to upgrade the skill sets of stakeholders through sustained capacity building system. Review of the standard operating manuals connecting the missing dots based on decided legal cases to strengthen the value chain can make IBC sturdier and result oriented. Thus, the stakeholders should work on turning this adversity into an opportunity engaging in the brick building to enhance competency in more effectively dealing with the emerging challenges, once the debt resolution process resumes.

Since the enactment of Insolvency and Bankruptcy Code – 2016, banks have been wrestling with the task of referring large identified NPAs to NCLTs for time bound resolution. RBI has been directing banks pinpointing NPAs where invocation of IBC is felt essential. Whenever recovery measures are initiated, mighty and strong delinquent borrowers identify weaknesses in the legal structure to seek asylum in courts. In many such litigations, the honourable courts have steered clear the recovery actions of banks in line with the provisions of IBC, much to the detriment of dodging borrowers. But still there was scope to meddle with its legal provisions.

As a result, some of the errant promoters of large defaulting companies were keen to bid for assets to be auctioned by CoC to realize their dues as part of debt resolution plan. The deep haircut in the resolution process may turn such assets cheaper than market price. The promoters of delinquent companies evince interest to bid for their own company assets as they are more familiar and understand how to resurrect them for gains. In such a milieu, the promoters can again buy back their own company assets at a discounted price regaining management control. In the process, banks have to absorb haircut while the defaulted promoters can get away easily meddling with the legal lacunae. There was no specific provision in IBC to bar promoters from buying their own company assets.

15.12 Amendment to IBC – 2016:

Recognizing such glaring legal gap, an ordinance amending the IBC has been approved barring errant promoters, wilful defaulters, guarantors to the debtors, those with poor credit worthiness and disqualified directors of the companies. It is the call of the committee of creditors to undertake due diligence of bidders under the resolution process. Penal provisions have been built into the system for violations, if any. The present amendment is a right step to abrogate the malicious move of delinquent promoters, who by their own act have brought the company to the brink of such ignominy. Even in such distress, some of the errant promoters find a way to dupe the banks and buy back assets at lower price. Henceforth, even practice of providing cross guarantees among borrowers will also be checked. A part of the due diligence will have to be done by guarantors as well. If they do not test the prudence of borrowers, such guarantors also will have to a pay price for their tacit role when the loan account turn sour.

While there could be exceptions, most of large NPAs are the result of unmindful and reckless diversification and misuse of borrowed money by the entrepreneurs. Had these funds been applied for the purpose for which loans were granted, the unit would have been operational. The diversification is the result of overleveraging and making greedy investment in real estate or other high-risk ventures. Genuine failure of business due to downside economic cycle are rare and can be taken care by banks with inbuilt handholding process/restructuring of loans. It is the wilful act to default bank loans that cannot be protected by systems and policies.

There has also been an increasing attitude among borrowers to seek enhancement of loans to accommodate such vilification. Banks having funded large sum is often left with no option but to continue the facilities with little enhancements now and then to ensure that loans continue to be serviced and remain standard as long as possible. Ever greening of loans by banks so as to maintain the relationship with borrowers also plays its own role in accumulating NPAs. Such forced accommodation with additional doses of loans ultimately led to steep climb of stressed assets in banks to over Rs. 12 trillion, majority of which are held by PSBs.

The present massive stock of NPAs in the banking system has to however undergo the gruelling process of debt resolution. Even finding eligible bidders as per new norms can now pose a great challenge as was experienced in SDR scheme of RBI. But the long-term impact of well amended IBC could be an elixir for the ailing banking system. The future generation of borrowers will understand that not honouring commitments to repay bank loans could deprive them of the continuity of business forever. Besides the ordeal of facing NCLT proceedings and dictate of committee of creditors, losing the commercial activity could put an end to not only their current span of business but can also cost very dear to their next generation.

The legal tool of IBC is well set to emerge as an invincible tool against future defaults. At the same time, introduction of various follow up measures by RBI since 2014 will develop better systemic controls in banks to bring the incipient sickness of accounts to the floor of lenders through joint lender forum. The combined impact will bring a tectonic shift in the attitude of borrowers towards loan repayment culture. Banks also would not hesitate in classifying bad loans in time to initiate available recovery measures. The crusade against toxic loans in banks would converge into an effective force to enhance the asset quality and stabilize a better credit culture much to the relief to banking sector.

With sizeable capital infusion by the government from time to time, if the existing pile of NPAs are taken to their logical end, the PSBs in particular can regain robust health to support economic growth with accelerated lending in the next two years.

Though the challenge for insolvency professionals and committee of creditors has gone up substantially in identifying new investors, the banks have been put on firm footing. The amended ordinance has thus removed an anomaly that could dissipate ethical dimensions of debt resolution. As a sustainable strategy, banks should have a firm and uniform policy to declare borrowers as wilful borrower as soon as possible in the usual course of business. Since there was no specific advantage for banks to declare borrowers as wilful defaulters, it was hardly pursued as a deterrent in managing asset quality.

Now, such classification will hold lot of significance. Since it can be challenged in a court of law, banks have to pursue strict policies in line with RBI guidelines. Though the ramification of amendments to IBC is open to challenges in implementing it, yet it has great potentiality to ring fence the moral standard of debt resolution process.

CHAPTER – 16

NPA MANAGEMENT – RECOGNITION TO RESOLUTION

In the credit administration in a bank, while lending is a complex function of credit origination, its recovery is much more significant to ensure that the cycle of banking operations remain sustainable. But in practice, lending looks easier than recovery for the reason that the commitment in later case is with the borrower. How the borrower keeps up the commitment will decide the recycling process of funds. Banks are always stressed under the weight of bad loans not only in India but across the globe. The biannual FSR of RBI has clearly highlighted the threatening proportion of NPAs in banks, more so in PSBs. Having unmasked the deplorable state of asset quality, the banks now need to focus on the resolution of toxic debt. Banks began to recognize the NPAs after RBI increased its surveillance to find out the actual state of asset quality.

Despite applying more rigor and interventions in the follow up for loan recovery at various stages driven even from the highest level, there has been no significant improvement in recovery performance. As a result, the GNPAs in banks have gone up from 7.8 percent in March 2016 to 9.1 percent in September 2016. The stressed assets have increased from 11.5 percent to 12.3 percent during the period. Looking at the status of Special Mention Accounts (SMAs), the pipeline GNPAs too is further set to exacerbate. The surprising part is the trend of slippage of assets which is beyond the watch list of banks that speak of lack of adequate surveillance on the quality of assets.

It is estimated that the GNPA ratio may increase from 9.1 percent in September 2016 to 9.8 percent by March 2017 and further to 10.1 percent by March 2018. Among the bank groups, PSBs may continue to register the highest GNPA ratio. Their GNPA ratio may increase to 12.5 percent in March 2017 and then to 12.9 percent in March 2018 from 11.8 percent in September 2016. Sectoral break up of NPAs indicates that 13 percent of it pertains to infrastructure loans where PSBs have a larger exposure.

The total stressed assets of infrastructure sector work out to 21 percent. Operating under the excessive weight of NPAs, growth in loans and advances of PSBs decelerated to 2.1 percent in 2015-16 from 7.4 percent in the previous year. On the liability side, moderation in deposit growth led to lower credit growth that further exacerbates the NPA position. The deposit growth and credit growth have a direct relationship. If deposit growth is fast, the resources have to be deployed and they may flow towards growth though banks may have the alternative to opt for investments. The accumulation of deposits after demonetization may set another new trend where lack of appropriate deployment opportunities may turn deposits into low yield liabilities eroding the already fragile Net Interest Margin (NIM) of banks.

16.1 Continuing uptrend

When it comes to assessing the stock of bad debts, the total stock of NPAs was at INR 3.3 trillion in Q2 of FY16. They jumped up to INR 6.5 trillion by March 2017. Some of the key rating agencies put the pipeline stress close to another INR 3 trillion. Despite massive efforts of RBI to empower banks in enforcing rigor in monitoring, control and recovery of loans, the slippages in the quality of assets still continue to outpace the recovery. Despite the introduction of graded credit monitoring measures by RBI to classify loan accounts into Special Mention Accounts (SMAs), the worrying factor is the slippage of loan accounts which are beyond the watch list of the bank.

According to RBI norms introduced in February 2014 under which, if the instalment and interest are overdue for over 30 days, the account should be brought under watch list as SMA-I. The preventive actions are prescribed if they slip into SMA-II (overdue beyond 60 days) to speed up debt resolution. Any consortium account migrating to SMA-II calls for collaborative action of forming Joint Lenders Forum (JLF) to find a solution to the impending problem credit. The pace of write-off of loans is yet another cause of concern that impacts the profitability of banks.

The operating results of some of the private sector banks were also clearly pointing towards exacerbating asset quality woes stretching fast across the sector. The systemic controls built by RBI as a preventive tool did not make much impact in controlling the trends. In order to tackle the menace of NPAs in the medium and long term, it is always essential to recapitulate the underlying reasons for the exponential rise in NPAs in banks. The reasons for surge in NPAs in PSBs could be different because the target group to whom lending is made is different. Since the magnitude of NPAs in PSBs was glaring, a further granularity of data will be able to explain the trend prevailing at that point of time.

Table-I: Trends of Movement of NPAs of Public Sector Banks – FY11-16

(Amount in INR Crore: Figures in bracket are in %)

Sr No	Parameter of NPAs	FY12	FY13	FY14	FY15	FY16
1	Opening NPAs as on April 1 of the Financial year	74616	117262	164461	227264	278468
2	Additions during the year (Slippages)	92808 (124)	119613 (102)	163546 (99)	177862 (78)	385962 (139)
3	Recovery	35321 (47)	45540 (39)	67915 (41)	75679 (33)	65029 (23)
4	Write-off	14841 (20)	26873 (23)	32828 (20)	50979 (22)	59445 (21)
5	Closing NPAs on 31st March of the year	117262	164462	227264	278468	539956

(Source: Statistical Tables Relating to Banks in India FY16 – RBI Publication, Mumbai)

Figures in bracket indicate the percentage of the parameter to opening balance of NPAs of the year.

16.2 Recovery position of NPAs in PSBs:

The analysis of NPA trends clearly indicates that the problem is more concentrated in PSBs. Hence, movement of NPAs in PSBs will be more pertinent to find out precise reasons and understand the gravity of the problem. Banks manage the NPAs by combining efforts for (i) recovery; (ii) write-off subject to internal policies and (iii) prevention of slippages to check deterioration of asset quality during the year that results in year-end NPAs. The outcome of the total thrust on NPA management lies in their ability to manage asset quality. Relevant data on NPA trends of PSBs of past few years will indicate how the NPAs were continuing to increase year after year (Table-I).

The granular data on NPA flow chart of PSBs of the last five years indicates the incipient weaknesses. The percentage of slippage, recovery and write-off has been worked out from the opening level of NPAs to compare the performance. The trend of new loan accounts becoming NPA has been steep. It ranges from 124 percent of NPAs to 139 percent (due to the impact of AQR). That means new NPAs are surfacing faster than they can recover. The recovery portion of NPAs varies from 47 percent of the opening level of NPAs in FY 12. The pace of recovery has been consistently receding down to 23 percent in FY16. Due to base and pace, the percentage comes down with the rise in NPAs. Therefore, the recovery efforts need substantial improvement to keep pace with broadened base. The amount of write-off of loan accounts is also high. It is in the range of 20 percent of the stock of NPAs which directly hurts the profitability.

Recovery and write-off put together are less than fresh slippage of NPAs. That means the net stock of NPAs is getting added year after year exacerbating the problem. The result of efforts for recovery is unable to keep pace with slippage and loan write-off figures are also on rise. Both recovery and write-off put together are less than slippage. PSBs have to necessarily focus more on prevention of additional loan accounts turning into NPAs adding to the outstanding level.

16.3 Slow recovery trends in NPAs

Besides normal recovery efforts, banks make every effort to reduce their NPAs using various legal channels like resolutions through Lok Adalats, Debt Recovery Tribunals (DRTs) and by invocation of SARFAESI. But the outcome has been lukewarm. These tools were not as effective as they should have been. The amount recovered by all SCBs through these channels got reduced to INR 227.68 billion in FY16 as against INR 307.92 billion during the previous year.

PSBs, which are burdened with a high proportion of the banking sector's NPAs, could recover only INR 197.57 billion as against INR 278.49 billion during the previous year. The deceleration in recovery was mainly due to a reduction in recovery through the SARFAESI channel which had dropped down by 52 percent from INR 256 billion in 2014-15 to INR 131.79 billion in 2015- 16. With the rise in the number of NPA cases, it is increasingly becoming difficult to speed up recovery by using SARFAESI Act. On the other hand, recovery through Lok Adalats and DRTs had marginally increased.

Banks also reduced their stressed assets by selling them to ARCs. This has been increasing since March 2014 because of the regulatory support extended to banks under the framework to revitalise the distressed assets in the economy. Even the heightened measures for recovery could not keep pace with the trends of slippage in asset quality. Greater legal reinforcement will be needed to augment recovery of dud loans.

16.4 Key reasons for slippage

There could be many reasons for surge in NPAs depending on the bank's (i) size, (ii) geographical reach, (iii) business mix, (iv) strategic approach towards credit growth, (v) strategic business priorities, its strengths, and (vi) market positioning and so on. But, some of the common reasons could be the following:

- There is no built-in fear of law for borrowers to repay banks' loans. Hence servicing bank loan ranks later in the order of priority in meeting payment commitments. There is neither social castigation of loan defaulters nor a barrier for continuing business/ enterprise except for limited restrictions for a proclaimed wilful defaulter.

- There is a distinct lack of rigour in the credit origination process of banks leading to a pile of systemically weak loan accounts, particularly belonging to large borrowers.

- Policy barriers and weaknesses in governance are resulting in a significant number of stalled projects hitting the banks which have exposure to them.

- The excessive exuberance of banks in lending to infrastructure sector with more focus on road projects, power and the like with inadequate due diligence that led to added pile of NPAs. The compounded annual growth rate of advances of 39.31 percent to the infrastructure sector affirms the excessive exposure with its repercussions. Credit risk management was not balanced with sectoral mix of exposure.

- External interference and / or entry of middlemen in credit decisions diluting the asset quality impacting a sizeable credit portfolio, particularly in large ticket advances. The intervention typically is seen in big advances to influential large borrowers.

- Diversion of loan funds by borrowers due to lack of bank's adequate post disbursement monitoring system of credit.

- Lack of enough manpower at branch/unit level to maintain follow-up and surveillance on the conduct of accounts and borrower rating.

- Inadequate use of technology in monitoring credit in many banks.

- There is a lack of enough sensitisation among even corporate borrowers towards hedging currency risk / business risk. As a result, the business risk gets transmitted to banks diluting the asset quality. Though RBI directs banks to monitor exchange rate risk of borrowers, the wherewithal of some of the banks is inadequate and needs to be upgraded to peep into the hedging policies of borrowers. Some banks are unable to adequately upgrade technology and skill sets of employees to efficiently handle the increased load of a number of borrowers / depositors. This impacts credit quality.

- Banks are yet to institutionalise a graded approach in credit origination, monitoring and debt resolution. The 'one size fits all' kind of policy in credit administration is leading to staff accountability issues. Banks should put in place an appropriately graded policy to protect employee interest. The fear of staff accountability has reduced the risk appetite of banks.

- The 'after action' of banks against employees in NPA accounts is diluting the culture of credit decision making. The fear psychosis among employees is impacting credit growth. So, even if NPAs remain same, the fall in advances increases the severity of asset quality and potential loss of interest income.

- There is no institutionalised protection against genuine and bonafide commercial decisions that may go wrong in due course due to external factors but such tendency can reduce the credit risk appetite of employees.

- The continuing fear of career-conscious employees towards staff accountability leads to a slowdown in processing and even compromise proposals detrimental to the asset quality of banks. Such undisposed compromise proposals prevent reduction of NPA levels.

- Lack of grooming and upgrading critical employees in credit risk assessment leads to dilution in asset quality. Training and encouraging development of sustained skills, lack policy focus to nurture competencies that leads to talent deficit.

- There is no pronounced reward and incentive for building credit risk appetite. There are neither incentives nor institutionalised disincentives that leads to a lukewarm attitude towards management of asset quality.

- The ecosystem in most of the state-owned banks is neutral to credit growth and NPA stock. Except for fear of staff accountability if loan accounts turn into NPA there no impact if credit does not grow.

- The sporadic announcement of debt waiver schemes benefitting the defaulters and not incentivising prompt repayment of bank's loans creates a detrimental culture of debt repayment. An honest borrower feels cheated when such schemes are announced that encourage borrowers to wait for opportunities to escape repayment of bank dues. This is a cultural issue where loan repayment should be respected instead of providing benefits to loan defaulters.

While sharing his mind on reasons for the current spate of NPAs, Dr Raghuram Rajan, former Governor, RBI described that 'Sensible lending means careful assessment up the front of project prospects, which have been marred by irrational exuberance or excessive dependence on evaluations by others (Banks / lead managers)'. Credit origination, therefore, lays the foundation for quality of assets. A compromise at this stage cannot be made up at later stages of loan life. The purpose of piecing together common reasons for the rise in NPA levels can enable policy makers in banks to devise such medium and long-term policy initiatives that can ring fence the asset quality of banks. An ecosystem needs to be cultivated where the professional approach to credit decisions and early identification and action for recovery of loans can be institutionalised on a sustainable basis. Incentives and disincentives must be built into the policy framework.

16.5 New debt resolution schemes

Besides the existing legal and institutional framework for enforcing recovery of bank loans, RBI has consistently been working on empowering banks. In this league, the recent softening and modification of norms of Strategic Debt Restructuring (SDR) originally introduced in June 2015, Sustainable Structuring of Stressed Assets (S4A) brought in by RBI in June 2016 may take considerable time to improve the ecosystem for enforcing recovery of loans and improving overall asset quality. Even the proposed recent approach of government to handover stressed units in power, steel and shipping to well-functioning public sector companies would be a protracted process to resolve the bad debts of banks.

Though the banks proclaim to have moved from the mode of recognition of bad loans to resolving them, their recovery action is not able to bring visible results. Debt restructuring schemes are not able to show positive results. Perhaps the efforts lack enough traction to make them work in the field? Banks had to begin classifying loan accounts brought under SDR as NPAs. Banks had 18 months of time after converting 51 percent of their debt into equity to find an investor to transfer its stake. However, later SDR scheme could not find significant favor in the industry as it is found difficult to find such an investor. Hence the scheme was scrapped but the bank employees should be conversant about the schemes that emerged and discontinued. Even when an investor is identified, there was a tussle for haircut (meaning the loan discount that investors seek on the value). Banks are usually not willing to take more than 25-30 percent haircut in most cases, but investors insist for a larger haircut even stretching to the extent of 50 percent depending upon the status of the project and loan account.

The haircut is least in real estate whereas in metal companies it is demanded in the range of over 65 percent where banks had to backtrack. In a bid to find a pragmatic solution, RBI refined the debt recast scheme with S4A under which the loans of companies are to be split into sustainable and unsustainable portions based on cash flows of the projects. But the sustainable part has to be more than 50 percent which is again a limitation for banks to work upon. Since banks are under severe pressure in dealing with such issues, haircuts can be viewed differently inviting not criticism for the decision but also issues of staff accountability. These are some of the reasons that efforts of banks made so far had a lukewarm response though some large defaulters proposed to sell their non-core assets to pay back loans. The follow-up actions in some large NPAs are only striking headlines with no real relief to banks. Thus, the build-up of NPAs seems to be unending with no visible respite. More autonomy is needed in enforcing recovery from NPAs. More important is to create systemic controls in disincentivizing the loan default.

16.6 Weak loan recovery ecosystem

It takes considerably longer time for resolution of bad loans in India compared to peer nations. Overall, it takes over four years to resolve debt in India compared to less than two years in China and US. It only takes close to a year in Germany, UK, Malaysia, Australia and the least time is taken in Japan where debt can be resolved in a short span of six months. Even the percentage of loan recovery (amount of loan recovered as percentage to loan outstanding) is too poor in India close to 25 percent compared to 40 percent in China and 42 percent in Thailand. It is as high as 85 percent in Singapore, 82 percent in UK, 80 percent in US and Malaysia. It only reflects that there is lack of sense of urgency in resolving debt in India and collaboration among various agencies involved in the process needs substantial improvement. At the end of the credit life cycle, if banks are able to recover only paltry portion of loan, it is difficult to keep lending as a commercial activity.

16.7 Better loan resolution system in making

The IBC – 2016 was passed by the Parliament on 11th May 2016, received Presidential assent on 28th May 2016. An IBBI became operational on December 1, 2016. The government notified rules for insolvency professionals, agencies, and devised model bylaws under the bankruptcy code. The NCLT is the adjudicating authority on such matters.

This new law aims to establish a transparent and time bound process for bankruptcies. The institutionalisation of resolution professionals and creating a cadre of debt resolution experts is in making. The time bound debt resolution that was 270 days earlier is now made to 330 days. Compared to the time that it used to take, even such time lines are a good beginning. Moreover, RBI is proposing to set up a financial sector resolution corporation to help speed up debt resolution process.

16.8 Immediate relief after demonetisation

Realising the practical constraints following demonetisation of high-value currency, RBI allowed certain relaxations in prudential standards as a temporary measure for banks and NBFCs. (a) The recent extra window of 60 days granted by the central bank for classification of loans as 'Sub- Standard' taking the period to 150 days from the present norm of 90 days due to the fallout of demonetised currency for loans of up to INR 1 crore. The relaxation in norms is to be applied for dues payable between November 1 and December 31 (b) In further relief to borrowers hit by demonetisation, RBI raised the tenor or relief of another 30 days over and above 60 days for repayment of housing, car, farm and other loans worth up to INR 1 crore. These measures cannot be a panacea for the woes but can provide some temporary relief and immediate saving of additional provisioning. Looking to the distress caused by the demonetization of high value currency notes, there were lot of disruptions in the economic activities with its cascading impact on the repayment capacity of loans.

16.9 Future policy shift

In the emerging ecosystem, the sustainability of the banks will rest on improved asset quality. It will need a multipronged initiative. In addition to legal reforms, it is felt essential to de-risk bank balance sheets by reducing excessive exposure to large corporate accounts. Consequently, RBI would cap banks' exposure to a group of connected companies at 25 percent of the lenders' core capital, seeking to reduce concentration risk in a banking industry laden with bad loans. The central bank lowered the limit of group exposure from 40 percent of the banks' total capital funds, which include both Tier 1 (core) and Tier 2 capital, and gave banks time until 2019 to meet the new norms of reduction to 20 percent of Tier 1 capital, compared to 15 percent of total capital funds (Tier 1 and Tier II) currently in force.

The new norms will make banks reduce their exposure to large corporate sector borrower and phase out even the existing exposures. It is set to develop bond and equity market to create alternate funding sources for the corporate sector. The introduction of Masala Bonds (where exchange rate risk is passed on to the investor) will help in accessing overseas funds by strong Indian entities.

16.10 Innovations in NPA management strategies

The current size of NPAs cannot be tackled with past organisational structure and/or point of focus. As part of the plan, banks will have to put firm, more robust and compatible organisational structure that can follow up with the delinquent borrowers. The three distinct phases of credit administration need upgradation of skill sets. While (a) Credit origination requires improved appraisal and market/economic intelligence techniques, (b) Credit monitoring will need perseverance and hand holding tact and (c) Problem of credit (NPA) resolution will need a grip on legal knowledge, latest provisions of seeking help of IBC-2016 and negotiating skills of the highest order.

The system of deployment of credit officers to handle any of its functions may not be effective when focused attention on every task needs specific knowledge and skill sets. Grooming of manpower is required on immediate priority to handle different phases of credit portfolio management. Internal training capability or taking help of external training organisations need planning and phasing of training. Realising such emerging need, RBI recently made it mandatory to plan 'Capacity building in banks and non-banks' as per the recommendations of Shri Gopalakrishnan committee. It requires certification of competency of bank employees in functional areas.

In the last few years, banks have formed new organisational structure to meet challenges of credit growth and NPA management, but that may not be sufficient in future. More specialisation will be needed for debt resolution. Managing standard assets and managing NPA portfolio are two distinct functions with a different set of rules. Removal of fear psychosis, fear of staff accountability and empowerment of line management in accepting compromise and quick settlement of problem loan accounts should be facilitated. Setting up back offices to manage collection of regular loan instalments can shed routine work at branches so that they can focus on granting new loans.

Asset recovery branches are now generally considered as parking slots for branded non-performing staff. This notion needs to be removed. Smart and career conscious executives with broad vision have to man these units to speed up the recovery of loans. Similarly, the negotiation skills have to be developed among executives who coordinate with ARCs for sale of NPAs or effective participation in consortium meetings and Committee of Creditors. Similarly, IT people will have to sit together with credit people to work out dashboard management system for timely interventions/guidance by organising data flow from field to controlling offices.

Banks need to tone up the administration of credit at every point with the help of technology to improve efficiency and reduce the cost of credit operations. It is important that the strategy has to be multi-pronged, intended to tackle the rise in the

(i) Volume of borrowers

(ii) Diversity of products

(iii) New empowerment for recovery of loans

(iv) Change in the legal structure

(v) Use of technology to monitor credit and

(vi) Coordination with a host of interdependencies.

The study of data on NPA, emerging regulations, legal empowerment and commitment of stakeholders on resolving the NPAs suggests a fundamental change in bank's approach for moving from recognition to resolution of credit. Realising the deeper impact of rising NPAs on the long-term financial stability, all stakeholders have been consistently working together to mitigate the menace. Regulatory, legal and systemic controls are increasingly getting tightened. But all these new norms of managing NPAs need to be implemented by the banks.

It is necessary for a stakeholder to look beyond enactment and prescription of a new set of measures and harp on strengthening the banking system from the point of their ability to work and implement them to get the desired results. The missing link seems to be the realistic inadequate ability of banks to implement the new measures with the necessary focus and skills sets. Since the funds of banks are struck, they are more concerned about the recovery aspects than any other stakeholder. But somewhere their ability to handle the volume of NPAs of the current magnitude and ability to use the new empowerment by regulators and laws are having genuine limitations.

It cannot be expected that the same set of bank employees with past skill sets and knowledge will be able to handle the kind of NPAs that pose new challenges. The stakeholder may have to do lot of homework to not only empower banks with regulations and new set of laws but also will have to guide the banks, more particularly in reforming and raising the wherewithal of the organisational structure, reporting relations, performance management system, adequacy of manpower, their skill sets, knowledge, compatibility of technology, rewards and incentive structure, promotions and deployment and so on instead of confining to directions and insisting for compliance.

Many banks might be genuinely serious in handling the NPAs and doing their best which may not be helping them to the optimum extent. Their limited abilities are also to be considered and need to be realised in expecting results. Keeping the realities away from the domain of problem solving will only take the NPAs further up. Hence going into NPA management pattern from recognition to move towards resolution would perhaps require a much larger methodology. Borrowing community should also join in NPA management to create a peer pressure and bring delinquency as a negative point in their business relationship management. Borrowers must understand that recycling of bank funds is in their long-term interest, and their next generation may not be able to avail funds for their projects unless a good credit culture is maintained. Therefore, the solution for NPA lies much beyond the scope of lending and recovering bank loans. The ecosystem needs a complete overhaul.

CHAPTER – 17

MANAGING CREDIT DELINQUENCY

Despite rigorous credit appraisal and monitoring system, banks had to manage large volume of problem loans as part of credit risk management. Globally, meeting the challenge of asset quality management is at the centre stage of banking operations. More so in densely populated countries where the cost of follow up of loan accounts is usually much higher due to low digital literacy of borrowers, low digitization of credit monitoring system and legal costs and weak recovery laws adding up to the woes. The credit cost tends to remain elevated where the digital component in credit administration is low.

In managing the cycle of credit risk management, the best option will be to (i) build a robust and healthy credit portfolio with right sectoral mix, right size of loans of borrowers so that even if one sector is in cyclical downturn, the other will be able to balance the health of the credit portfolio. (ii) The next step is to strengthen internal credit monitoring system so as to make slippage of loan account into NPA difficult. (iii) The competency at the end of the credit risk spectrum is to handle problem account, in case a loan account turns into NPA. The bank should have skilled manpower to manage problem credit.

An existing or prospective credit analyst or the credit management leadership should develop all the three skill sets to be able to manage credit risk. Banks need to groom its human resources to pick up skill sets that are strong enough to manage all phases of credit risk management. Let us look at how important it is to improve the asset quality management keeping in view the immense scope of credit growth with increasing growth aspirations. The growth of the economy is to be supported with adequate credit flow.

17.1 Risk in scope for credit growth:

In addition to the gradual reduction of statutory pre-emption of funds by the central banks of many countries by reducing Cash Reserve Ratio (CRR) and Statutory Liquidity Ratio (SLR), additional liquidity windows have been opened. The thrust on financial inclusion also opens up more scope for deposit accretion. The challenge is tougher to tackle the collateral damage due to coronavirus pandemic. As a result, banks have more lendable resources. But banks are not having the credit risk appetite to lend. They need to develop it. Since, bank credit to GDP ratio in India in December 2019 was at 56.2 % that has now come down close to 50 %. In Japan it is 163 %, UK -164 %, US – 150 %. Among BRICS economies, China -204 %, Brazil – 74 %, Russia – 73.1 % and South Africa – 73.1 %. Australia – 191 % and Thailand – 116 %. Compared to many economies, the volume of flow of bank credit to industry is still low with vast untapped potentiality and is set to increase in the years to come. Scope for bank credit growth is more in economies wherever the penetration of credit is low.

Moreover, in bank led economies, when the growth aspirations are high, increase in credit growth is imminent. When the credit growth picks up, the bank is exposed to higher credit risk and consequently, the problem loans may tend to rise unless the entire spectrum of credit governance is made amenable to handle higher growth trajectory. The corner stone of credit governance is based on the capital adequacy and robust loan policy to set right risk appetite supported by qualitative credit evaluation process, to begin with.

17.2 Credit Risk Management:

Institutionalization of effective Credit risk management (CRM) processes across the organization will be an important need when increased credit portfolio is to be handled. Preparing the organization to systematically manage CRM is an inclusive task that encompasses harnessing technology, market intelligence and credit analytical skills. Credit risk is defined as the potential that a bank borrower or counterparty will fail to meet its obligations enshrined in the loan agreement between lender and borrower. As an institution, the bank has to constantly prepare itself for any default by a borrower. The goal of CRM is to maximize a bank's risk-adjusted rate of return by maintaining credit risk exposure within acceptable parameters and protecting the quality of assets.

Banks need to manage the credit risk inherent in the entire portfolio as well as the risk in individual credit transactions. Banks should also consider the relationships between credit risk and other risks. The effective management of credit risk is a critical component of a comprehensive approach to risk management and essential to the long-term success of banking entities.

Credit (loans) are the largest and most obvious source of credit risk; however, other sources of credit risk exist throughout the activities of a bank, including in the banking book and in the trading book, and both on and off the balance sheet products. Since exposure to credit risk continues to be the leading source of problems in banks worldwide, regulators and banks should be able to draw useful lessons from the way in which credit has been managed in the past. In order to effectively manage credit risk, banks need to identify, measure, monitor and control credit risk as well as to determine that they hold adequate capital against these risks and that they are adequately compensated in the form of risk adjusted returns for undertaking credit risks. In order to pick up the nuances of CRM, a granular understanding of various steps in lending will be essential.

The capability of banks to handle CRM at all levels shall need institutionalization of best methods to step up (i) Credit origination – improved credit appraisal techniques (ii) Robust credit sanction process, documentation, stamping, charge creation legal compliance statutory compliance in line with the bank's loan policy (iii) disbursement of loan in accordance with terms of sanction, end use verification, site inspection, asset verification, post sanction scrutiny etc (iv) monitoring of credit – off-site by keeping a close watch on the loan account operations, stock statements, financials, trends of utilization of working capital funds, discipline and response of the borrower in the conduct of the loan account. – On-site by bank officials visiting the unit and discussing with the borrowers and staff working to ensure that there is general orderliness in unit's operations.

17.3 Changing gear of Credit Risk Management:

Despite best monitoring, if the loan account slips into NPA, there is a clear case of gaps in monitoring system. Hence, the skill sets of CRM need to be upgaraded. Now the aim is to delicately handle the situation in such a way that bank is able to recover maximum of its dues in the given circumstances of the borrower/unit. It includes options such as (a) bringing borrower to negotiating table, hand holding by restructuring the loan account to ensure that the unit keeps running and the borrower comes out of the financial difficulty of fund mismatches (b) If the borrower is unable to run the unit or is not viable to do so – negotiating for a quick compromise within the 'compromise policy' of the bank also referred as 'one time settlement (OTS) of loan account can also be an option. Any delay in recovery action will reduce the value of underlying assets financed by the bank and *haircut* for the bank tends to increase. In India, the *Debt Recovery Tribunals (DRTs)* hold out of court loan recovery camps known as 'Lok Adalat'. Banks can use it for small size accounts, say up to Rs. 10 million. (c) If the borrower is not forthcoming for a compromise and is not agreeable to settle the loan account of the defunct unit, legal action is the only necessary course of action to enforce recovery.

Among the various tools of recovery, the lender has to choose the one that is fast, effective and cost efficient. In India, if there is mortgage in favour of the banks for land and building, Securitization and Reconstruction of Financial Assets and Enforcement of Security Interest Act (SARFAESI Act) 2002 can be used or Insolvency and Bankruptcy

(IBC) Code – 2016 could be invoked. The NPAs can also be sold to Asset Reconstruction Companies (ARCs).

In a more holistic perspective, comprehensive credit risk management will call for (1) establishing an appropriate credit risk management environment; (2) operating under a sound credit-granting process; (3) maintaining an appropriate credit administration, measurement and monitoring process; and (4) ensuring adequate controls over credit risk.

Although specific CRM practices may differ among banks depending upon the nature and complexity of their credit activities, a comprehensive CRM system will address these four areas. As part of toning credit risk management, banks need to acquire greater skills in not only in lending and monitoring but also in handling problem credit – finding viable ways of debt resolution till the problem loan account is fully liquidated.

17.4 Learning from Case studies:

Drawing cue from past problem loan cases that have actually happened and whose outcome are already known will help understand the nuances of missing actions or actions that could have been taken. It will add to the new perspectives with different kinds of cases throwing up different solutions. It will add to the body of knowledge in handling live problem situations. let us look at brief facts of the two problem loan case studies of large corporate loan accounts that have become NPA and have gained prominence for the way in which they gained quick success and then failed as enterprises putting banks in an irreparable loan loss. They can provide more learning points to help banks avoid such pitfalls in future.

In order to illustrate the sequence of events tracing the decision system, following case studies have been discussed:

(I) Jet airways – Aviation industry

(II) Bhushan Steel Ltd – a steel industry

(I) Case study – 1:Jet Airways – excerpts:

Jet airways was started by Mr. Naresh Goyal on a modest note on May5, 1993 as a modern airline with a tag line – Joy of flying. In next 3 years, it went zooming to capture 23 percent market share by 1996-97. Soon banks queued to increase finance to the entity and a consortium of banks led by State Bank of India pitched in with greater thrust. Jet airways went international in March 2004 connecting many overseas hubs. It went in for an IPO in December 2004 to gather more equity. Ambitiously, it acquired Air Sahara and floated 2 low-cost services – JetConnect and JetLite to capture better market share. It has rebranded its low-cost products and tried to reposition Air Sahara acquisition as strength but it did not work. Jet Airways, known as a full-service airline by middle and upper middle-class flyers were not able to appreciate the difference in service levels and costing.

As a result, it had to drop its fares to match its fares with low-cost airlines like Indigo, Spicejet etc. Jet Airways merged its two low-cost subsidiaries with itself in March 2012. Jet Airways soon ventured into a partnership with Etihad Airways ceding 24 percent equity stake in November 2013 retaining 51 percent share by Mr. Naresh Goyal. Looking to the success and popularity, banks went on lending its growth. As a result, the bank loan liabilities of Jet Airways reached Rs. 112.61 billion, of which Rs.72.51 billion by domestic banks and others accessed through other entities. The intense competition, government policy to connect un-remunerative airports, uneconomical routes, rise in crude prices and normal hike in operating costs led to financial stress. Early signs of weakness began to manifest in 2017. It posted a quarterly loss of Rs.10.45 billion during January – March 2018 and losses went on increasing to Rs.13.23 billion in April- June 2018. The July-September 2018 losses worked out to Rs.12.97 billion.

The recurring losses quarter after quarter led to default in salary payment to employees and to vendors. In addition to the external factors related to crude price, compulsion to fly to un-remunerative sectors, the wrong business strategies and highhanded management by

Mr. Naresh Goyal led to collapse of the premier airline. Though no conclusive evidence could be found but Mr. Naresh Goyal diverted funds of Jet airways to create own assets and began to work with vested interest. Many attempts to rescue the airline ended in fiasco causing immense collateral damage to employees, investors, overseas entities, vendors and other stakeholders. It is a classic case of rise and fall of Jet airways engineered by the disproportionate urge to grow. The banks and management of Jet airways missed the action at a point when their low-cost operations were eating into their hitherto established full scale services. When customers start getting similar facilities at a lower cost, it is unlikely that they would fly on full-service airlines. The acquisition of Air Sahara and introducing a parallel low-cost service was a strategic move that did not work in its favour. It pulled the airline by its own subsidies and due to the unintended consequence of wrong decisions. The competition from other low-cost airlines which were not active hitherto will become active if a well branded airline starts showing signs of withdrawal. Banks should have taken a stand at an appropriate time to cut losses. In this case, throwing good money after bad money ended the whole lending process in a fiasco inviting huge pile of additional bad loans. Banks desperate to recover their loans invoked Insolvency and bankruptcy code- 2016 and is admitted on June 20, 2019. Looking to the negative net worth and poor asset value, banks will have to incur huge loan losses on this problem account. A timely intervention and coordination with the borrower would have averted such crisis.

(II) Case study – 2:Bhushan Steel Ltd (BSL)

BSL was a good performing steel unit with completion of Phase –I of the Orissa project with production of Sponge Iron. It gained success and quickly acquired a major stake in Brown Energy Ltd of Australia through its 100 % subsidiary Bhushan Steel (Australia) Pty Ltd. It entered into a joint venture to develop their coking coal and thermal coal projects in Australia. Lured by the success story and good going of BSL, banks increased their exposure. In fact, banks were looking to fund good projects and in 2010, the loans reached Rs.114 billion. The overseas market crashed and steel prices slumped. The massive debt burden and cost of servicing it fell high on the unit struggling with low overseas prices of steel.

But BSL continued its aggressive tone in borrowing and banks were willing to take credit risk. By 2012, the steel industry was slipping fast and steel prices in overseas markets fell from a high of US $ 1265/ton to US $ 300/ton. Such steep fall could not be made up with reduction of production cost. The losses were imminent. Banks were in a fix. If they pull the plug and stop working capital finance, the unit will collapse and banks were expecting its Odisha plan to reach full capacity that did not happen. By 2014, BSL was on the brink of loan default. Having already provided huge loans, SBI had to muster courage to provide fresh loans in a bid to rescue it.

The burden of interest cost was high and company's total debt increased by 30 % in 2 years to reach Rs. 357.10 billion in 2014 to Rs. 460.62 billion by March 2016. At this stage, there was no way in which BSL can repay loans. Ultimately on July 26, 2017, banks invoked Insolvency and Bankruptcy Code- 2016 and approached National company Law Tribunal (NCLT) for debt resolution. Corporate insolvency and Debt Resolution Process (CIRP) began and Tata steel submitted its resolution plan and bid for it. Ultimately, Tata Steel acquired BSL at a price of Rs. 352 billion while the outstanding loans stood at Rs.560.79 billion.

It led to a haircut of 37 percent. But the unit could be saved and it merged with Tata Steel. The case study highlights how the external factors could be overwhelming leading to collapse of even good units. Banks have missed the game changing points. When the price of steel was crashing, the production should be reduced and cost of production should be closely monitored. The lending spree of the unit should have been checked to prevent piling of debt burden. The management should be able to take a cue from external developments and tuned its internal growth policies accordingly. Even when the steel prices were crashing, some of the steel plants could function well and sustain the shock whereas, BSL could not withstand the market turmoil. The entrepreneurs and banks should be able to see the emerging crisis much before it manifest to take protective position. If timely action is missing, the disaster hits more sternly.

17.5 Broad reasons for Problem credit:

While every loan account will have its own reason to turn into problem credit but there are certain common significant reasons that gradually builds up tendency of delinquency. The art and science of CRM is to capture such nascent developments to counsel the borrowers and challenge their business strategies, mould them to adopt best practices. Based on the excerpts of the two classic problem accounts discussed here, let us summarize key reasons for fall of the loan accounts so that in managing CRM banks will be able to take care and avoid pitfalls.

(1) Internal factors:

- Borrower's lack of experience with ambitious business aspirations much beyond the industry trends are usually responsible for build-up of adversities. It should be accompanied by an urge to upgrade managerial and risk assessment skills and entrepreneurs should acquire knowledge of management of finance.
- Lack of diligence in the end use of loan amount and imprudent operations during the course of business operations.
- Taste of early success in business sometimes leads to reckless expansion of lines of business exposing the business to more risk of failure.
- Diversion of bank loans to purposes other than, for which it is granted.
- Tendency to invest business funds into other unconnected purposes or into personal accounts/creating family assets.
- Lack of attention towards developing management skills and

lack of respect for proper governance, ethics and principles. A business not firmed up on basic tenets of ethical management principles can be damaging that is found in case of both the case studies.

- Centralization of decision-making authority – arrogance of quick success
- Not listening to good counselling by managerial staff – adoption of authoritative management systems. Experts in the organisations are meant to manage risks, if their counselling is not taken into cognizance, the outcome can be devastating.
- Not analysing/reviewing key strategic decisions from sustainability angle and carried away by emotional factors.
- Over emphasis on building brand image
- Ambition to be ahead in the industry without developing wherewithal for it.
- Not taming the growth despite clear adverse external factors.
- Not consulting bankers for guidance in managing debt and debt burden.
- Inability to develop a realistic vision for the organisation can be counterproductive.

(2) External factors:

- There could be many other reasons to list out from the case study but let us look at some of the external factors that could be beyond the control of entrepreneur and bank.
- The prices of inputs could go up substantially high like crude oil prices, operating costs etc when the internal costing and production activities cannot be proportionately fine-tuned, like what has happened in the case of Bhushan steel limited. The global prices of steel plunged from a high of US 1300 per ton to Rs.350 -400 per ton.

- Geopolitical developments and international trade disputes could bring down demand and price of products like the price of steel crashing in international markets.

- Government policies could be sometimes unfriendly to the business. It is necessary to balance the stakeholder interests by realigning business policies. Operation of unremunerative air routes that impacted the Jet airways but it is noteworthy that other airlines could survive the regulations.

- New taxes could be imposed adding to the cost not factored while starting the business entity.

- The economy could go into slow down phase like what has happened in global financial crisis and now during coronavirus pandemic. The business units have to adjust to the new norms.

- Banks should keep a watch on various sectors of the economy and change the exposure norms to align with the business prospects.

- The business cycles may change from boom to bust and entrepreneurs will have to adjust its policies

- Failure to read the trends and adopt to changes may lead to collapse/loss to even the mighty institutions and the losers could be banks and financial institutions that are exposed to them.

17.6 Regulatory changes:

Once a loan is granted, bank has to live with it during its tenure by constantly monitoring the loan account. The full repayment of loan can only be the end of the loan contract. It has to ensure that it runs well and bank earns risk-adjusted return on the exposure as envisaged while taking a lending decision. The central bank – RBI in case of India keeps modifying and improving monitoring tools to guide banks to prevent slippage of loan accounts into NPAs. Rigor in its implementation can be the differentiator.

Beginning with red flagging of loan accounts from the list of 45 early alert indicators of irregularities in any loan facility. RBI brought out a guidance on 'Early Recognition of Financial Distress, Prompt Steps for Resolution and Fair Recovery for Lenders: Framework for Revitalizing Distressed Assets in the Economy' in 2014. Banks had to closely watch the operations in the loan account – drawings and deposits and point out any sign of weakness to address it.

The concept of special mention accounts (SMA) was introduced to detect early sign of delinquency – SMA – 0 with loan accounts overdue up to 30 days, SMA – 1 with over dues from 31 days to 60 days. SMA -2 having over dues from 61 days to 90 days before the loan slips to NPAs. In all loan accounts of Rs.50 million and above, banks have to report to RBI under Central Repository of Information on Large Credits (CRILC) so that large loan accounts are under scanner. A close connect with the borrower following the monitoring framework can help banks detect the irregularities at a stage where it could be reversed with proper intervention and understanding.

The discussion of credit risk management techniques with focus on management of problem loans with the help of excerpts from the case studies and RBI dispensation on monitoring of loan accounts from time to time will be able to provide a better insight into the management of asset quality in banks. A loan account turns into problem loan either due to unexpected external developments like the subprime crisis 2007-2008 or internal mismanagement. Both these developments are gradual. They do not happen suddenly except a natural calamity led collapse. An alert bank with proper coordination with borrower's understanding should be able to tackle the problem loans at an early stage where debt resolution becomes easy well before the value of collaterals and underlying assets shrink.

The onus of a bank is to ensure early intervention so that the borrower unit is able to function with little tweaking of terms of loans and timely handholding to the borrower. More than the ecosystem of CRM, development of skill sets and competencies will be important as the economies tread the path of growth in the years to come.

CHAPTER – 18

BAD BANK – LONG TERM IMPLICATIONS

Banking system continues to suffer with shocks of asset quality woes. The collateral damage caused by such high volume of toxic assets impinges upon the overall efficiency of banks. More so in PSBs that have larger share of bad loans. Whenever banks accumulate large toxic assets attracting the attention of stakeholders, the issue of hastening resolution comes to the center stage of policy debate. RBI has armed banks with several tools to undertake proactive monitoring of loan accounts to prevent slippage. The information submission, collection and collation has also been made compatible to capture early signs of sickness of loans.

Coming down heavily, the 'Economic Survey 2021' rightly attributed inefficient bank boards, poor governance structure and the failure of auditors to understand and dissect the 'ever-greening' problem added to bad-loan mess. Besides recapitalizing banks, enhancing governance in banks is held essential to improve the stability of the banking system. Going by the past experience of ever greening, the survey suggested for another round of AQR after the current Covid induced forbearance is phased out to assess the correct state of asset quality. It also supported the idea of setting up a bad bank to rescue the banks in near term. These policy perspectives led the union budget 2021-22 to provide for setting up a NARC – also known as Bad Bank to take over the large stock of NPAs from banks. This can free banks to concentrate on fresh lending instead of grappling with the stock of NPAs. Bad bank structure and its expected functioning, modus operandi of dealing with bank NPAs and wider connotation of it will be discussed in the later part of this chapter. Before that, let us understand why the dire need to set up a bad bank has arisen.

Of course, the once in a century kind of pandemic has created many historical firsts in the world. Lockdown, staying at home, work from home (WFH), online classes, largescale webinars, digital payments, reduced currency usage, deserted schools, Parks, cinema halls, public places. Mandatory wearing of masks, using immunity boosters, measuring oxygen levels with oximeters, large scale hospitalization, dedicated Covid19 hospitals, isolation, quarantine, separating sick and healthy people, banning domestic/international flights, stopping trainings, closing temples. The situation is such that own relatives are not ready to help sick people, fear of flu, owning personal oxygen cylinders, not meeting and talking to people, not attending even funerals of closest relatives, no travelling, washing all packages, using hand sanitizer, fever check at entry points in shops, fear of crowd, trimming gatherings, restrictions on social functions and many more. The present generation have never witnessed such developments. Coming to the economy, tolerance for larger fiscal deficits, negative GDP, higher inflation, low interest rates, more liquidity, moratorium on loan repayments, restructuring of loans, government guaranteed loans to entrepreneurs, soft loans for restarting activities and many more which have not happened in the past. The only good part of the pandemic is the show of caring society with increased generosity and philanthropy. In this kind of unprecedented covid induced developments, opting for a bad bank to deal with NPAs is not a bad idea.

18.1 Deterioration of asset quality:

Besides many interconnected factors, the prime reasons for deterioration of asset quality of banks leading to spurt in NPAs is a function of combination of factors (i) lack of adequate focus on the quality of credit origination. It is linked to the autonomy in credit decisions, risk governance and effectiveness of systemic controls. (ii) Intensity of post sanction monitoring and follow up of credit, effectiveness of monitoring tools – ability to sense incipient sickness. (iii) Effective and speedy debt resolution ecosystem to hasten loan recovery and to dissuade loan defaults. Its demonstrated impact should be able to transform the credit culture in the society. A deep dive into the state of these asset quality drivers can help identify the gaps.

Having seen several swings of bad loans – gross non-performing assets (GNPAs) in banks, the recent spike to 11.2 percent in 2017-18 can be considered part of its fluctuating tendency. Out of them, PSBs had more GNPAs at 14.58 percent. Contrary to the rising trend, the private banks could however contain them at 4.62 percent. Due to the consistent efforts of banks, GNPAs were brought down to 8.5 percent by March 2020 and to a further low of 7.5 percent by September 2020, partly due to regulatory forbearance and standstill clause in the asset classification.

RBI in its Financial Stability Report – December 2020 clearly flagged its concern that once the standstill clause is lifted, the GNPAs can climb back to 13.5 percent by September 2021 in baseline stress and to 14.8 percent if the stress is severe. They are expected to touch a high of 17.6 percent in PSBs. The state of asset quality continues to be of great concern though they stand masked at a low level now as all NPAs were not accounted for.

As a result of such deterioration in asset quality, the capital to risk weighted assets ratio (CRAR) at 15.6 percent in September 2020 may drop down to 14 percent in base line stress and to a low of 12.5 percent if the stress is severe. It is expected that 4-5 banks may even breach the minimum benchmark of CRAR of 11.5 percent in baseline and 9 banks in severe stress situations.

RBI has taken probability of a 'zero' GDP in 2021-22 as baseline stress and -7.6 percent GDP as severe stress. Incidentally the latest views of RBI, Economic Survey and International Monetary Fund (IMF) indicates that such a stress may not manifest looking to the green shoots in the economy unless a second wave of new virus strain causes massive disruption. Later after February 2021, the ferocious attack of the virus in the second wave caused massive loss in many ways pulling back the revival of the economy. The loss of life and livelihood shook the economy once again due to resurgence of its brutality in a more furious form.

18.2 Global trends of asset quality:

The asset quality data of IMF indicates that though there is no official 'acceptable' limit for level of GNPAs, it is considered manageable if the banking industry in any country has GNPAs below 3% mark and net NPAs close to 1 % of assets. In this context, India does not compare well even with BRICS members.

According to IMF, India ranks at 33 among 137 nations in a global list of countries with bad debt ratio in a descending order based on data of September 2018. Out of 32 countries having more bad loans than India, 16 are in Africa and rest is in Asia, Europe and Caribbean. China's GNPAs stand at 1.75%, Brazil's at 3.69%, South Africa's at 2.83% as against Indian GNPAs at approximately 9.85% in 2017. Only Russia is worse in the tally with 10.7 percent.

The best asset quality in banks is maintained in Canada at 0.4 percent, Republic of Korea at 0.50 percent and Switzerland at 0.6 percent. Ukraine with 54.3 percent, Greece – 44.1 percent and Cyprus at 36.4 percent are struggling with high component of bad loans. The balance of power between debtors and lenders decides the tilt of bad loans. The ecosystem in India is gradually moving power from debtors to lenders that can set a better trend in future with potentiality to improve the asset quality.

18.3 Credit Risk Management:

As part of credit risk management, banks improve the asset quality using various strategies. By (i) proactive prevention of slippage of assets –

tackling borrowers to prevent accumulation of over-dues. (ii) Recovery of bad loans through persuasion and constant follow up (iii) Many times banks may have to enter into compromise for one time settlement (OTS) of bad loans sacrificing a part of defaulted loans.

Banks go for technical write off of aged bad loans against which 100 percent provision has already been built up. Such write off can reduce its burden on bad loan portfolio and conserves capital while keeping the recovery options from borrowers open. Banks are forced to completely write off loans when (a) there are no realizable securities (b) borrowers are not traceable (c) loan recovery is not viable where administrative cost of enforcing recovery is more than the potential recovery, (d) fraud perpetrated by borrowers has made it impossible to recover and many such compelling internal reasons.

Recent RBI report on *'Trend and progress of banking in India – 2019-20'* indicates that banks have written off Rs. 8,83,168 crores in the last ten years. The share of PSBs in the write off is Rs. 6,67,345 crores working out close to 75 percent. Government has infused Rs.3.5 crores into PSBs in last five years. Effectively, the entire chunk of capital provided is drained out to cover the bad loan losses. Banks can also sell bad loans to ARCs, other financial institutions or can enforce recovery through DRTs or by invoking IBC -2016.

The continued erosion of asset quality reduces share of interest earning assets, increase provision requirements and bring down profitability of banks. The resultant impact truncated the capital adequacy ratio (CAR) of some of the PSBs. The overall deterioration in the performance of banks led to RBI imposing prompt corrective action (PCA) on 11 banks. It also led to hesitancy of banks to expand fresh credit that made bank dependent borrowers at the bottom of the pyramid to suffer.

18.4 Loan Recovery tools:

The government and RBI in collaboration with other stakeholders have been building robust debt resolution framework to improve credit culture. Beginning with the enactment of 'Recovery of Debts Due to Banks and Financial Institutions Act (RDDBFI Act), 1993' Debt Recovery Tribunals (DRTs) and Debt Recovery Appellate Tribunals (DRATs) were formed. It began with formation of first DRT at Kolkata on 27th April 1994. There are at present 39 DRTs and 5 DRATs in India. DRTs while speeding up loan recovery have also enabled setting up of 'Lok Adalat', an informal forum for out of court recovery of bad loans of banks.

Later the Securitization and Reconstruction of Financial Assets and Enforcement of Securities Interest Act, 2002 (SARFAESI Act) enabled banks to deal with NPAs without court intervention. It also paved way for setting up Asset Reconstruction Companies (ARCs) that needed license to operate and are regulated by the RBI. Since the promulgation of SARFAESI Act 2002, 29 ARCs got registered. The latest addition to ARCs is the NARC set up to take over bad loans of banks. RBI also permitted sale of NPAs of banks to other banks, non-banks and financial institutions wherever possible to improve the asset quality. Recently, RBI issued guidelines for transfer of exposure of banks that opens up trading in standard loans as well – opening up secondary sale of loans. These supportive institutions/guidelines will be playing a strategic role in accelerating debt resolution and easing liquidity flows.

The promulgation of Insolvency and Bankruptcy Code – 2016 and setting up IBBI hastened the debt resolution in some large borrower accounts. Going forward, the biggest impact of IBC stems from section 29A that can develop a well behaved "credit-culture" in the corporate arena.

Every defaulter, by now understands that if one does not repay what one has committed to pay in liquidation of loans, one will lose the reins of control over business forever. This eventually should lead to a new cult of healthy borrowing – where borrowers shun over-leveraging, over-borrowing thereby tempting to diversify. It should be able to address the chronic problem of rising willful defaulters in banks.

The new legislative tools are helping banks to recover loans faster. The bad loan recovery by invoking IBC worked out to 45.7 percent and 45.5 percent of total recovery made during the year whereas it was 15 percent and 26 percent by invoking SAERFASI Act 2002 during the year 2018-19 and 2019-20. It shows that IBC is proving to be a more effective tool in resolving bad loans. But despite all efforts, the accretion of fresh bad loans has been higher than recovery of loans adding to the total stockpile of bad loans. Despite such legal tools and institutions dedicated for recovery of bank's bad loans, the tendency of built of stock pile of toxic assets did not abate significantly.

Despite improvement in internal credit administration needed to prevent deterioration of quality of assets in banks, asset quality woes continue to mar the bank's capacity to recover bad loans and consequently unable to take up fresh lending. The fact that some of the delinquent, disgruntled large borrowers are still able to play around with legal framework to escape from the obligation to repay loans and cause mayhem in financial intermediation shows that credit quality assessment/appraisal in banks needs to be sturdier.

18.5 Reasons for rise in bad loans:

According to RBI, a rapid bank credit growth during 2005-12 and massive built up of restructuring of loans led to spike in bad loans. The forbearance to restructure loans at a concessional provision of 5 percent might have led to 'ever greening' of loans. Hence, RBI withdrew the restructuring facility at concessional provision in April 2015.

It led to sizeable divergence in the asset quality data of banks and RBI. Concerned over the inconsistency in the classification of GNPAs, tendency to shield impairment by restructuring assets, sporadic ever greening of loans and such unhealthy practices made RBI to introduce AQR during 2015-16.

As a consequence, banks began to reclassify the assets and many restructured loans classified as standard loans slipped into GNPAs exacerbating the asset quality woes. RBI highlighted, among others, the absence of strong credit appraisal and monitoring standards that have led to steep deterioration in asset quality in banks. Coming from the regulators, the comments have to be taken up by the banking system with seriousness.

Toning up credit administration and internal credit risk management is vital to the sustainability of the business model of banks. With technology able to support augmentation of market and economic intelligence, banks may have to revisit their internal credit handling processes, procedures and systemic controls related to quality of credit origination.

Bank for International Settlement in its document on credit risk management outlined sound practices – (a) appropriate credit risk environment (b) sound credit granting process (c) maintaining appropriate credit administration and finally (d) ensuring adequate controls over credit risk. If the cue of BIS is implemented and lending infrastructure is strengthened, the quality of credit origination will improve significantly when the loan recovery tools developed thus far will be enough to manage the credit risk.

18.6 Shape of asset quality:

Banks already loaded with high level of bad debts are further stressed due to the impact of pandemic induced challenges. The potential large-scale rise in GNPAs in the coming fiscal 2021-22 needs to be tackled well with multi-pronged strategy. Granting additional loans and restructuring of the existing loan facilities will provide borrowers enough time to recoup from the ongoing stress. While RBI in its recent FSR acknowledged that whenever the standstill clause in asset classification is lifted, banks will witness rise in GNPAs to 13.5 percent by September 2021 in baseline stress that can further slip to 14.8 percent in severe stress situation.

Looking to the extraordinariness of the ongoing crisis, while it is necessary to focus on near term challenges, at the same time, banks should not lose sight on the long-term systemic approach to improve the asset quality. While all the stakeholders are working together to tackle near term challenges, when additional capital infusion and even setting up of a bad bank could be a possibility.

18.7 Sustained Strategy to rein in asset quality:

Working out process reengineering of credit origination, monitoring and quick debt resolution can be an integrated long-term approach to improve the quality of assets in banks. Going by the size of bank borrowers, collateralized loans – farm loans, retail loans, MSME loans, many of them having an add on cover of collateral securities are large in numbers and low in value. Whereas large loans and corporate sector loans, mostly secured by primary securities built with loan funds are low in number of borrowers but high in value.

According to the size wise distribution of borrowers, out of 27.25 crore bank borrowers in March 2020, only 6,79,034, much less than one crore borrowers have borrowed Rs. One crore or more from banks sharing 56.3 percent of total outstanding bank loans of Rs.105 trillion. Loans of Rs. 47.38 trillion are spread among 89473 borrower who have borrowed more than Rs. 10 crores. 95.7 percent of borrowers have loan limits up to Rs. 10 lakhs. 77 percent borrowers have loans below Rs. 5 lakhs.

The crux of the problem may be due to engagement of banks in handling large number of loans of small value – less than Rs.10 lakhs. In an effort for equitable distribution of resources, banks may not be able to balance the interest of few large size loan accounts. If the proportionality of focus on few large loan accounts is ensured, the quality of loan portfolio can improve.

While improving credit appraisal and follow up techniques, it may be necessary to ear mark certain bank branches for small value loans while loans of Rs. One crore and above to be handled by few branches where the compatible talent pool can be parked. Even alliances with non-banks for small size loans can be worked out so that more time can be devoted to better manage large size loans and organize credit risk management accordingly.

Post sanction scrutiny of borrowers conduct and account operations need more attention. Technology can be better used to follow up loan accounts of Rs.1 crore and above with enhanced oversight to prevent down grade of loan accounts. If due to any external or internal cause the account goes out of order, quick action to retrieve it can be planned.

However best, the external legal ecosystem is improved, unless the credit origination and internal follow up methodology of credit is improved, the asset quality standards cannot sync with best practices. Unless credit quality improves, banks will not have enough latitude to compete in terms of risk-based pricing and market share. Any temporary solution like formation of a Bad bank/Alternate Investment fund (AIF) can be a 'Band-Aid' and not a panacea against the ills of present state of credit risk management in banks.

18.8 Origin of Bad Bank:

Given the inevitable potential rise in toxic assets, stakeholders were considering various alternatives to resolve the woes of crisis-ridden banks. Despite the government exchequer – under tremendous pressure to carve out allocations amid the truncated revenues, Union Budget – 2021-22 had provided Rs.20000 crores for capital infusion in PSBs during the fiscal.

It has also mooted formation of a separate special purpose vehicle (SPV) – Asset Reconstruction Company (ARC) on the lines of Bad bank to take over the bad loans of banks. Post the budget proposal, it is expected that the newly formed ARC (Bad Bank) will have capital coming from various banks.

Many banks contributed to the capital of bad bank amounting to Rs.6000 crores to start operations. A bad bank is a corporate structure that isolates risky assets held by banks in a distinct entity, relieving the banks from the burden. It would enable the banks to offload bad debts to a separate entity, and thus banks can concentrate on new business.

18.9 Pandemic shifted policy stance:

The proposed structure of a bad bank is based on the earlier recommendations of a panel headed by the former Chairman of PNB, Mr. Sunil Mehta, called project 'Sashakt' two years ago. However, it did not go through. It perhaps did not merit consideration at that point of time as asset reconstruction companies (ARCs) formed for this purpose have been in operation with similar objectives. It was decided at that time to strengthen the existing ARCs instead of bringing a new entity. However, even ARCs could not come to the rescue of banks in a big way in tackling the bad loan menace. Participating in the discussions on setting up a bad bank, Arvind Panagariya (former Vice Chairman, NITI Aayog) affirmed *"there is no need for India to set up a new state-run fund manager to resolve the world's highest stressed assets ratio as it already has institutions that can deal quickly with the problem"*.

But looking to the current situation of NPAs and banks' inability to muster enough capital for fresh lending, the policy stance on bad bank is undergoing a change. Recently the RBI shared its opinion on the issue: *"A bad bank has been under discussion for a very long time. We have regulatory guidelines for Asset Reconstruction Companies (ARCs). If any proposal [for setting up a bad bank] comes, we are open to examining it and issuing required regulatory guidelines"*.

Ostensibly, the extraordinary stress situation arising due to the Covid-19 pandemic is leading to the change in perception to provide an out-of-box solution. Hence, setting up a bad bank can be a plausible strategy. It will enable banks to hive off toxic assets out of their credit portfolio to the bad bank. Circumscribed with a potential rise in NPAs, threat of a truncated CRAR, and the need to pump prime credit flow to salvage ailing enterprises in the larger interest of the economy, a policy change was inevitable.

18. 10 Self-liquidating transitory structure:

The business model of banks, regulatory rigour, corporate governance structure and its implementation strategies, effectiveness of monitoring, and control of credit, should be well-integrated with normal operations to enable banks to lend and recover loans in normal course of business. Banks should be capable of managing the level of NPAs arising from usual lending operations invoking normal recovery tools with their prudence and credit administration skills. Depending on external institutions in perpetuity cannot be a sustained model. If the current legal and institutional support is not adequate to recover loans, they need to be reviewed and their power to enforce recovery must be increased instead of shifting the onus of loan recovery to another agency.

A recent RBI report on "Trend and Progress of Banking in India" highlighted that the absence of strong credit appraisal and monitoring standards have been the key reasons for the spike in NPAs in banks. Coming from the regulators, these comments must be taken seriously by the banking system. Strengthening credit administration is vital to the sustainability of the business model of banks. With the support of available technologies to augment market and economic intelligence, banks may have to revisit their internal credit-handling processes, procedures, and systemic controls on quality of credit origination.

Among the available recovery tools, two important ones are the Securitisation and Reconstruction of Financial Assets and Enforcement of Securities Interest Act (SARFAESI), 2002, and Insolvency and Bankruptcy Code (IBC), 2016, which have shown clear signs of effectiveness.

Hence, a bad bank driven by the impact of Covid-19 had been set up with a clear agenda that NPAs will be permitted to be pooled over say, the next 2-3 years. A timeline of about five years can be fixed for the bad bank to completely resolve the pooled stock of NPAs – say by 2025-26 –beyond which it should stop accepting toxic assets. Once the shadow of the pandemic recedes into history, the bad bank should wind up.

Therefore, the terms on which the bad bank will be formed will be critical in shaping the banking system going forward. In seeking to resolve near-term instability, we ought to be mindful that the fear of incapacitating banks with a sense of complacency, abdicating the onus of responsible lending, can trigger long-term financial instability in a bank-led economy.

The mandarins of the financial sector should therefore be cautious and opt for a one-time self-liquidating structure for the bad bank. It should be very clear that banks are not allowed to kick the can of NPAs down the road. Building resilience of banks with compatible regulatory oversight, and ability of banks to handle the credit administration as an integral part of their operations, is essential to foster efficient financial intermediation.

18.11 Imparting Financial Education:

Another constant endeavour is that of financial-sector regulators, who are working in close collaboration with banks, to develop a positive credit culture. The National Strategy for Financial Education 2020-25 of the RBI has a long-term agenda to spread mass awareness about financial and digital literacy. It is intended to help people manage money more effectively to achieve financial well-being by accessing appropriate financial products and services through regulated entities with fair and transparent machinery for consumer protection and grievance redressal.

Going forward, every borrower should realise that a delinquent loan is not only a threat to the bank, but it also adversely effects the prospects of their own future enterprise. Banks muddled with large NPAs are unable to recycle loan funds. The pain of asset quality erosion prevents banks from lending to the next generation of entrepreneurs, therefore depriving them of business opportunities. In the larger interest of ensuring seamless opportunity to access loans from banks as a means to economic development, it should be clear to the borrowing community that loan delinquencies can result in a permanent blot to their credit history, making it more difficult for them to be in business.

Robust credit intelligence is meticulously built up by the RBI by introducing systemic controls/information systems e.g. (i) through CRILC data on borrowers of Rs. 50 million and above, (ii) Special Mention Accounts (SMA) for data on early signs of stress (not yet classified as an NPA), and (iii) the Central Registry of Securitisation Asset Reconstruction and Security Interest of India (CERSAI) to identify frauds in lending against equitable mortgages. Banks now will have access to a wider range of data/ information to better administer credit.

In the future, the PCR of the RBI, which is currently being built, will add on as another tool in the armoury of the financial system to control NPAs. These systematic efforts, together with rising financial and digital literacy levels, will hopefully improve credit culture to make the bad bank irrelevant in the long run. Hence, the bad bank can be a transitory solution with defined timelines but cannot be a panacea against fault lines in the quality of credit administration. Hence, bad bank as a good idea in bad times cannot be good in perpetuity.

18.12 Differentiated approach:

In a bold move to clean up bank's balance sheets, a process that started with AQR of RBI in September 2015, formation of NARCL will be able to realize its end state objective of *'distressing the banking sector'*. It came up as part of 'Indradhanush' the next generation 7 – pronged bank reform package articulated after the first banking conclave – Gyan Sangam held in January 2015. The urgency to address the bad loan menace exacerbated due to the onslaught of the pandemic that badly marred most sectors of the economy. Their revival and ability to repay bank loans are likely to take time for which RBI has provided restructuring windows.

Unlike the large number of 28 ARCs operating now as non-banks to buy NPAs from banks and resolve them, the NARCL is differently designed to make it work quickly and efficiently to unlock the value of underlying impaired assets. The stakeholders have rightly diagnosed the reasons for the lull in the performance of ARCs and reinforced the new entity with a host of enablers and systemic controls to make it more efficient. (i) Government guarantee of Rs.30,600 crores available for invocation to make good the difference between value realized from the NPAs and face value of SRs. It will provide a huge comfort to banks. (ii) Formation of IDRCL to operationalize the process of debt resolution with cross section of experts working on it to realize better value. (iii) the progressive increase in guarantee fee from 0.25 percent from second year onwards to 2 percent in third/fourth and fifth year on the outstanding unrealized SRs that can hasten resolution. (iv) The government support may end in five years by when most of the proposed total NPA stock of Rs. 2 trillion, the target amount will get resolved.

18.13 A near term solution:

At a time when the faster slippage of retail and MSME loans are expected to increase the level of NPAs of banks from Rs. 8.35 trillion in March 2021 to Rs.10 trillion by March 2022, formation of a Bad bank can be essential as a near term measure. But it cannot be a panacea against the tendency of built up of bad loans in the normal course of banking operations. Credit risk management is an integral function of banks that includes recovery of loans. It is necessary for banks and regulator to find out the precise reasons for rising trend of NPAs and its management cannot be shifted to another entity.

Banks should be capable to lend and recover the loans as part of regular banking operations. The legal framework including insolvency and bankruptcy code – 2016 has to be revamped. The borrowing community should be made accountable for repayment of loans in time so that seamless flow of credit to ensure sustained growth of the economy can be ensured. The five-year validity of government guarantee of SRs is a clear sign that banks have to reform their credit management systems in the next 2-3 years so that accumulation of NPAs do not become an inhibitor for their growth and sustainability.

18.14 Structure of Bad Bank:

Finally shaping up the Bad Bank as envisaged in Union Budget 2021-22, RBI granted a licence to the Rs 6,000 crore NARCL on October 4, 2021 to start its operations as the bad bank. The licence was granted under Section 3 of the SARFAESI Act, 2002. IBA has been entrusted with the task of setting up the Bad Bank. Unlike the other existing private sector Asset Reconstruction Companies (ARCs), NARCL has more credibility with government guaranteeing security receipts (SRs) to be issued in lieu of transfer of NPAs from banks to NARCL to the tune of Rs.30600 crores in next five years – a contingent liability of the government. It is akin to some of the global practices to use government backed ARCs like the one formed in South Korea and Thailand after the banks were hit by global financial crisis – 2008.

Another unique move is to set up India Debt Resolution Company Ltd (IDRCL), an operational entity meant to manage assets and collaborate with market professionals and turnaround specialists to unlock optimum value from the underlying assets. Public and private banks together will hold more than 51 percent in NARCL – the bad bank and up to 49 percent in IDRCL. The capital of NARCL initially put at Rs. 6000 crores will be used to buy NPAs from banks by paying 15 percent upfront against cost of acquisition of NPAs with SRs to be issued for the rest. The proposed transfer of high value NPAs – Rs. 500 crores and above amounting to Rs.90000 crores against which full provision is already made will enable banks to trim down their assets and improve capital adequacy ratio creating additional room for fresh lending.

Besides making use of NARCL to create new lending capability, banks should look into their methods of follow up of loans. Despite institutionalization of early alert system – data on special mention accounts, the slippage of loans into NPAs continue to cause great concern. Either the quality of credit origination is not up to the mark or the subsequent monitoring of credit is not adequate to improve the quality of credit risk management. Banks have to introspect and fix the missing gaps in credit risk management taking bad bank as a temporary, one-time respite so that dependency on it could be reduced in the next five years. The long-term sustainable policy is not to rely on bad bank but to improve its own efficiency in managing credit.

CHAPTER – 19

POLICY INNOVATIONS IN MSME SECTOR

Deposit growth in banks has been picking up faster than credit growth during the current fiscal, at a point of time when crisis needs credit flow to ailing sectors, more importantly to MSME sector. Many banks including newly entered small finance banks are eyeing on lending opportunities to the sector that can provide better risk adjusted return to augment better profitability. The massive capital infusion in PSBs, three PSBs coming out of the PCA mode, many banks posting better asset quality status in Q3 of FY19, the recent repo rate cut, improved macroeconomic dimensions on the back of benign inflation and crude prices are some of the positive headwinds that can be harnessed to support growth. Based on the evolving macroeconomic setting, RBI has projected GDP growth in FY 2019-20 to be at 7.4 percent. It should range between 7.2 -7.4 percent in H1 and 7.5 percent in Q3.

The capacity utilization in the manufacturing sector is showing a shade higher at 74.8 percent in Q2, up from 73.8 percent in Q1. The Gross Value Added (GVA) during the year is expected to be 7 percent in FY 19 compared to 6.9 percent in FY18. The RBI industrial outlook survey (IOS) for Q3 indicates weakening demand conditions in manufacturing while the business expectations index (BEI) points towards improvement in Q4. Similarly, the uptick in manufacturing purchasing managers' index (PMI) for January 2019 is stacked with increased output supported by new stream of orders.

Among the sector specific credit growth, the lingering impact of asset quality woes and ongoing litigations surrounding debt resolution cases pending in NCLTs and NCLAT under IBC – 2016, banks are apprehensive in taking exposure to corporate sector. The ongoing spree of debt waivers and agitating mood of farm sector is making it difficult to lend to large size agro-based loans. Seen from prudent perspectives, the most attractive sector to diversify credit growth is to target MSME. It has immense scope after many of the MSME units are digitally connected with the formal economy after introduction of GST. Connecting with GST has multiplier impact on business growth and MSME forums are educating them to make the units 'Future ready'.

19.1 Growth and prospects of MSME:

In view of immense employment potentiality and prospects in MSME sector, the strategies for growth and sustenance of MSMEs continue to be at centre stage of the new policy initiatives. Looking to the added challenges arising from demonetization and implementation of GST, the industry forums and representative bodies have been harbouring increased support and the regulators are receptive to it. Moreover, MSME sector is globally acknowledged as the lifeline of the economy with immense employability and an estimated 90% of all enterprises falling in this segment. The reforms in the MSME centric policies have been a continuous journey with federal and state governments providing compatible ecosystem to take care of their needs to fulfil the unfinished agenda for growth of MSME sector. It is daunting to revamp MSME, which is mired with several challenges that calls for deep-rooted simplification to reach out to them.

The latest data suggests that the number of working MSMEs in India stands at around 63 million units. The crux of the problem lies in the fact that, of these, a whopping 96% are unregistered. In terms of size of enterprises, 89.6% are micro enterprises, 10% are small enterprises and 0.4% is medium sized industrial unit. During FY15, the sector accounted for 7-8 % of the GDP, 33% of the manufacturing sector output and about 45% of the country's exports. It provided employment to 117.1 million people in FY15. Employment in MSMEs grew by 4.9% per annum during FY11-15. The investment and capacity expansion of the sector in the form of fixed assets had worked out to annualized growth at 7.2 percent.

There are 205 SMEs listed in BSE and 94 in NSE having a combined market capitalization of Rs. 175.9 billion by October 2017. Considering their pain points and employment intensity, relief is accorded to the sector at various points of time. Similarly, the recent spate of relief should have multiplier impact.

19.2 Global status of SME:

Though enactment of MSMEAct 2006, changed the nomenclature of SMEs in India into MSMEs from June 16, 2006 but globally they are recognized as SME sector and many economies use the sector interchangeably – SME or MSME. A report on the MSME country indicators released by International Finance Corporation (IFC) a World Bank group publication (December 2014) that reflects the growing significance of the sector. The global network of formal MSME units were 162.8 million, of which 96.3 million units are in emerging market economies reflected in the report of December 2014. There were about 28.7 million formal SMEs, with about 18.6 million of them were operating in emerging markets. Similarly, of 131.4 million formal microenterprises, 77 million of them were in emerging markets.

It accounts for a very large share of world economic activity in both developed and developing countries. The SME share of economic activity is typically larger in OECD economies rather than in emerging-market economies, reflecting a mix of stronger SME productivity levels in the former and higher rates of economic informality in the latter. In emerging-market economies, SMEs are responsible for up to 45% of jobs and up to 33% of national GDP. These numbers are significantly higher when informal businesses, which are often more than half of the total enterprise population, are included in the count.

When the informal sector is included, SMEs in emerging-market economies account for 90% of total employment. Continued thrust on MSME sector will enable reaching Sustainable Development Goals (SDGs) launched by the United Nations in 2015 and can help reduce inequality and unemployment. When a comparison is made, majority of MSME units in India are not in formal map that deprives them from the multiplier impact of various supportive policies enunciated from time to time. It is therefore essential to educate and bring more units under formal sector to tap the growth opportunities.

19.3 Multiple Policy initiatives:

Taking a cue from the global best practices and in order to empower the sector, a multifaceted outreach program was launched on November 2, 2018 with comprehensive make over plan. It encompasses steady focus on five key aspects that include: (i) access to credit, (ii) access to market, (iii) technology up-gradation, (iv) ease of doing business and to provide (v) sense of security for employees of MSME sector. In order to broaden these five areas – 12 point 'Support and Outreach' (12SO) policy has been initiated and has been well calibrated. As part of access to credit, 2% interest subvention for all GST registered units was proposed to MSMEs, on fresh or incremental loans. Accordingly, a new scheme – "Interest Subvention Scheme for Incremental credit to MSMEs 2018" was implemented over 2018-19 and 2019-20 rolled out by RBI on February 21, 2019.

Recently RBI also permitted a one-time restructuring facility to the sector for loan accounts up to Rs.25 Crores to be implemented by March 31, 2020, the time line was extended from time to time due to persisting covid induced stress. The identified loan accounts should be standard as on January 1, 2019 and registered with GST. The banks and NBFCs should have an internal board-approved policy to undertake such restructuring. They will be downgraded and may slip progressively to lower asset classification if they are not revived by the end of restructuring period of one year.

In the same league, in order to further support MSME sector, RBI had already granted forbearance in their classification of non-performing asset (NPA). It relaxed recognition criterion for banks and NBFCs for some of their exposure to the sector. Banks and NBFCs can continue to classify loans to MSME as a standard asset even if the dues are paid within 180 days from their respective original due dates instead of 90 days and 120 days respectively.

The relaxed NPA classification norms shall apply if (i) the aggregate exposure, including non-fund-based facilities does not exceed Rs 25 crore on January 31, 2018; (ii) the loan account should be standard on August 31, 2017. In addition, the cap on loans to the sector that can be classified as priority sector loans has been removed. However, a provision of 5 percent is to be made by banks/NBFCs against such loan accounts falling in the relaxed category.

As broader frame of 12SO initiative, MSME entrepreneurs can seek loans up to Rs. One crore through a specially designed electronic portal which provides *'in-principle'* sanction of loans in 59 minutes by collecting and collating borrower credit history and turnover data from income tax and GST portals online, evaluating credentials, and it summarizes the credit worthiness of the borrower. The portal generates an 'In principle sanction letter' to the 'entrepreneur – applicant' which can be taken to a bank for further processing to take credit decision. However, it will then be up to the lender to take a credit decision on the pre-processing done by the portal. How it pans out as a speedy credit dispenser has to be watched. But an innovation is always welcome to reach out to the ailing MSME sector that calls for special treatment.

Similarly, the interest rate subvention on pre/post shipment export credit is raised from 3 percent to 5 percent. It is also suggested that public sector units should buy a third of their products from MSME units increasing it from 20 percent. They should also procure 3 percent of their needs from women MSME entrepreneurs. All central public sector entities will have to procure through *'Government's E-Market* place (GeM)' where 1.5 lakh suppliers are registered, of which 40000 are MSME units.

The government has allocated Rs.6000 crores to upgrade technology of MSME units. The spent will be routed through 20 hubs and 100 tool rooms to be set up for the purpose. Moreover, efforts were made to address cash flow problems of MSME units with 'Trade Receivables e-Discounting System (TReDS)' that can allay fears of delayed payments by companies.

Going further, the government has raised the exemption limit from GST for units with annual turnover from Rs. 20 lakhs to Rs.40 lakhs. The corpus of the Credit Guarantee Trust Fund for Micro and Small enterprises (CGTMSE) has been raised from Rs. 25 billion to Rs.75 billion. CGT coverage of loan limits under the guarantee is raised from Rs. 10 million to Rs.20 million now. Such CGT cover is available to NBFCs. The government has implemented various schemes for the promotion of MSMEs. The total expenditure on these schemes as on Oct 31, 2017 was Rs. 33.5 bn as against RS.4.5 bn till Oct 2016.

With the kind of policy reinforcements now put in place, MSME sector can be transformed into a robust economic vehicle to increase employment and contribute in augmenting exports and enhance its share in GDP. But these can happen, provided lenders recognize the merits in financing them. Since MSME is a buoyant portfolio with large number of borrowers having their own challenges, banks will have to find out ways and means to use technology to service them. Otherwise, the MSME portfolio could have larger transaction cost which banks may not be able to afford.

19.4 Diminishing flow of Credit:

Bank credit to MSMEs sector currently works out to about 15% of total credit that is far less than its potentiality. The reason for subdued credit is lack of financial literacy among the large number of unregistered units who access credit from informal sources. But another added cause of concern is the diminishing flow of bank credit to MSME sector. RBI data indicates that in the last two years, the absolute amount of flow of bank credit to the sector could post merely a shade higher from Rs.25793 billion in November 2016 to Rs. 27084 billion in November 2018. Effectively, the growth rate of credit to MSME units is just at one percent in FY17 and four percent during FY18 as against overall credit growth of 8.5 percent and 13.5 percent respectively during the same period. Compared to other sectors, the flow of credit has been low to MSME.

In its FSR – December 2018, RBI cautioned about the spike in bad loans of the sector, more coming from Mudra loans. The stakeholders should take a cue from the RBI concern and improve quality of credit origination but should not slow down flow of credit to the sector that can exacerbate gaps in cash flows to the detriment of their long-term interest. Credit worthy borrowers should not be deprived of timely credit fearing rise in NPAs. NPAs should be dealt independently by intense follow up, disseminating financial literacy on how to inculcate better lending practices and in ensuring end use of funds. The budding enterprise should not be curbed just that the business of lending is risky. Risk mitigation is to be professionally tackled and lenders must develop compatible skill sets and acumen to manage it. The status of the sector needs to be gauzed in the context of how it thrives globally to assess its significant role in strengthening the economy.

19.5 Challenges of MSME entrepreneurs:

Among a host of challenges, critical challenges of MSMEs are well in the knowledge of major stakeholders. They relate to (i) Non-availability of adequate, timely and affordable credit, (ii) lack of skilled manpower, (iii) lack of basic managerial traits and knowledge in dealing with government agencies, banks and tax matters – the people management skills (iv) unable to comprehend account keeping and cannot afford engaging subject experts – financial literacy (v) inadequate marketing support and infrastructure facilities to take the products to the right spot to get right price and profits. (vi) lack of understanding of merits of digitization and modernization of production methods. (vii) The degeneration of unique geography specific art, culture and skills by next generation micro entrepreneurs due to continued poverty and suffering witnessed in their family. They prefer to turn out to be labor in cities than continuing making of artefacts in hinterland based on their lineage. (Viii) Lack of supply of water, electricity and civic amenities to host MSME units in hinterland. (ix) lack of road connectivity and transportation facilities from point of manufacturing to point of sale leads to proliferation of middle men who eat into the fragile profits of the entrepreneurs. (x) lack of free access to raw materials and accessories to improve productivity and lower input costs. These challenges have turned out be the major dampener for the growth of MSMEs in India, and hence need to be resolved.

19.6 Emerging lending opportunities to banks:

Access to finance is one of the major challenges faced by the MSME sector in India. The MSME Census of 2006-07 revealed that almost 87% of MSMEs did not have access to secure formal finance. They are constrained often to rely on meagre internal sources or approach friends or relatives to meet their financial requirements. Alternately to borrow from local moneylenders on exorbitant terms that takes away the benefits of enterprise. One of the major reasons for this demand-supply mismatch in MSME financing can be seen as an opportunity to lend where the credit risk is well disbursed. This is primarily due to non-availability of valid invoices, proper accounting systems and dearth of known buyers. In order to mitigate such perceived credit risk, higher collateral is sought, which cannot be brought in by many MSMEs.

In order to assuage such protracted sufferings, simplification of formal lending systems and dissemination of financial and digital literacy to entrepreneurs will be needed. The financial literacy and credit counseling centers set up by RBI should be utilized and lead bank of the district must take up responsibility to educate masses on bank's various schemes and how they can be connected. Even the large base of PMJDY can be used as leads to reach out to the budding entrepreneurs. The more important is to bring informal units into formal domain with simpler registration process. They should know the various schemes of the government and banks to shed inhibitions to approach the formal channels. The litmus test for the government agencies/NGOs will be to convert informal MSME units into formal registered units so that they can avail finance from banks, expand their operations to prosper. It is necessary to look beyond policy formulation to ensure that more units get connected to the system to avail the various government supportive schemes. Extending facilities to existing small base of entrepreneurs will not serve the larger purpose of expanding MSME base to harness full potentiality of the sector.

Using the synergy of such strong and supportive policy framework put in place; SIDBI and commercial banks can lead coordinated action at various levels so that the intended outcome of transforming MSME units into economic growth centers could be achieved. But such a move is not simple. While accelerating lending to MSME, banks will have to coordinate with many stakeholders and work together. Most important is to rope in services of local NGOs to educate entrepreneurs.

With the help of education department, the industries department should use the government schools should as 'MSME Pathshala/ Entrepreneurial Schools' in the evening or weekends to teach them the nuances of using simple arithmetic and use of digital devices so that they are made capable to interact with formal government and financial system. The skill development corporation should also coordinate with these agencies for faster dissemination of knowledge and know-how. The available lending schemes and subsidies, interest subventions should be explained to them so that more and more bankable projects reach bank branches. The financial and digital literacy must be able to change the mindset of MSME units and drift them from informal high-cost finance options to formal low-cost funding.

Banks should be able to identify the potential MSME clusters and maintain liaison with industries department and SIDBI to intensify financing activity. With such robust banking system and differentiated banks, a credit growth of one to four percent in a year indicates lot of unfilled gaps in extending loans. Banks should find out methods to float several activities specific *'over the counter'* – ready to use low value MSME loan products of say up to Rs. 1 Crore with simplified procedures, so that loan growth picks up speed. It is the immense cross selling opportunities that can help in augmenting savings deposit growth. Looking to the interest evinced by the government and regulators, it is the right opportunity for banks to step up MSME credit growth and help the economy realize its potentiality.

CHAPTER – 20

REINVENTING MSME SECTOR

Significant role of MSME is well recognized due to its high employment intensity and umbilical connect to the macroeconomic growth and ultimately, the well-being of the entrepreneurial society. Sops form part of every policy dispensation to accelerate economic growth. As part of industrialization policy, during post-independence era, several sustained efforts were made to nurture the sector. If the growth potentiality of the sector is fully unleashed, it can eventually reduce the yawning income inequality. Keeping such buoyancy of the sector in view, the Sustainable Development Goals (SDGs) of United Nations (UN) highlighted the need for different economies to consider sustained growth of MSME, more popularly referred globally as SME in all forms of policy interventions and allocation of resources/priorities. Accordingly, even NIti Ayog, in its mapping of SDGs with different functionaries had incorporated it as an important performance milestone rightly mapped to the ministry of MSME. Hence MSME continues to occupy the center stage of government policies to revive entrepreneurial appetite.

Despite such continuous efforts, the plight of MSME sector has not improved concomitant to the policy support. Many premier educational institutes/think tanks have undertaken lot of research and suggested ways and means to tap the immense potentiality of the sector. It is further supported by various institutions such as Non-Government Organizations (NGOs), associations and public forums that have been working together with the units to bring them out of lurch. But the outcome is not significant. There is a consensus that the sector needs to be strengthened on a sustainable basis to increase its role in accelerating growth and ameliorating poverty. In order to diagnose the crux of the issue, it will be necessary to look at how entrepreneurship and industrial climate has been built.

20.1 Genesis of industrial thrust:

Post-independence era concentrated well on development of Small-Scale industries (SSI) with the enactment of 'The Industries Development and Regulation Act of 1951'. Small Industries Development Board was formed in 1954 and subsequently Small Industries development Organization (SIDO) had begun to function under 'Development Commissioner – SSI'. Similarly, Directorate of Industries was responsible for developing SSIs at state level and to coordinate with the federal government.

In order to innovate better policies, Karve committee (1955) was the earliest known committee to recommend protective environment for growth of SSIs. In order to step up flow of credit to SSI sector, RBI introduced priority sector lending norms in November 1974 calling for certain mandatory lending to hitherto deprived sectors. Banks had to necessarily extend loans to identified sectors up to 33.3 percent of their total credit by March 1979. Such mandatory loan limit was raised to 40 percent by March 1985. Over a period of time, several committees, working groups, study groups have worked at various points of time to develop policy framework for growth of industries. Prominent among them can be Shri P.R. Nayak Committee set up by RBI to examine difficulties confronting Small Scale Industries (SSI) in the matter of securing finance (1991), Dr.Abid Hussain Committee (1997), Study group on Development of Small Enterprises under Dr. S.P. Gupta (1999), Working Group on Flow of Credit to SSI sector (Chairman: Dr. A.S. Ganguly) that was formed by RBI in 2004. Among several measures to step up SSI, there was a consensus opinion of experts to provide for a proper legal framework for small sector to relieve it of the requirements to comply with multiple rules and regulations that led to enactment of Micro, Small and Medium Enterprises Development (MSMED) Act, 2006.

20.2 Transition from SSI to MSME:

Better reinforcement of industrial growth began with formation of a dedicated Ministry of MSME on May 9, 2007 with merger of erstwhile Ministry of Small-Scale Industries (SSI) and the Ministry of Agro and Rural Industries. Such strategic move began to improve industrial climate evolving new policies for promoting, facilitating faster implementation of programs/projects/schemes and close monitoring of outcome. Quickly thereafter a legal framework was provided with enactment of MSME Development Act -2006 on 16th June 2006 to facilitate the development of these enterprises as also enhance their competitiveness. Incentives, allocations, subsidies and other benefits were focused from a single vantage point.

As a follow through action a number of statutory and non-statutory bodies were brought together under single control to converge their synergy into a reckoning force. These include the Khadi Village Industries Commission (KVIC) and the Coir Board besides National Small Industries Corporation (NSIC), National Institute for Micro, Small and Medium Enterprises (NIMSME) and Mahatma Gandhi Institute for Rural Industrialization (MGIRI). In all its forms, the industrial ecosystem has been strengthened to take MSME to next trajectory of growth. It also led to formation of National Board for Micro Small and Medium Enterprises (NBMSME). The role of the Board is to examine the factors affecting the promotion and development of MSMEs, review the policies and programs of the Central Government and make recommendations in regard to facilitating the promotion and development to enhance their competitiveness.

Even after formation of MSMED act several committees have worked to improve the sector. A Prime Minister's Task Force on MSMEs (Chairman: Shri T.K.A. Nair, Principal Secretary) was formed in 2010 to increase flow of credit to the sector. Shri Prabhat Kumar committee

(2017) was formed to make recommendations for national policy for MSME. Their valuable inputs/recommendations led to policy changes to benefit the sector. Many of the recommendations of such eminent groups were pieced together into the policy framework, some of them were implemented, some of them were work in progress but still MSME sector continues to dither.

20.3 Recent Key initiatives:

The latest Report of the Expert Committee on MSME (Chairman: Mr. U.K. Sinha) is thought provoking with several measures to create perpetual momentum to turbo charge the sector. Among many far reaching recommendations, the game changing proposals could relate to (i) formation of Stressed Asset Fund of Rs.5000 crores for units impacted by change in external environment (ii) setting up an apex National and State level council for MSMEs (iii) doubling of limits of collateral free loans under Pradhan Mantri MUDRA Yozana and Start up India to increase flow of funds (iv) expansion of scope of SIDBI to work as the fulcrum to steer the sector to next level of growth (v) creation of incentives and disincentives to lenders by introducing Rural Infrastructure development fund (RIDF) scheme that suggests that banks should deposit amount equal to shortfall in achieving MSME targets with SIDBI akin to RIDF scheme with NABARD. (vi) making it mandatory to source 25 percent of PSU needs from MSME units through GeM portal (vii) expansion of number of MSE Facilitation Council (MSEFC) to help address the delayed payment conundrum of the sector. Strengthening of Trade Receivables electronic Discount System (TReDS), a secured digital trade receivables exchange for quick financing of MSMEs against pending invoices for which supplies have already been made to large industries.

At the same time, the government has also directed PSBs to assign credit availability aspects of MSME sector to GM level executive for accelerating flow of credit. It also suggested a well-calibrated monitoring mechanism to institutionalize weekly feedback in a bid to improve accountability for performance.

Earlier, the government had rolled out 12-point MSME outreach initiatives in November 2018, the impact of which may trickle down in future. Another important initiative was the introduction of *'in-principle'* sanction of loans to MSME units up to Rs.1 crore in just 59 minutes. The intending borrower should log into a dedicated website – *'psbloansin59minutes'* which will collect borrower details online from various digitally connected sources such as income tax department, GST portal and other interdependent sources to provide an 'in principle sanction' with which the potential borrower can approach any PSB to get the loan. Its effectiveness can be assessed in due course but a supportive exercise has well begun.

20.4 Union Budget – FY 2020:

In order to further push MSME and *'Startups'*, measures were proposed in the union budget 2020 to increase flow of credit. The angel tax has been addressed and a two percent interest subvention is allowed on fresh loans to be granted to GST registered MSMEs for which an allocation of Rs.350 crores is made. Rationalization of labor laws can help them accelerate formalization of the economy. Corporate tax rate is brought down to 25 percent for firms having turnover of up to Rs.400 crores, raised from Rs.250 crores which will provide relief to 99.3 percent of the 1.5 lakh companies incorporated so far according to the data of Ministry of Corporate Affairs (MCA).

In order to reinforce *'Make in India'* campaign to pump prime manufacturing activity, the import tariffs are calibrated to boost local manufacturing. Increase in customs duty of certain automobile components and electronic devices will increase local manufacturing activities. MSME units will be encouraged to increase production by taking benefit of concessions using digital mode.

20.5 Lending to MSME:

Lack of funding to MSME units is considered as the biggest impediment for their growth and lack of competitiveness. Besides lending to MSME from all its branches, commercial banks have set up dedicated MSME branches close to 3000 (March 2017). Forming part of 40 percent of Priority Sector Lending (PSL) targets, banks should lend a minimum of 7.5 per cent of Average net bank credit (ANBC) or credit equivalent amount of off-Balance Sheet Exposure, whichever is higher to MSME units.

The total demand for credit for MSME sector is close to Rs. 37 trillion as estimated by the expert panel (Mr. U.K. Sinha 2019). But as against such demand, the formal credit flow is currently put close to Rs.15.50 trillion that hardly meets much less than half its needs. The trends of flow of bank credit to MSME in the recent years is as under:

The trends of bank credit indicate that from FY16 onwards, the rate of growth of MSME loans were far less than industry level growth rate. It had fallen steeply after AQR implemented by RBI in September 2015. Recognizing the potential gains from transition of MSMEs to the formal sector through GST registration, RBI allowed banks to restructure loans of GST-registered MSMEs units whose aggregate exposure was of less than Rs.250 million (as on January 31, 2018), which was standard as on August 31, 2017.

In order to encourage lending to MSMEs, RBI has taken a number of steps, including issuing banking licenses to ten Small Finance Banks. These banks are expected to lend to un-served and under-served enterprises including small business units, small and marginal farmers, micro and small industries and un-organized sector entities (Mundra, 2017).

Trends of bank loans to MSME sector

₹ Billions

Sr. No.	Sector	2012-13	2013-14	2014-15	2015-16	2016-17	2017-18	2018-19
1.	Total Bank Credit	48696	55296 (13.55%)	60030 (8.56%)	65469 (9.06%)	70945 (8.36%)	76884 (8.37%)	86334 (12.29%)
2.	Micro & Small	2843	3482 (22.48%)	3800 (9.13%)	3715 (-2.24%)	3697 (-0.48%)	3730 (0.89%)	3755 (0.67%)
3.	Medium	1247	1241 (0.48)	1245 (0.32%)	1148 (-7.79%)	1048 (-8.71%)	1037 (-1.05%)	1064 (2.6%)
4.	MSME (Under Priority Sector)	5623	7078 (25.88%)	8003 (13.07%)	8476 (5.91%)	9020 (6.42%)	9964 (10.47%)	10672 (7.11%)
5.	Total Credit to MSME	9713	11801 (21.5%)	13048 (10.57%)	13339 (2.23%)	13765 (3.19%)	14731 (7.02%)	15491 (5.16%)

(Figures in the bracket indicate (%)Growth Rate)

Source: Source: https://rbi.org.in/scripts/PublicationsView.aspx?id=18511

20.6 Booster dose for MSME:

Irked by the continuous slowdown in the economy due to geopolitical tensions, ongoing global trade war and domestic apprehensions of the industry, the government had rolled out a 32-point relief package on August 21, 2019 to revive the morale of various sectors of the economy. As the known anchor of economic growth, MSME sector too is provided with supportive measures to revive its momentum of growth.

All pending GST refunds due to MSME will be paid in 30 days and future such refunds will be on auto mode within time lines of 60 days. Banks to pass on lower lending rate benefits by linking it to variable repo rates of RBI. Violations of spend on corporate social responsibility (CSR) activities will henceforth be a civil offense under 'Companies act 2013'. There are several indirect measures to benefit MSME sector. Most important is the release of capital infusion of Rs.70,000 crores in one go to PSBs to enable them to accelerate lending speed, a part of which should logically flow to MSME.

20.7 Some missing links:

The narrative of consistent development of industrial growth in the last seven decades clearly indicates that there were steady efforts to extend policy support, that got accelerated in the last decade and more after formation of exclusive ministry of MSME. Despite such efforts, the pace of growth of MSME sector is ostensibly far less than its potentiality. Serious introspection into efforts and outcome points towards some glaring missing links (i) lack of organized thrust on disseminating entrepreneurial literacy and capacity building (ii) the improvement in the 'ease of doing business' did not adequately ease the life of MSME units. (iii) Monitoring of performance of MSMEs and handholding has not been effective. (iv) the supportive coordination work of associations/ MSME forums/non-government organizations (NGOs) could not assist/ educate mass of potential entrepreneurs. (v) The efforts of National skill development mission are still a work in progress. (vi) the efforts of banks to reach out to MSME units were not sufficient and recent financial inclusion efforts have not been adequately tapped.

According to Standard & Poor's Global Financial Literacy Survey – 2014, 33 percent of adults in the world possess Financial Literacy (FL). As a result, majority of adults across the globe, most of them from developing economies do not have any understanding of financial products and services. In the same way, lack of literacy among MSME entrepreneurs that have to collaborate with various agencies to excel in manufacturing and business becomes a stumbling block for growth. The average FL rate works out to 28 percent of adults among the BRICS (Brazil, Russia, India, China and South Africa) economies. In the league of financial literacy, 24 percent of Indian adults possess some sort of FL while; China has 26 percent and 42 percent in South Africa. In the absence of FL, it will be impossible for entrepreneurs to understand the intricate MSME policies, products and benefits. It results in 86 percent of MSME units remaining out of the purview of formal financial system and most of them remain as unregistered units. They depend on moneylenders and indigenous barefoot financers charging usurious interest rates.

Literacy becomes much more significant with spread of digital network/operating space including need to interact with complex GST portal and submission of online returns. Proliferation of virtual banking system accessible round the clock across geographies can transform the convenience of the new age entrepreneurs. But it is not happening because of lack of focus on financial and digital literacy. The ATM base, POS terminals and debit card base can indeed make a big difference to users but it is not delivered to the entrepreneurs because of their inability to understand the nuances of digitalization. With MSMEs gradually getting connected to GST portals, more digital literacy is imminent.

20.8 The diagnosis:

The distilled views emanating from various committees /public debates/ conclaves/discussion forums collectively point out some common broad-brush age-old deficiencies such as lack of (i) Easy access to institutional finance from commercial banks/NBFCs (ii) Ease of doing MSME business. The sector has to still deal with cumbersome government procedures to register, obtain/renew licenses, get environmental clearances wherever needed, deal with labor laws, taxation and a host of other regulatory compliances not understandable to many of the entrepreneurs without seeking help of experts. Hence, they are in despair. (iii) Adequate transport infrastructure to take products to markets/buyers (iv) Adequate training in financial literacy and credit counselling to access credit from formal sources. (v) Knowledge of latest technology despite availability of government's Technology up-gradation fund (TUF) scheme. (vi) Systemic compulsion for large industries/corporate sector to make timely payment for accessories sourced from MSME units. Having done huge policy making groundwork so far, with an integrated approach of government, regulators, banks and other stakeholders in creating the MSME value chain; the next task is to take the value proposition to the entrepreneurs. It can commonly be observed that many supportive measures address short-term impediments.

20.9 Long term solutions for MSME:

But real solutions to bail out ailing MSME sector would lie in adopting multipronged strategy with its far-reaching long-term ramifications. Single window simplified procedures for registration, finer turnaround time in licensing (if any), quick granting of environmental clearances, rewarding reduction of carbon emissions, providing amenities for improving production, quality focus, transport facilities and marketing assistance and so on will be essential.

Long-term efforts should include a greater dissemination of knowledge to the last entrepreneur in the value chain by coordinating with district/block/gram panchayat levels to set up entrepreneurial literacy touch points. The business correspondents (BCs) of banks could be made to share knowledge on how to approach banks for loans. Schools, colleges, institutes and premier universities should be persuaded to undertake coaching and mentoring of entrepreneurs in their areas. The stakeholders will have to look beyond policy interventions and create a learning dissemination structure to make them reach the beneficiaries. Globally, literacy is occupying center stage in ensuring inclusive growth in the economy.

In a bid to further resuscitate the sector on a sustainable basis, it may also be pertinent to use the model of self-help groups (SHGs) for MSME entrepreneurs operating in clusters/industrial estates working at the bottom of the pyramid. They can be organized by proactive non-government organizations (NGOs) or extended outfits of voluntary forums of MSME associations to work towards seeking institutional credit. The entrepreneurial literacy, financial and credit counselling support should make these clusters capable to draw up their financial statements and deal with government agencies in compliance. It will be essential to improve their financial capability and work towards capacity building right from availing loans from banks/non-banks/alternate funding agencies, apply those funds for the purpose for which it is borrowed so that repayment of loans from out of unit's operations become seamless.

So long as the entrepreneurs are educated only on accessing credit, it will be insufficient. They need to be educated on holistic pattern to include on the significance of utilization of funds, quality consciousness in production, compliance and adherence to tax laws, repayment of loans in time so that banks get an assurance that the sector is credit worthy.

Even the best of ideas, policies of liberal funding, subsidy schemes rolled out in the past could not reach the target group and improve their wellbeing. It remains the stakeholders' puzzle that the whole ecosystem is designed to support MSME but it still languishes in the same old sub optimal trap. May be the solutions lies in innovations and shifting the gear. Drawing spirit of SHGs in improving MSME sector could be a way to unleash its potentiality to contribute to GDP growth. Lot of follow up actions and end use of solutions mooted at public debates will be necessary if MSME is to deliver its full value.

20.10 Inclusive participation:

Every able stakeholder, more importantly the stronger MSME units themselves have to come forward to create a better productive ecosystem. There are some good MSME units and even larger export-oriented units capable to fund CSR activities. They should be the harbinger to write the fortune of disadvantaged units of the sector. More plough back of resources, willing commitment and resolution to resurrect MSME sector from better performing units in coordination with government and voluntary agencies will be able to make a difference.

Government can take a cue from the economic survey that suggested use of the behavioural economics concept of 'nudge' to encourage desirable social and economic change. Nudge theory is based on the rationale that human resources often need encouragement or intervention – a nudge – to get going and to enable them to do their best.

With best entrepreneur friendly policies consistently built, the next phase should therefore be dedicated to educate, enrol, handhold, ease the life of entrepreneurs and groom them to improve productivity and raise quality of output to international standards. Financial capability of entrepreneurs must be targeted to enable them to demand services and get funding so that MSME can play a greater role in achieving higher GDP growth and can employ a greater number of people. Thus, the thrust should shift to providing financial capability to entrepreneurs to make policies work and to lend sustainability in its journey to support growth.

CHAPTER – 21

CHANGING CREDIT RISK MANAGEMENT POLICY

The Financial Stability Report (FSR) – June 2021 released by RBI indicates that banks are on a stronger footing with capital adequacy ratio edging up by 130 basis points during FY21 reaching 16.03 percent from 14.7 percent recorded during FY20. The GNPA has slowed down to 7.48 percent in FY21, down from 8.2 percent a year ago. Despite severe disruption caused by the second wave of coronavirus, the damage is likely to be slower than previous year. The provision coverage ratio is getting close to 70 percent from 65.4 percent of last year.

Despite increasing robustness of banks and ample multipurpose liquidity provided by RBI under Targeted Long Term Repo Operations (TLTRO), there is no perceptible improvement in the credit growth, as yet. The nonfood credit growth of banks has been down to 5.56 percent in FY21, at a 59 year low as against 6.14 percent recorded in FY20, an analysis by SBI Research showed recently.

Even amid such fragile credit growth, the recent 'Coalition Greenwich Report' – a Division of CRISIL on *"Future of Corporate & Transaction Banking Operating Models"* brings some cheer that big banks are gaining better share in corporate lending. SBI, ICICI Bank and HDFC Bank have emerged as '2021 Greenwich Share Leaders' while Axis Bank was the '2021 Greenwich Quality Leader'. This sounds good as they need to do heavy lifting for the revival of the economy.

The report further observes that market penetration of SBI and private banks in corporate banking improved in the last five years. SBI is providing credit to 32 percent of corporates in 2020, up from 30 percent in 2016. Private Banks are providing services up to 24 percent of corporates in 2020, up from 17 percent in 2016. It is beginning of a good trend that large banks with sound capital base should develop strong risk appetite to lend to large sector and have accordingly moulded their risk management strategies.

The very purpose of merger of banks is also to make them big enough to improve their lending capacity. According to Bank for International Settlement (BIS), the credit to GDP ratio in India, though marginally improved to 56 percent in 2020 up from 52.4 percent in 2019 but continuous to be way behind its peers and just half of the G20 average and is second lowest among its Asian peers. It is down from 64.8 percent in 2015 indicating that banks were unable to align pace of credit flow in sync with the rise in GDP. A diagnostic look into the reasons will be interesting.

21.1 Asymmetric distribution of Bank Credit:

Logically large banks with better capital base and credit risk management capacity should take up large size loans. But a look at RBI's *Basic Statistical Report – 2020'*, indicates a different phenomenon. According to the size wise distribution of borrowers, out of 272.5 million bank borrowers, only 6,79,034, much less than a million borrowers borrow Rs.10 million or more from banks. Bulk of the borrower accounts are small loans of less than 10 million. 95.7 percent of number of bank borrowers have loan limits up to Rs. 1 million. Strikingly 77 percent borrowers have loans below Rs. half a million.

The policy of assuming credit risk by commercial banks are yet to align to the size of loans. There is no obvious connect between capacity to lend – assuming credit risk to the size of loans. As a result, the load of small and tiny borrowers with low credit risk propensity is taking away the bulk of time of banks and is adding to the intermediation cost that is disproportion to the competence of large banks. Moreover, almost a similar loan dispensation procedure loaded with paper intensity is adding to the turnaround time of loan processing. Recent adoption of lending automation systems has, of late, started de-cluttering the procedure and improving the operational efficiency but it is a long way to go to optimize time utilization in banks. More reforms in articulating sector specific credit risk management policies and procedures and linking them to the size of loans will have to be thought through.

21.2 Uniform lending system:

Though Indian banks work on universal banking system is having banks of as large as SBI with huge credit risk appetite on one side and a small bank with low-risk appetite – a cooperative bank operates on the other hand predominantly in hinterland. There is no defined policy of what kind of borrowers can approach which kind of bank branch. Universal lending policy provides an ecosystem where any kind of borrower can borrow any amount from any bank branch and there is no way they can be encouraged to choose a right kind of bank that suits to their requirements in terms of size of loans and inherent risk appetite of the underlying bank. Proximity to a bank branch is the only guiding factor as of now.

A three-tier banking structure is gradually evolving with the recent spate of mergers in banking space. Large banks with international presence with asset size exceeding Rs. 10 trillion are operating in both public sector and private sector group of banks. There are some banks with medium asset size as national level commercial banks. There is a third rung of banks – Regional Rural Banks, Small Finance Banks, Payment Banks, Cooperative banks and Cooperative credit societies with their intense presence in hinterland. These categories of banks are in line with the spirit of recommendations of Narasimham Committee – I (1991). These banks have, over a period of time developed different capabilities in terms of credit risk appetite that can be well harnessed for faster credit expansion. Even the skill sets for credit appraisal of medium and large loans are different whereas small loans can be template driven. Sheer volume of borrower base mixed with large number of small loans can be impacting quality of lending, so is the need to handle bad loans of the segment. Every kind of bank getting into every size of loan may therefore be counterproductive when seen with their credit risk management skills and risk appetite.

21. 3 Reforms in policies:

It is therefore a time to debate if large commercial banks can focus on loans above a million rupees while the second set of banks can serve the retail community. The purpose is to improve the quality of growth and equitable use of credit risk management skills and risk appetite. It can create concomitant resources for closer post sanction monitoring of credit to tackle asset quality woes in long term. Banking system on the cusp of transformation can debate on the idea of big banks shedding low ticket size lending to its other peers and use the time to concentrate on developing robust large size credit portfolio better using their credit risk management skills instead of withering their competence in routinely handling whatever size of loans that drop in the branches.

According to analysts, bank credit growth is a key indicator of economic growth and a credit-GDP ratio of 100 per cent is the ideal, which indicates robust demand for credit without the fear of a bubble in the making. A higher credit-to-GDP ratio indicates aggressive and active participation of the banking sector in the real economy, while a lower number shows the need for more formal credit.

If Indian banking system is to reach a credit to GDP ratio anywhere closer to its peers in Asian region, a new way of thinking will be needed. The age-old lending practices cannot serve a growing society that too in the midst of strength of demographic dividend providing an opportune time. Mining the capacity of banks by allowing them to choose the right size of lending activities aligned to their innate specialized credit risk management capacity in place of the present implied 'one size fits all' approach can be a possible solution to the sluggish credit growth.

Though it may not look compatible when every bank has presence in every location metro, urban, semi-urban and rural centres but, to begin with, an informal agenda not to load large banks with international presence in metro and urban areas with low ticket loans but to allow them to take up large lending project by pooling credit risk management experts at such prime centres. The present arrangement of lending to all segments can continue at Semi-urban and Rural Centres.

There is no point in exceptionally large banks figuring in top 100 global banks in metro centres entertaining a home loan of Rs. One million. Eventually, such mega banks should be used to fund large projects of over Rs.10 million or more. There are enough compatible institutions to take care of lower segment of borrowers to fund MSME and Small businesses. Credit risk management policy and using of risk appetite need to be scaled up differently to support revival of the economy. Fintech and non-banks can also use technology and collaborate with middle order banks to fund in hinterland.

21.4 Increasing synergy between banks/ non-banks:

The growth of global banking system is a function of synergy between banks and non-bank entities. They coexist and complements role to support the growth of the economy. As a result, many times, banks have to enter into dealings even with less regulated /unregulated financial entities. Alternatively, the prime customers of banks may in turn be in business league with such entities transmitting their inherent risks on to banks. The experience of global financial crisis in 2008 leading to collapse of Lehman Brothers, indicated that interdependency of banks on non-bank fragile financial entities led to crystallization of systemic risks that eventually led to its dubious collapse. As a consequence, the Basel Committee on Banking Supervision aimed to evolve an appropriate framework in October 2017 to mitigate potential spill over effects from such interconnectedness between banking system and financial entities forming part of shadow banking system.

Bank for International settlement (BIS) terms such non-bank entities as unconsolidated entities, defined as a non-bank unit not falling within the scope of regulatory consolidation. According to Basel Committee framework, the regulatory consolidation includes all banking and relevant financial entities meeting prescribed regulatory criteria of the Central Bank. The existence of such informal financial constituencies in any economy cannot be ruled out. The financial intermediation by such entities leads to shadow banking. Since banks have to coexist in such systems, it is more important to be able to apprehend and manage such risks. Since they are not compliant to regulatory dispensation of the standards banks follow, they tend to be riskier.

21. 5 Shadow banking:

Thus the shadow banking system is business done by a set of institutions that carry out functions very similar to those of traditional banks but that are largely unregulated and can potentially carry larger risks. They perform the same kind of maturity transformation traditionally performed by commercial banks. Thus, the shadow banking system, despite its somewhat unwholesome sounding name, provides a useful service to society. Thus, shadow banking is not necessarily a bad thing. The problem is that, under certain circumstances, these financial institutions can become fragile — that is, subject to panic professing incomprehensible risks to regulated entities. Its collateral damage is a worrying factor.

An important fact about the shadow banking system is that it has grown significantly in the last 30 years and is serving a large sector of grassroot level population. It is estimated that just before the financial crisis of 2007-08, the assets of the shadow banking system began to grow as fast as the assets of commercial banks. Thus informal and unaccounted financial intermediation began to add to risks. Another important fact about the shadow banking system is that it has grown outside the oversight of regulators. As banking and finance in general have expanded in recent decades, part of that growth has occurred in the shadow system, largely to avoid the costs associated with regulation. Banks have to protect themselves from such risks.

21.6 Global Surge in Volumes:

The Financial Stability Board (FSB) measures shadow banking as "credit intermediation involving entities and activities (fully or partly) outside of the regular banking system". Some authorities and market participants prefer to use other terms such as "market-based finance" instead of "shadow banking". The use of the term "shadow banking" is not intended to cast a pejorative tone on this system of credit intermediation.

However, the FSB uses the term "shadow banking" as this is the most commonly employed and, in particular, has been used in earlier G20 communications. According to its Global Financial Stability Report – 2016, out of the total global financial assets of US $ 321 Trillion (based on the data from 27 jurisdictions and Euro Area representing 80 per cent of global (GDP), the volume of shadow banking assets is put at US $ 34 trillion as of end 2015. The data only provides an inkling of emerging trends of share of shadow banking as a global phenomenon.

No economy, including South Asian Association of Regional Cooperation (SAARC) nations, of which Sri Lanka is a member cannot be completely immune from shadow banking practices. Thus banks operating in different economies will have to be aware of risks but need not necessarily be averse to such risks. It needs to be better managed by understanding its nuances. Wherever non-bank financing is involved in bank-like activities, transforming maturity/liquidity and creating leverage like banks, it can become a potential source of systemic risk, both directly and through its interconnectedness with the banking system. Such risk is broadly associated with 'Step-in-Risk'.

21.7 Step in Risk:

It is the risk when a bank decides to provide financial support to a shadow banking entity that is facing stress, in the absence of, or in excess of, any contractual obligations to provide such support. The main reason for step-in risk might be to avoid the reputational risk that a bank might suffer were it not to provide support to an entity facing a stress situation. Indeed, the experience of past financial crisis provided enough evidence that a bank might have incentives beyond contractual obligation or equity ties to "step in" to support such non-bank financial entities to which it is connected.

In this context, the Basel Committee defined reputational risk that automatically emanates from Step in risk. In fact, it is effectively the risk arising from negative perception on the part of customers, counterparties, shareholders, investors, debt-holders, market analysts, other relevant parties or regulators that can adversely affect a bank's ability to maintain existing, or establish new business relationships and continue access to sources of funding. As such, step-in risk is associated with a possible source of reputational risk as well. It arises when a bank considers that it is likely to suffer a negative impact from the weakness or failure of an entity and concludes that this impact is best mitigated, by stepping in to provide financial support to bail out the entity.

21. 8 Mitigation of Step in Risk:

The Central Bank and banks in the ecosystem *mutatis mutandis* endeavour to ring fence the financial system against such precipitating risks. It is more important for individual banks to be aware of risks associated with shadow banking and those transmitted from the financial derivatives. The systemic controls have to be more robust in dealing particularly with risky investment products, financial pawnshops and loan shark operations and informal peer to peer lending that is not adequately insulated by the regulatory authorities. The common narrative is that these products and practices thrive outside the regular banking system threatening the safety and soundness of financial architecture. Many times, the shadow banking may be able to escape regulatory lens exacerbating the risks but banks dealing with them continue to confront risks.

In developing economies, market players have to be mindful about the step-in risk and its impact on the stability of banks and financial entities. Shadow banking proliferates for a reason: free from regulation, funds flow to where it is needed but can jeopardize the interest of regulated entities like banks. Hence, it may not be possible not to deal with non-bank entities creating shadow banking but what is more important is to be aware of extent of step-in risk and take appropriate preventive measures. More so when the financial system is on upsurge to support the burgeoning economies.

CHAPTER – 22

RISK MANAGEMENT IN FINANCIAL SECTOR

Amid the fast-transforming financial sector, the interconnectedness and rising spill over risks among financial intermediaries may exacerbate unless they adopt robust risk management practices. In the fast-diversifying financial landscape, NBFCs including Fintech companies are fast inundating financial intermediation space creating intense competition and accentuating business risks. While providing more autonomy in operations and diversification of lines of business, the regulatory glare is yet to be well aligned to balance risks from the sustainability angle.

RBI, SEBI, Insurance and Regulatory Development Authority of India (IRDAI), Pension Fund Regulatory and Development authority PFRDA and IBBI are working in their sphere to ring fence financial sector against risks as part of their continuous journey. More important is for financial intermediaries to enhance risk management standards.

The experience of IL & FS, DHFL and recent SREI financial services fiascos continues to haunt the NBFC sector as reminders against the missing links in risk governance and its consequences. NBFCs handling additional activities must be mindful about the associated risks and its potential impact on the sustainability. With the divide between functions of banks and NBFCs beginning to shrink, the standard of their risk sensitivity and nuances of managing it needs careful scrutiny. The commercial interests of new found activities of NBFCs should not be allowed to dilute risk management practices, more importantly keeping the knowledge levels and outsourcing practices in some such financial entities.

22.1 Changing trends:

Between March 31, 2009 and March 31, 2019, the total assets of NBFCs grew at a compounded annual growth rate (CAGR) of 18.6 per cent, while the balance sheets of SCBs grew at a CAGR of 10.7 per cent. Consequently, the aggregate balance sheet size of NBFCs increased from 9.3 per cent to 18.6 per cent of the aggregate balance sheet size of SCBs during the corresponding period. The asset size of NBFCs measured as percentage of total bank's balance sheet has almost doubled during the decade. In absolute terms, the asset size of NBFC sector (including HFCs), as on March 31, 2020, is Rs.51.47 trillion as against the asset size of banks standing at Rs.180 trillion. The balance sheet size of NBFCs now works out to 28 percent of that of banks. The number of NBFCs currently regulated by RBI is close to 10,000 and their scope of activities and last mile connect with the hinterland is clearly on rise helping to take the financial inclusion to next level.

As part of it, NBFCs including about 1200 Fintech companies are set to expand their operations with innovative products. RBI had already set up a framework for a regulatory sandbox in August 2019 that allows Fintechs to test their products without any regulatory requirements before they are commercially rolled out. It will help existing and upcoming Fintechs to pre-test the efficacy and build solid products that can enable them to earn bigger space in financial intermediation.

Among them, Fintechs, engaged in digital lending may assume an aggressive tone once they adopt RBI regulations on fair practices for digital lenders issued in June 2020. The recent incidents of excesses used against borrowers in recovering loans by digital lenders attracted the ire of the regulators leading to issue of fair practices guidelines.

22.2 Increasing penetration of NBFCs:

Beginning with RBI allowing co-origination of loans by banks and NBFCs in September 2018 under priority sector, the role of NBFCs is enhanced. The 'Co-origination Model' should involve sharing of risks and rewards between the bank and the NBFCs. The arrangement of working together on the mutually decided agreement between the bank and the NBFCs will help them realize their business objectives while providing choices to customers. The joint-origination model will enable NBFCs to depend largely on funding by banks that have greater access to low-cost deposit resources. It will enhance the synergy enabling NBFCs to bank on banks for funding their impressive credit growth.

But the risk management systems and procedures of banks are known to be more methodical and system driven as they are better regulated entities. NBFCs may have to improve their internal risk management systems to handle larger volumes and diversified products, in the long term, akin to banks.

In a bid to further widen the scope and diversity of financial sector, RBI has been shifting its reform gear to involve non-banks in a broader frame. In its recent monetary policy – 2021-22, RBI (i) opened up remittances facilities through Real Time Gross Settlement System (RTGS)/National Electronic funds transfer (NEFT) to entities other than banks. (ii) While making the interoperability among Prepaid Payment Instruments (PPIs) mandatory for full – KYC accounts, the limit of outstanding balance in such PPIs has been raised from Rs. 1 lakh to Rs. 2 lakhs. (iii) Inducing greater interoperability and full-KYC, cash withdrawal subject to a limit will be allowed against PPIs through ATMs/ POS terminals.

Loans extended by banks to NBFCs for on lending to underserved and unserved community will continue to be classified as priority sector lending till March 31, 2022.

RBI continued its digital payment thrust by increasing transaction limit in IMPS from Rs.2 lakhs to Rs.5 lakhs, geo tagging of payment system touch points, introduction of retail digital payment solutions on offline mode. With increasing role and penetration of NBFCs, it is necessary to protect consumer interest. Therefore, RBI introduced internal ombudsman scheme (IOS) for certain categories of NBFCs having higher customer interface. Efforts and guidance of RBI to financial intermediaries are clear on the need for increasing risk management capabilities.

The digital thrust brought through these measures will fine tune not only quality and efficiency of financial services but also shall open up stiff competition for banks for float funds and cross selling of products. With NBFCs entering into more permitted activities the interconnectedness and associated risks are on rise. Hence, the financial entities have to understand and confront the vulnerabilities and risks and constantly assess the impact of shocks transmitted to or from the sector to ring fence them.

22.3 Global trends:

Though the role of NBFCs in India is beginning to rise, way forward, its poised to occupy a formidable share in financial intermediation in the coming decades that needs sustained focus on building integrated organizational competency. A global cue in impending shift of roles of banks and non-banks can be perceived. The global data trends of banks and NBFIs provided by BIS will be able to corroborate the emerging trends. During the decade 2008-18, the combined assets of NBFIs stands at US $ 184 trillion as against US $ 148 trillion of banks.

While the non-banks could provide additional sources of finance to trade and industry, it can also contribute to systemic risks through links and interconnectedness with the banking system. BIS observes that in the wake of Great Financial Crisis, G20 leaders urged the financial Stability Board to strengthen the oversight and regulation of shadow banking. While the regulators will be doing their bit, it is incumbent on the part of financial intermediaries to act fast to brace for shifting roles.

22.4 Thrust on Governance, Risk and compliance (GRC):

With the increasing role of NBFCs in direct credit intermediation, RBI has been reiterating that NBFCs should augment risk management practices at the board level to imbibe best practices in risk management. They need to strengthen the architecture of governance, risk and compliance to bring about awareness and sensitize them towards better risk management practices. In May 2019, RBI directed NBFCs having asset size of over Rs.50 billion to appoint a Chief Risk officer (CRO) with clearly specified roles and responsibilities. The CRO should function independently so as to ensure highest standards of risk management.

RBI also introduced Risk based internal audit (RBIA) in February 2021 for institutionalizing an independent and effective internal audit function in a financial entity to provide vital assurance to the Board and its senior management regarding the quality and effectiveness of the entity's internal control, risk management and governance framework.

The essential requirements for a robust internal audit function include, inter alia, sufficient authority, proper stature, independence, adequate resources and professional competence. All deposit taking NBFCs, all non-deposit taking NBFCs with asset size of Rs 5000 crores and above, all Urban Cooperative banks having asset size of Rs.500 crores and above are covered under the RBIA of RBI.

There could be regulatory arbitrage in the functioning of NBFCs compared to banks that should be navigated with caution. The addition of activities to the scope of NBFCs is allowed but many of them may not be well versed in managing associated risks. Therefore, RBI is proactive in issuing a discussion paper on revised regulatory framework for NBFCs on a scale-based approach in January 2021 that is still in a consultative process. Peer to peer lenders – (P2P), the, NBFC segment is brought under RBI regulations in October 2017. All the Housing Finance Companies (HFCs) are brought within the regulations of

RBI in February 2021. Cooperative banks are now brought under the regulatory purview of RBI.

RBI has been consistently issuing new guidelines to enable financial entities to cope with the new range of business risks emanating from the diversified activities. But it is financial entities that should be working meticulously to act upon the regulatory dispensations to build risk management capabilities in letter and spirit. RBI has now mandated the Risk Based Internal Audit (RBIA) system to all deposit taking Non-Banking Financial Companies (NBFCs) irrespective of their size, on-deposit taking NBFCs (including Core Investment Companies) with asset size of ₹5,000 crore and above and Primary (Urban) Co-operative Banks (UCBs) with asset size of ₹500 crore and above, vide circular dated 3rd February 2021.These new directions should create better risk culture in these financial institutions in the larger interest.

22.5 Capacity building:

Based upon the recommendations of RBI Committee on Capacity Building' (July 2014) under the Chairmanship of former Executive Director, Shri G Gopalakrishna, banks should identify specialized areas for certification of the staff manning key responsibilities.

As part of capacity building activities banks should make acquiring of a certificate course mandatory in critical areas (i) Treasury operations – Dealers, mid-office operations. (ii) Risk management – credit risk, market risk, operational risk, enterprise-wide risk, information security, and liquidity risk. (iii) Accounting – Preparation of financial results, audit function. (iv) Credit management – credit appraisal, rating, monitoring, credit administration.

It is time that it should be made mandatory for NBFCs to expose its human resources including line management to upgrade skill sets in specific areas. Such professional certification will ensure sustained capacity building to equip them to protect the interest of consumers better and manage risks more efficiently.At the same time, the financial entities should create proper infrastructure to disseminate financial and digital literacy to harness the full potential of digital power. The digital infrastructure has to be put to vulnerability test from time to time to protect against cyber threats – the biggest operational risks. Financial entities should look beyond the commercial angle of increasing scope of activities and build a step-by-step metrics for enhancing comprehensive risk management capabilities.

CHAPTER – 23

DEVELOPMENTS IN LENDING RATES

Low lending rates, low inflation and adequate supply of institutional credit is broadly meant to create demand for credit, spur investment, revive consumption demand and create buoyancy in the economy to spur growth. That precisely is the reason for reining in inflation within the bandwidth fixed in the glide path of inflation 4 percent with +/- 2 percent. Effectively the desirable range of inflation should lie between 4 percent and 6 percent in upper end. With inflation presently within the comfort zone of RBI, recently repo rate has been cut to its historically low level due to the pandemic and its after math. It created a spur of optimism towards lower lending rates so that credit could be made more affordable to trade and industry.

Logically therefore, every repo rate cut raises the conventional debate about effective transmission of monetary policy signals leading to lowering of interest rates, more importantly the lending rates. But discussion on lending rates cannot be in isolation. It has to be linked to interest rates on liabilities (deposits and borrowings) of banks and other financial intermediaries. Even interest rates on small savings in post offices also has an influencing impact. Financial markets are so integrated that interest rates get transmitted from banks to other intermediaries.

But in a bank led economy like India, interest rates ruling in banks assumes greater significance now, though regulatory changes are set to shift the trend gradually in future. Whenever the discussions are centred around interest rates, the banks are at the epicentre. They broadly mean lending rates which are of immediate interest to trade and industry should be lowered. But it must be kept in mind that repo rate cut is more symbolic of an evolving climate of economic well-being but may not necessarily lead to drop-in interest rates, though cheaper bank loans may add to the optimistic fervour.

Therefore, industry forums, regulators, government and other stakeholders pushes and prods banks to cut lending rates. But the algorithm of interest rate determination in banks has many dimensions, of which repo rate could be one but it cannot be the sole basis to soften lending rates. Therefore, the repo rates cut may not necessarily and immediately change the cost – income equation of banks in near term that is critical for transmission of lower interest rates. The cost of resource mobilisation, regulatory costs on account of CRR/SLR, cost of intermediation and many other factors related to balancing of business mix rule the equation.

23.1 Equation of pricing:

Banks are commercial entities engaged in financial intermediation. They source liabilities (deposits) and create assets (loans and investments) to augment profitability. The cost of liabilities and yield on investments are important factors in determining the pricing of products. They operate and survive on the arbitrage earned in the process. The simple arithmetic suggest that sourcing cost (cost of resources) has to be less than yield (earnings on assets) so as to absorb costs of financial intermediation and leave a small margin enough to sustain as perpetual institutions.

But the trends of data on cost and yield indicates that intermediation cost to assets ratio is on rise from 1.77 percent in FY 2013-14 to 1.85 percent in FY 2017-18. At the same time, the NIM too has dropped from 2.70 percent to 2.50 percent adding to the earning crunch. The additional burden of making provision against rising bad debts since FY 2016-17 and spree of write off of loans after introduction of AQR by RBI is another debilitating factor impinging upon the fragile profitability. Many PSBs are reeling under negative return on assets due to high share of NPAs. In such state of elevated establishment costs and depleting earnings, it will be difficult for banks to lower the lending rates in near term.

23.2 History of deregulation:

None of the lending rate models evolved after deregulation of interest rates in post reform phase that could speed up transmission of interest rates. Marking the end of administered lending rate regime, RBI deregulated lending rates for loans of over Rs. 2 lakhs way back in October 1994. It introduced Benchmark Prime Lending Rate (BPLR) system in 2003 to create competition and bring better transparency in computation. Lower BPLR becomes a sign of better efficiency of banks. But it suffered due to major weaknesses that banks could even lend below BPLR. This has made BPLR irrelevant as banks began to quote different interest rates according to the perceived risk and to maintain better clout on industry. It created scope for bias and opaqueness and unruly competition. Mighty borrowers got loans at cheaper rates while the other industry players were either deprived or had to borrow at elevated cost. There developed a tendency of price neutralization from marginal borrows to wealthy borrowers, a situation not warranted in interest rate administration.

In order to improve the lending rate framework, based on the recommendations of the Working Group on BPLR (Chairman: Shri Deepak Mohanty), Base Rate system was introduced with effect from July 1, 2010 with specific provision that banks cannot lend below the base rate. Introduction of base rate system removed the possibility of lending at ultra-low interest rates to mighty borrowers. It worked for some time but a problem had come up. Whenever base rate was changing, loans were getting repriced due to floating rates but the term deposits had to wait till their maturity of contractual period to get into lower interest rates. In the meantime, banks were not able to pass on the benefit of low interest rates to its borrowers. Therefore, over a period of time, even the Base rate system was replaced with Marginal Cost of Funds Based Lending Rates (MCLR) from April 2016 to overcome the slow transmission of lending rates.

Banks were unable to reduce interest rates under Base Rate System as most of their term deposit commitments continued at old interest rates and cut in repo rate had nominal impact on its cost structure. Even the MCLR system is now undergoing change. Beginning April 1, 2019, all floating rate new retail and small business loans extended by banks will be linked to any of the three benchmark – repo rate/treasury bills (91 days and 182 days yields)/any other benchmark interest rates indicated by Financial Benchmarks India Pvt. Ltd (FBIL). The reason for unsatisfactory exit of each successive lending rate model is perhaps not that it is unfit but that the solution of transmission of interest rates lies elsewhere.

23.3 Repo linked lending rate (RLLR):

From October 1, 2019, all new floating rate personal or retail loans such as car or home loans that are sanctioned by banks will have to be linked to external benchmarks, and the central bank's repo rate is one of them. Every bank will have its own Repo linked lending rate or RLLR which will keep varying each time the RBI revises the repo rate. Repo rate is the rate at which banks borrow from the RBI. The central bank reviews the repo rate by its Monetary Policy Committee or MPC at its bimonthly meets.

The computation of risk premium loaded above the benchmark rate will always be open to debate. Better regulatory lens on computation methodology may resolve the issue.

Hence, repo linked lending rate or RLLR is the lending rate which is linked to the RBI's repo rate. However, the effective RLLR interest rate depends on multiple factors. For example, the RLLR-linked home loan interest rate will depend on several factors such as what the loan amount is, the loan-to-value of the loan and even the risk group of the borrower, amongst other things. There can be a Spread or Margin charged by the bank. To explain, a bank may have an RLLR of 6.5 per cent, but the actual home loan interest could be 7.5 per cent, of which I per cent will be the Spread or Margin of the bank. Banks are free to fix Margin while lending to the borrowers.

23.4 Viability of Interest rate Models:

Irrespective of interest rate models that are put in place, the crux of its viability will rest on its cost-income metrics. Logically, banks should be able to save on costs arising from lower repo rate to share the benefit with borrowers. But the major source of funds for banks are deposits which have slowed down. Credit growth has now overstepped deposit rates creating liquidity crunch with volatile cost burden. Moreover, only close to 3 percent of resources of banks are accessed through repo route. Therefore, change in repo rate effectively has a benign impact on cost of resources that ultimately culminates into lending rates.

Even if deposit rates are reduced on term deposits, it will take time for them to get repriced to create room to lower lending rates. Term deposits forming 58 percent of deposit base will continue at old interest rates till they mature delaying cost reduction depending upon the tenor and mix of deposits. Rest of 32 percent of Current account and Savings accounts (CASA) – low-cost resource is cost neutral unless even deposits are also linked to an external benchmark and made into floating rate deposits.

Otherwise, reduction of deposit rates by any bank may lead to loss of deposit base when more and more newly opened payment and small finance banks may offer differentiated liability products at attractive rates. When interest rates on employees' provident fund is poised to rise and post-office savings deposit rates remaining intact, it will not be tenable to reduce deposit rates with risk of losing deposits to other intermediaries.

23.5 The SBI Move:

The surprising move of SBI has proposed to link savings bank (SB) interest rates on accounts having balances of over Rs. One lakh with repo rate is a tectonic shift brought about in the history of SB deposit rate determination in a PSB. Floating rate savings bank interest rate is a new phenomenon. Though SB interest rates were deregulated for depositors maintaining balances of over Rs. I lakh way back in 2011, such latitude was rarely used for fear of losing market share in low-cost resources, the most sought-after segment of deposit. SBI brought down SB interest rates down to 3.5 percent for all SB accounts having balance of above Rs. I lakh and below Rs. One crore and pays 4 percent on accounts maintaining balances above Rs.One crores since 2017. However, some private peers have used the same autonomy to woo the upper end customers to boost SB deposits. While deregulating interest on savings bank deposits, RBI stipulated a condition that there should be no discrimination in paying interest on savings deposits for deposits of up to Rs. I lakh, the majority segment of the portfolio.

Starting May 1, 2019, SB account holders with balances of over Rs. I lakh will get interest rate at 275 basis point below repo rate that works out to 3.50 percent. It will bring down SB interest on accounts with balances of over Rs. One crore to 3.5 percent as against 4 percent received till then. The reduction of interest rate on SB accounts of SBI will impact 80 percent of deposit base. It may also prompt some of the depositors to move to fixed tenure deposits. Similarly, on short-term working capital loans/overdrafts of over Rs. I lakh, SBI will charge 225 basis points above repo rate and shall bring lending floor rate to 8.5 percent which was close to Marginal Cost of funds-based lending rates (MCLR) ruling at 8.55 percent at that time. Till now SBI has kept retail lending out of its purview. Risk premium above such threshold will however be based on risk perception of the borrower.

The innovative approach of SBI to convert SB deposits of over Rs. I lakh into floating rates and linking it to repo rates is designed to suit its asset liability structure. It may not be feasible for other competitors with fragile CASA base to adopt it. But the move of SBI shall herald a new way of thinking that can eventually create a low interest rate regime pertinent to support growth of the economy. Even while experimenting with new lending rate models in quest to find the ideal system, the need to work on its viability for banks should not be lost sight.

CHAPTER – 24

IMPLICATIONS OF LIBOR TRANSITION

London Inter-bank Offered Rate (LIBOR) is a reference rate used in the calculation of interest and other dues on interbank lending and borrowings, derivatives, bonds and other financial transactions, both in the UK and in many other parts of global markets. LIBOR is set to exit from global financial markets by December 31, 2021, a big change in the global financial markets. LIBOR is benchmark interest rates that provided an indication of the average rates at which panel banks could borrow wholesale, unsecured funds for set periods in particular currencies.

It is calculated and published daily by the Intercontinental Exchange (ICE); the International Benchmark Administrator (IBA) based on submissions from a panel of banks. The task of fixing LIBOR moved from British Bankers Association (BBA) to ICE in July 2017. It is published across a range of currencies (GBP, USD, EUR, JPY and CHF) and maturities (overnight, one week, one month, two months, three months, six months and one year).

LIBOR serves two primary purposes in modern markets: as a reference rate and as a benchmark rate. A reference rate is a rate that financial instruments can contract upon to establish the terms of agreement. A benchmark rate reflects a relative performance measure, oftentimes for investment returns or funding costs. It thus serves as the primary reference rate for short-term floating rate for financial contracts like swaps and futures.

In LIBOR-based cash products, interest rate payments are known at the beginning of an interest rate period. Most variable rate cash products are based on quarterly payments, where three-month LIBOR allows pre-determining the interest rate payment of the counterparties at the beginning of an interest period. These obligations are then paid at the end of the interest rate period. LIBOR has the desirable feature of being pre-determined, which in turn has had an influence on how some of the market's 'plumbing' has been set up.

However, pre-determinedness is not the only feature of LIBOR. LIBOR also reflects interest rate expectations for specific longer-term tenors and is therefore a so-called forward-looking term rate. This feature could lead to evolution of risk-free rates (RFRs). Although RFR has matured well, it is unlikely that the bulk of transactions will match the maturity of the forward-looking RFR based term rates. Such circumstances would thus require a rather complex methodology for term rate construction. At this stage, it will be necessary to understand how LIBOR gets constructed.

24.1 A Peep into LIBOR History:

LIBOR's origination has been credited to a Greek banker by the name of Minos Zombanakis, who in 1969 arranged US $ 80 million syndicated loan from Manufacturers of Hanover to the Shah of Iran based on the reported funding costs of a set of reference banks that led to the institutionalization of LIBOR. In addition to providing loans at rates tied to LIBOR, banks whose submissions determined the fixing had also begun to borrow heavily using LIBOR-based contracts by the mid-1980s, creating an incentive to set standards in interest rates in determining funding costs. LIBOR has been serving the financial system for over 50 years.

As a result, the BBA took control of the rate in 1986 to formalize the data collection and governance process. In that year, LIBOR fixings were calculated for the U.S. dollar, the British pound, and the Japanese yen. Over time, the inclusion of additional currencies and integration of existing ones into the euro left the BBA with oversight of fixings over ten currencies as of 2012.

Eventually, fifteen maturity terms were reported for each currency, ranging from overnight to a 1-year term. However, the number of currency-maturity pairs has fallen in the aftermath of the LIBOR probes.

24.2 Composition of LIBOR:

LIBOR served for decades as a benchmark rate as unsecured market rate, a risk-free rate for interbank lending and borrowing. LIBOR can be thought of as a combination of term and risk spreads: where LIBOR = overnight risk-free rate over the term + term premium + bank term credit risk + term liquidity risk + term risk premium. The first term is the traditional hypothetical overnight interest rate at which a riskless institution could expect to borrow over the LIBOR for a fixed period. The term premium represents the inter-temporal rate of substitution for the term of the loan. Even when lending rates are linked to LIBOR, lenders must understand that banks are not inherently risk-free borrowers. Therefore, adding on the borrower's counterparty credit risk premium is necessary to manage credit risk that commensurate with loan maturity. The term liquidity risk compensates for maturity risk incurred by the lender by tying up funds for a longer period of time, which could include market illiquidity for interbank funds that may increase the lender's rollover refinancing costs. Finally, the term risk premium builds in compensation for the risk that any of these components may have realizations that differ from their expected amounts.

24.3 How LIBOR is fixed:

LIBOR fixing is based on 'Ask James' model. A clutch of suit-clad bankers is asked – at what rate are you likely to borrow money of a reasonable quantum before 11 am. The average of their quoted rates becomes the

LIBOR. The LIBOR then becomes risk free borrowing/lending rates for the day. LIBOR may change every day depending upon the perception of the markets and market players. BBA has been assuming the responsibility to administer LIBOR and publishes the rate each business day at approximately 11:30am GMT (6:30am EST). Actual collection of responses and calculations are performed by Thomson Reuters.

The official LIBOR fixing for each currency-maturity pair is calculated as the interquartile trimmed mean of submissions: the set of individual bank submissions are ordered, then the top and bottom four responses are discarded, and the remaining values are averaged to arrive at the LIBOR fixing for that currency-maturity pair. The banks that comprise the LIBOR panel tend to be the largest and credit worthiest ones with London operations, with the constituents varying based on currency, though changes in composition within currencies occasionally occur.

Of the ten LIBOR currencies that were reported in recent years, nine had panels consisting of 16 respondents, yielding precisely an interquartile trimmed mean. The USD panel, on the other hand, has 18 respondents as of October 12, 2013, yielding a 23% trimmed mean after the top and bottom four submissions are discarded.

The survey question posed to the panel banks relates to seeking response to the simple issue. *"At what rate could you borrow funds, were you to do so by asking for and then accepting interbank offers in a reasonable market size just prior to 11am?"* Hence, LIBOR is fixed on a consensus of prime banks using averaging methods while removing top 4 and bottom 4 offerings to keep outliers out of reckoning.

24.4 Wider use of LIBOR:

LIBOR's growth to prominence as a reference rate is closely tied to its historical popularity of unsecured risk-free term borrowing rate used for determining interbank borrowing rates. A BIS working group notes that these rates were the first to be introduced and have evolved over time into the industry standard because of early adoption by market participants (BIS 2013). More generally, however, reference rates allow for easier standardization of financial contracts while reducing the complexity with which terms on floating rate legs are determined.

The rationale for the wider usage of LIBOR in financial contracts is based upon its fixing pattern and globally acceptable rate. Because LIBOR represents the terms at which the world's largest and most financially sound institutions are able to obtain funding on a short-term basis. It serves as the lower bound for the borrowing rate of other less creditworthy institutions and individuals, *ceteris paribus*.

Rates are typically expressed as "LIBOR + x," where x is the premium charged in basis points for each particular borrower on top of the LIBOR rate of the corresponding maturity term. The financial contracts most commonly tied to LIBOR include interest rate swaps and other derivatives, fixed income securities and other similar financial products where interest rates are to be quoted. In this sense, banks extending variable rate loans can guarantee a positive net interest margin by ensuring that the interest rates they charge are tied to their cost of funds, with a positive premium built in. In addition to LIBOR there have been other reference rates in use in different financial markets.

24.5 Alternate benchmark rates in use:

Looking to the limitations and potential weaknesses of a universally adopted reference rate – LIBOR, there were other reference rates that began to emerge in financial markets. Adequate market liquidity and depth – a rare concern prior to the financial crisis – has emerged as a top criterion for regulators to provide leeway for alternate benchmark rates. Prudent oversight, resilience and robustness are now necessary components of any conversation about reference rates. Though the USD LIBOR fixing is the most dominant and widely recognized benchmark rate in the world, many other reference rates exist that seek to capture funding conditions in global financial markets.

EURIBOR is perhaps the second most widely used benchmark rate next to LIBOR and is calculated based on the funding abilities of a larger panel of European banks. Other financial centres like Tokyo, Mumbai, Singapore, and Hong Kong have developed their own internally calculated rate fixings in TIBOR, MIBOR, SIBOR, and HIBOR, respectively. These benchmark rates also employ similar methodologies, though they have, on some occasions arrived at different fixings.

Another strand of unsecured interbank borrowing rates relies on past transactions for quotes. The Euro Overnight Index Average (EONIA) is perhaps the most well known in this set and serves as a complement to EURIBOR since the panel of banks were historically the same for the two rates. Though both rates reflect measures of term borrowing for wholesale Euro deposits, EURIBOR is more widely used.

24.6 Why LIBOR lost sheen:

Beginning in June 2012, LIBOR came under public scrutiny due to controversy over individual panel bank submissions during the height of the financial crisis. Allegations arose that bank had purposefully underreported their borrowing costs by significant amounts in order to project financial strength amidst market uncertainty. In addition, banks were alleged to have manipulated the rate to realize gains on LIBOR-based contracts. Whereas underreporting one's own submission can signal financial strength, gains in LIBOR-based contracts often involving concerted action by multiple individuals to influence the final fixing.

Though many banks were allegedly involved in misreporting, the most prominent to have reached settlements to date are Barclays, UBS, RBS, and Rabobank. Commodity Futures Trading Commission (CFTC) probes ultimately concluded that the firms had acted in violation of the Commodity Exchange Act's false reporting provision. In addition to paying a settlement of $453.6 million to U.S. and British financial authorities, Barclays also lost a number of senior executives in the aftermath of the scandal.

Further controversy arose in the U.S. when it was revealed that the Federal Reserve Bank of New York had first become aware of manipulative activities in 2007. Though the Fed had neither regulatory responsibility nor jurisdiction with regard to LIBOR but US Federal Reserve communicated to Bank of England authorities in June 2008 urging it to enhance the credibility of LIBOR.

It urged Bank of England to establish best practices for calculating and reporting rates, the expansion of the USD LIBOR panel to a broader set of banks, the addition of a second USD LIBOR fixing to reflect transactions that occur during US market hours, the specification of the transaction size at which submitted rates are applicable, the reduction of the number of maturities reported, and the elimination of incentives to misreport.

During the course of investigation, Barclays pointed out that allegations of rate fixing during the peak of the crisis were inconsistent with the fact that its submissions were often in the top quartile of survey responses and thus omitted in the calculation of the interquartile mean. It is important to note, however, that misreporting did not imply that the individual LIBOR submissions were consistently lower than those of competitors, but rather that submissions were lower than the bank's true cost of funding in the interbank market.

Barclays, as well as any financial institution, could misreport and still have rates among the highest submitted because of its borrower risk profile. The system's design, in which rate quotes are provided by market participants who hold large financial positions indexed to LIBOR, introduces an inherent conflict of interest.

Net creditors benefit from higher fixings, while net debtors benefit from misquotes in the opposite direction. Though the rate calculation via a trimmed mean reduces the market impact of each individual submission, individual behaviour and collaboration among panel banks can still result in meaningful divergences from true rates. While statistical evidence of wrongdoing by banks both in isolation and in tandem remains difficult to pinpoint even today, internal communications unearthed during the probes proved instrumental in showing purposeful intent to misreport.

24.7 Volatility and Divergence of LIBOR:

Prior to mid-2007, LIBOR tended to move closely with other short-term interest rates such as Treasury yields and the Overnight Index Swap (OIS) rate. However, LIBOR began to display greater volatility in August 2007 with the onset of the financial crisis. A combination of counterparty credit and liquidity concerns drove the 3-month USD LIBOR to 5.62% on August 31, 2007, compared to an average of 5.36% in the six months prior, during a time of stable expectations for the overnight federal funds policy target rate for the Federal Reserve.

The maturity-matched OIS rate measures expectations over the tenor of unsecured overnight bank borrowing rates, which in the U.S. correspond to the effective average federal funds rate. Such global experience of manipulative LIBOR led to the need to change the reference rate.

Beginning in 2007, regulators and market observers noted that LIBOR had failed to behave in line with expectations given other market prices and rates. Investigations by U.S. and foreign regulators have uncovered explicit manipulation by banks to influence rate fixings with the intent of projecting financial soundness during the crisis and benefiting proprietary trading positions. Four banks – Barclays, UBS, RBS, and Rabobank – have combined to pay settlements upward of $3.5 billion.

24.8 Reference rate reforms:

What started out, as the LIBOR scandal has not been confined to the one rate or the one market? Regulatory inquiries have abounded amidst heightened sensitivities in the post-crisis environment. EURIBOR has experienced similar rate manipulation allegations, while several banks are under investigation for manipulative practices in the energy, commodity and foreign exchange markets.

Financial regulatory bodies across the world including the International Organization of Securities Commissions (IOSCO) and BIS have joined in a coordinated effort toward reference rates reform in the wake of the LIBOR scandal.

At the heart of these deliberations sits the Financial Stability Board (FSB), an international body established in 2009 to oversee global financial system reforms. The FSB has convened an Official Sector Steering Group composed of central bankers and other regulators to coordinate consistency of reviews of existing reference rates.

UK's Financial Conduct Authority (FCA) announced that LIBOR panel bank submission would become discretionary from end 2021, which means availability of LIBOR as a benchmark rate becomes completely uncertain. This will have a significant impact on the banking and financial services industry. Thus a collaborative effort on the part of policymakers internationally is underway to reform the reference rate.

24.9 Move towards alternate benchmark rates:

Since 2017, the regulators and market players across the globe felt the need to move from LIBOR to a more sound and resilient financial system and undertook a significant, coordinated effort to evolve a better system. The UK's Financial Conduct Authority (FCA) responsible for regulating LIBOR indicated that the publication of LIBOR is not guaranteed beyond 2021. So, time is of the essence to prepare for the possibility that LIBOR is presumably on way to cease permanently. The transition from LIBOR is important because the potential disruption or cessation of LIBOR poses a financial stability risk as well as a risk to the individual firms with LIBOR exposures.

The Alternate Reference Rate Committee (ARRC) has after considerable debates; brainstorming and consultations identified the Secured Overnight Financing Rate (SOFR) as the rate can represent best practice for use in certain new USD derivatives and other financial contracts. In order to transition to SOFR, the ARRC developed the Paced Transition Plan with specific steps and timelines designed to encourage adoption of SOFR.

In order to develop sufficient liquidity, the ARRC is focused on supporting the launch and usage of SOFR-based financial products in the market and creating a forward-looking term rate based on SOFR. The ARRC suggested market players and financial intermediaries to customize their internal systems that outline key transition milestones that market participants should aim to meet across floating rate notes, business loans, consumer loans, securitizations, and derivatives. These are some of the countries specific benchmark coming up as alternates. SOFR is most likely to replace LIBOR as international benchmark rate while individual countries can choose its own benchmark as well.

24.10 Secured Overnight Financing Rate (SOFR):

Beginning December 2021, the U.S. dollar LIBOR may cease to be in use. The ARRC has identified the Secured Overnight Funding Rate (SOFR) as the recommended alternative reference rate to replace USD LIBOR. SOFR is calculated as a volume-weighted median of transaction-level U.S. Treasury repurchase agreements data, reflecting borrowing cost in overnight borrowing collateralized. SOFR is a broad measure of the cost of borrowing cash overnight collateralized by U.S. Treasury securities in the repurchase agreement (repo) market. This rate is robust and meets international standards. It is reckoned as an alternative to LIBOR in collaboration with New York Federal Reserve. New York Fed publishes SOFR each business day at approximately 8 am EST.

SOFR is a much more resilient rate than LIBOR because of how it is computed and arrived at taking into account the depth and liquidity of the markets that underlie it. As an overnight-secured rate, SOFR better reflects the way financial institutions fund themselves. The transaction volumes underlying SOFR regularly are around $1 trillion in daily volumes. The volumes underlying SOFR are far larger than the transactions in any other U.S. money market. This makes it a transparent rate that is representative of the market across a broad range of market participants and protects it from attempts at manipulation. Also, the fact that it's derived from the U.S. Treasury repo market means that, unlike LIBOR, it's not at risk in the hands of few.

It is thus broad based. In cooperation with the Treasury Department's Office of Financial Research, the New York Fed is publishing three daily compounded averages of SOFR: "30-day Average SOFR," "90-day Average SOFR," and "180-day Average SOFR," in addition to a daily index that allows for the calculation of compounded average rates over custom time periods: the "SOFR Index". By providing calculated term rates that can be easily cited in contracts, these averages are facilitating the adoption of SOFR.

In addition, Federal Reserve Board includes data on indicative compound averages of SOFR and, based on a methodology they have proposed, estimated forward-looking term rates that will be updated periodically. The data of SOFR so arrived at is for informational purposes only and are intended to help market participants better understand how forward-looking term and compounded SOFR may behave over time. The ARRC has set a goal of seeing a robust, IOSCO – compliant forward-looking term rate produced by a private administrator that could be used in commercial contracts once the SOFR derivatives markets that the term rate would be based on have grown to sufficient depth.

Moreover, at some point of time, in evolving alternatives, lack of consensus about a single global reference rate has resulted in a number of bodies such as the ARRCs and benchmark regulation and working groups defining a slew of alternative reference rates (ARRs) in various jurisdictions. These rates could be secured but are usually unsecured; however, secured overnight lending is perceived by market participants as more robust in the long term than unsecured overnight lending rates.

24.11 Preparedness for transition:

The impact of benchmark interest rates on the financial services industry and innumerable market participants is immense given that LIBOR/SOFR is key to be the pricing and hedging a slew of cash and derivative instruments. Since the new rate is set to come into force in 2022, banks must take steps to assess the impact of LIBOR transition and initiate measures to address them depending upon the volumes of internal exposures.

Banks will need to adopt SOFR as an alternative for LIBOR, build spread and term structure on par with LIBOR, determine LIBOR exposure, and efficiently manage the transition across different risk areas. Way forward after transition, the systems shall use advanced cognitive automation techniques and AI that will facilitate a smooth transition and help banks realize the desired outcomes.

The risk-free rates – SOFR is typically overnight and collateralized, which means that credit and liquidity risk premium must be added on as a spread adjustment factor to bring it at par with an unsecured reference rate such as LIBOR. The rates must be based on legitimate transactions and not on professional judgment. This means substantial transactional liquidity needs to be built up on these rates using both cash and derivative products before the substitute reference rate can be adopted as the official reference rate.

24.12 Role of Market Players:

There are a number of steps that markets may have to initiate.

- Review information available on LIBOR and other legacy benchmark transitions (including through the selection of links that are available)
- Undertake a review of transactions that are based on LIBOR and other legacy benchmarks;
- Consider the potential impacts that the discontinuation of LIBOR and other legacy benchmarks may have on the overall business;

- Consider the potential impacts that the transition to alternative interest rate benchmarks may have on financial markets and its outstanding commitments.

It may be necessary to consider seeking advice from the domain experts/ financial and/or legal advisers. The transition of existing LIBOR based contracts to contracts referencing alternative interest rate benchmarks may involve the payment of a spread adjustment and may impact the operation of certain financial covenants. There may also be cash flow and hedge accounting impacts if a mismatch arises on transition between a loan and a related derivative.

24.13 Impact of LIBOR transition on customers:

The transition to alternative interest rate benchmarks will impact a range of transactions and products. Customers should expect to be affected if they have a floating rate loan or credit facility, deposit or derivative that has or may have payments linked to LIBOR or other affected legacy benchmarks that mature after 2021. There are several differences between LIBOR and the proposed alternative interest rates – SOFR and, as a result, the transition may have pricing, cash flow, accounting and operational implications for customers and their business. Authorities and industry groups are still working through the implications and issues generated by the transition, including how best to move to new and existing products and transactions to the alternative interest rate benchmarks across the range of products by the end of 2021, if not before.

24.14 RBI Road Map:

Transition from LIBOR to alternate reference rate is a huge task. Way back in August 2020, RBI urged banks to frame a Board-approved plan, outlining an assessment of exposures linked to the LIBOR and the steps to be taken to address risks arising from the cessation of LIBOR, including preparation for the adoption of the ARR. Taking cognizance of the fact that Financial Conduct Authority (FCA), UK has announced on March 05, 2021 that LIBOR will either cease to be provided by any administrator or no longer be a representative rate:

(a) Immediately after December 31, 2021, in the case of all Pound sterling, Euro, Swiss franc and Japanese yen settings, and the 1-week and 2-month US dollar settings; and

(b) Immediately after June 30, 2023, in the case of the remaining US dollar settings.

With the objective of orderly, safe and sound LIBOR transition and considering customer protection, reputational and litigation risks involved, banks/financial institutions are encouraged to cease, and also encourage their customers to cease, entering into new financial contracts that reference LIBOR as a benchmark and instead use any widely accepted ARR, as soon as practicable and in any case by December 31, 2021. While certain US dollar LIBOR settings will continue to be published till June 30, 2023, the extension of the timeline for cessation is primarily aimed at ensuring roll-off of USD LIBOR-linked legacy contracts, and not to encourage continued reliance on LIBOR. It is, therefore, expected that contracts linked to LIBOR should not be undertaken after December 31, 2021, except for the purpose of managing risks arising out of LIBOR contracts (e.g. hedging contracts, novation, market-making in support of client activity, etc.), contracted on or before December 31, 2021.

India's exposure to borrowings linked to the benchmark is estimated to be around $331 billion in January 2021. Individual institutions have to take stock of their own exposures to manage their risks – post LIBOR. The RBI permitted authorized dealers to extend pre-shipment credit in foreign currency to exporters for financing the purchase, processing, manufacturing or packing of goods prior to shipment at Libor, Euro-Libor and Euribor related rates of interest. The first change is that banks can now extend export credit using any other widely accepted alternative reference rate in the currency concerned.

SOFR, one such alternative reference rate, is based on transactions in the US Treasury repo market and is being widely used as a substitute for Libor in dollar-denominated loans and derivatives across the world. Secondly, as per existing guidelines, changes in any of the parameters of an original derivative contract is treated as restructuring and the resultant change in the mark-to-market value of the contract on the date of restructuring is required to be settled in cash.

For derivative contracts, as per extant instructions, change in any of the parameters of the original contract is treated as restructuring and the resultant change in the mark-to-market value of the contract on the date of restructuring is required to be cash settled. Since the impending change in reference rate from LIBOR is a "force majeure" event, banks are being advised that change in reference rate from LIBOR/LIBOR-related benchmarks to an ARR will not be treated as restructuring. RBI has been changing the regulatory norms to ensure transition from LIBOR to ARR like SOFR. It is now up to the financial entities to make use of the latitude granted by RBI to ensure that risks arising out of ending of LIBOR regime should be managed well.

When the global financial system has been working with LIBOR at its epicentre for five decades, transition to a new reference rate – like SOFR will need coordination among banks, non-banks and other financial intermediaries and business houses to readjust with the transition to a new benchmark. With the most widely used financial benchmark, LIBOR to cease after end-2021, the market players should identify issues around the transition from LIBOR to alternative benchmarks that can pose challenges as well as opportunities and stakeholders need to be aware and prepared. Crystallization of risks is most important in managing the transition. The financial intermediaries will have to work out the implications of the change, reckon the outstanding financial commitments linked to LIBOR and remain in preparedness to settle the claims and re-price with the other benchmark.

The RBI has been participating in and monitoring global developments related to LIBOR transition and has tasked the Indian Banks' Association

(IBA) to consult on relevant issues. The IBA has since formed three work streams on (i) LIBOR transition arrangements, (ii) rates and methodology and (iii) outreach to market participants. IBA has also circulated a guidance note among its member banks to enable them to assess their preparedness for LIBOR transition on various parameters, viz., exposure and risk assessment and assessment of the outstanding liabilities, assets and to work out syncing information technology (IT) related implications and regulations.

The related financial sector regulators and market players are actively developing an acceptable alternative for Mumbai Interbank Forward Offered Rate (MIFOR) while the outreach Work stream is reaching out to stakeholders through webinars and conferences to create awareness about the upcoming challenge. It is high time that employees of the financial system start understanding the dynamics of transition to make it seamless as and when it is necessary but well before 2021 ends. The entities exposed to LIBOR and finance professionals should coordinate with peers to navigate the transition– an experience rare to acquire.